AMERICAN CATHOLICISM
AND NOW WHERE?

JOHN DEEDY

PLENUM PRESS • NEW YORK AND LONDON

Library of Congress Cataloging in Publication Data

Deedy, John G.
  American Catholicism.

  Includes bibliographical references and index.
  1. Catholic Church—United States—History—20th century. 2. United States—
Church history—20th century. I. Title.
BX1406.2.D42 1987   282'73   87-12765
ISBN 0-306-42706-0

© 1987 John Deedy
Plenum Press is a division of
Plenum Publishing Corporation
233 Spring Street, New York, N.Y. 10013

Printed in the United States of America

For Bill Buckley, the Good
W.T.B., of Worcester

PREFACE

THE AMERICAN CATHOLIC church is a remarkable institution. Its people worship in numbers that dwarf figures from elsewhere. It has one of the most vibrant of Catholic school systems, perhaps *the* most vibrant. It is by and large an obedient church, some would say docile— controversies of recent years notwithstanding. It is a church characterized by great loyalty to the pope and by unstinting financial generosity to Rome. Still, the American church is a church in transition. There has been erosion in areas of church life. Yet more is likely. The

American Catholic church, in sum, is a ready-made subject for analysis and study.

When this book project on American Catholicism was first broached, no particular time urgency seemed to be involved. In recent years, nuns and priests had exited the religious life by the thousands, and their ranks were not being refilled. Many seminaries and convents had been closed for lack of need, then sold off to meet the financial imperatives of the respective religious communities. The administration of Catholic hospitals in several cities had been turned over to lay boards, and a few Catholic colleges had shut their gates. A number of Catholic publications had disappeared from view, and in many Catholic parishes, focuses shifted, often to activities of apostolic inconsequence, as emphases drained away from diocesan schools, very many of which had closed for good. Still, on the institutional level, it was pretty much business as usual. The church had problems, but Peter's American bark was not about to keel over like some shaky ship in a rough sea.

Administratively, many of the problems of the American church could be attributed to zealous, indeed reckless, overextension during the years of rectitude-confirmed that followed World War II, those years coinciding roughly with the Eisenhower administrations, a time when everything was right with America and everything upbeat for American Catholicism.

Thus, when slippage began occurring during the latter 1960s, it was easy enough to interpret much that was happening as part of a natural process—the laws of evolutionary selectivity translated to the ecclesiastical sphere. If a few spoke of crisis, no one was pressing a panic button—at least no one high in authority was. The American church was in change, and if certain changes did not always seem for the better, at least they could be rationalized.

But in Rome, the American situation was not viewed so casually—or so placidly or benignly, as the case may be. So it was that under a new pope, John Paul II, a pope from a country quite different from the United States or, for that matter, any other in the world where Roman Catholicism was strong, Rome entered upon a program to right what it saw as wrong with the church beyond the Alps, including eventually the American church. Maybe it is unfair to suggest that this was a culture-gap pope, or to suggest, as does James Carroll in his roman à clef *Prince of Peace*, that this was—nay, is—a pope who would rule the church as the Communist Party would the pope's native Poland. But it is not unfair to say that this was and remains a pope with a very conservative agenda, call it traditional, if you will—except, of course, in Roman Catholicism, *traditional* pretty much translates as *conservative*.

It quickly became clear that very high among John Paul II's worldwide concerns was the state of the American church. In fact, as event piled on event, it was obvious that this pope, in the phrase from a *U.S. News & World Report* cover story on American Catholicism, was "taking dead aim at the American church,"[1] initiating disciplinary actions and setting in motion institutional reforms that, if not unique in the history of American Catholicism, were without parallel in some seventy-five years. In the first decade of this century, while Pius X was pope, the modernist controversies took their toll on the American church, virtually paralyzing Catholic life in the United States for decades. Milwaukee's Archbishop Rembert G. Weakland, O.S.B., recalled the times and their consequences in a remarkable column in his archdiocesan newspaper, questioning the wisdom of efforts by Rome to impose a stricter orthodoxy on the American church: "Seminaries were closed, theological periodicals were suppressed, a network of 'informers' in each diocese was organized, oaths were repeatedly taken, intellectually rigid bishops were appointed, and fear and distrust were everywhere in the U.S.A."[2] Those steps in the early century were taken to cope with a heresy that history knows as *Americanism*, but that was largely phantom so far as the church in America was concerned. In any instance, the repressions and the intimidations accomplished little that was positive. They stifled theological creativity, stunted intellectual growth of a religious kind, and ultimately left the American church unprepared for Vatican Council II—and, as Weakland would add, "unprepared" as well for "the dramatic changes of the 1960s."[3]

For Rome, the challenge to it these days does not apper to be substantively different from what yesterday's Rome deemed it to be during the days of the "Americanism" controversy. Once again, the issues involve discipline, theological and doctrinal orthodoxy, and the problem of ideological separatism. Elements of the American church might want more room in adapting the church's traditional teachings to their existential religious and cultural situations, but authority belongs to Rome and Rome is not about to surrender it or relax it beyond the measure already in effect. As Rome took a hard line in the early century, so it takes a hard line today. Who says history does not try to repeat itself?

These are different times, however. Yesterday, Rome could pretty much control new theological and doctrinal directions—and such internal matters as it needed to—simply by issuing an encyclical or an authoritative directive of one kind or another. Rome spoke; Catholics fell in line. Gone are the days!

Rome speaks, but the words fall on many deaf ears belonging to Catholics, so many, in fact, that the Rome of John Paul II obviously feels impelled to act directly to assert control, to quash dissent in order to maintain, reaffirm, and reestablish its hegemony over the 841 million Catholics of the world. It will take on a whole church in those countries whose house it deems out of order. It acted firmly and decisively a few years ago in terms of the Dutch church, and soon after, it took on the Brazilian church in the context of liberation theology.

It can no longer be doubted that Rome has now decided to come to grips with what it sees as the problem of the American church. The disciplining of so many American Catholics, from relatively anonymous nuns to prominent priests, including even an archbishop, allows no other conclusion. Confirming the impression further are actions such as the withdrawal of the imprimatur (the church's seal of approval on a published work) from several books and catechisms that enjoyed an earlier clearance, as well as the tightening of reins generally over U.S. dioceses, seminaries, colleges, and universities. The pope, in the words of *U.S. News & World*

Report's headline, has got tough—and he remains tough, so tough, in fact, that it sometimes appears that his reach or the long arm of one of his lieutenants is now everywhere in American Catholicism, and seemingly elsewhere as well, with the sweeping doctrinal statement of 1987, which would theoretically extend the church's reach beyond Catholics and the church to science and the state, and which would impose on political authorities and others strict limitations on the usage of new technologies in human reproduction, including, among much else, virtually all forms of artificial fertilization and embryo transfer.[4] The statement is seen as particularly applicable to countries such as the United States, where technology is moving so rapidly.

Returning to religion itself, the large wonder of it all is that, until fairly recently—up to the late 1960s, in fact—the American church could pass as one of the most trouble-free churches of Christendom. It so passes even today with many observers, whatever the current controversies. This is the church that was. Nonetheless, this church has its problems. At the same time, however, it is not one of the great problem churches of Christendom, although it often appears that Rome regards it as such. The worry is that an overbearing Rome might exacerbate such problems as exist and, in fact, create more of them by imaging or exaggerating the condition of the American church. Radical surgery is not the cure for relatively minor complaints. One doesn't go after a gnat with an elephant gun.

So rapidly have events involving Rome and the American church moved that what started as a leisurely writing project changed virtually overnight into something of an urgent one. Suddenly, there seemed the need for a book that reviewed events, placed them in some kind of historical and existential context, and speculated on their consequences. This is that book, or so it is hoped.

The book, be it said immediately, is not intended as a polemic or a diatribe, though it does build on an admittedly controversial proposition—specifically, that modern American Catholicism has evolved into something of a double-tiered institution, a church comprising people on two levels of membership: belief and worship. On the one hand, it is comprised of the orthodox—people who live, believe and worship by and of the institution, and who take the institution and its fortunes seriously. On the other hand, it is a church of the heterodox—people who are indifferent about ecclesiastical fiat, who live their spiritual lives on their own terms, and who are oblivious to most of what transpires in the institution except for such information as they might come across in the secular media.

Now, as always, Rome's reforms have a direct effect upon institutional Catholics. At the same time, those reforms do not begin to touch the large and growing numbers of detached Catholics—those noninstitutional Catholics whose interest has flagged, whose religious observance has become less theologically conforming, and whose Catholicism has evolved into a cultural rather than a deeply felt spiritual thing.

Appreciated by Rome or not, it is that situation which, so far as the church in America is concerned, constitutes its real challenge—if not also its dilemma. Disciplinary actions and institutional reforms affect the loyalists, those within the perimeters of the orthodox. They have the effect of correcting the course of some of the wayward and of making the saved a bit more saved, even while many of those actions and reforms risk the alienation of some Catholics, whether saved or unsaved, who regard indiscriminate disciplining and reforming as unnecessary and unfair. What is probably more to the point is that most, if not all, of the disciplining and reforming never even reach the detached, having little impact on them, beyond perhaps confirming many of the detached in their detachment.

The ranks of the detached seem to grow by the day. The great issue is whether their presence can be recovered, their involvements reclaimed by a tightening of the running of the ship. Or could it turn out that the tightening process will only accelerate the disembarkation process and quicken the detachment of the passengers? Time has that answer, not this book—though the book has thoughts on the subject.

Before I get to that discussion, a few acknowledgments are due, first to Linda Greenspan Regan of Plenum Press, who initiated the project, rode herd on it, and saw it to completion. Cornelius M. Buckley, Maurice Adelman, Jr., Owen Murphy, John Sprague, James Douglass, Herbert A. Kenny, and John Wilkins, the latter by telephone and letter from London, helped with counsel and information. Many people responded to requests for data, including Dean Hoge of the Department of Sociology at the Catholic University of America, and their cooperation is appreciated and explicitly credited by way of the footnotes. Jim Carroll, the Paulist who became a novelist of the first rank, was especially helpful, providing the text of his address ''The Lord of Disbelief,'' delivered 11 October 1986, to priests, sisters, and lay ministers of the archdiocese of Chicago—and in addition, offering to discuss his ideas further over espresso in a cafe in Boston's North End. And of course, the research facilities and helpful ministrations of the personnel of Sawyer Free Library in Gloucester and of my town's Carnegie Library were indispensable. I am grateful to them and to others, including many friends wearing the cloth, who are perhaps best left unnamed for their peace of existence within the institution.

Finally, a word about the second half of my title: *And Now Where?* The words are borrowed from the title of a Rockwell Kent lithograph done in 1936. Rockwell Kent was by no means a Roman Catholic, but his print of a man and woman in transit, seemingly searching for their directions—the woman resting on a rock, the man standing with his hand on her shoulder, their knapsack on the ground by their feet—is remarkably evocative of current Catholicism. Kent's concept conjured the hard times of the country and the agonies of a depression that routed old complacencies, uprooted families, and put many people on the road. Yet so much of the symbolism of the lithograph is exact for present-day American Catholicism: the rock, the figurative sign of Christ's church; the couple in transit, the embodiment of a pilgrim people, a people searching, which coincidentally happened to be a persistent Vatican Council II image. That woman, back of head to viewer—Is she concealing longings that her expression might betray? That man, his face in profile—Is he looking backward, or forward? That's the mystery, his the intriguing question, although the answer is easy enough to guess.

The parallelism of the print with present-day Catholicism breaks down there.

Or does it? For although many Catholics are looking forward, not all are, by any means.

That some are looking forward and some backward makes the times fascinating, but also a little bewildering.

JOHN DEEDY

Rockport, Massachusetts

CONTENTS

1

CRISIS, NOT QUITE; PROBLEMS, VERY MANY

BY ANY YARDSTICK, American Catholicism is one of the great success stories of religious history—an ancient faith transplanted to a new and at times unreceptive environment, and acclimating itself with the facility of...well, the starling, that rapacious bird of the Sturnidae family that was also a later arrival. Like the starling, American Catholicism has thrived, too.

The starling gained an American habitat, because around 1890, one Eugene Scheifflin thought it would be nice if every species of bird mentioned in Shakespeare's

1

plays could be found in the United States. So, in New York City's Central Park, he released several pairs of that passerine bird cited in Part I of *Henry the Fourth*.[1]

There was nothing so idyllic—and, be it hoped, much that was more benign, comparatively speaking—for the country and the human species in the arrival of Catholics, at first by a trickle in the eighteenth century, then by a virtual flood on the nineteenth century's great tides of immigration. In any instance, Catholics are here—52,654,908 strong, according to a 1986 count. They comprise almost 25 percent of the national population, and as an institutional entity, they check in as one of the largest in the land.

Indeed, so large, so entrenched, so influential is American Catholicism, it is hard to appreciate that it was only in relatively recent years—within, in fact, the lifetimes of its most senior members—that this church was accorded full "adult" status within Roman Catholicism itself. For portions of three, maybe four, centuries—from colonial times, to the founding of the Diocese of Baltimore and the naming of John Carroll as the first American bishop in 1789, through the entire nineteenth century, and into the first decade of the twentieth—the American church belonged in Rome's blunt and not exactly felicitous Latin phrase *in partibus infidelium*, "in the lands of the unbelievers." The American church was a missionary church, and it remained a missionary church until 29 June 1908 when the reigning pontiff, Pope Pius X, subsequently sainted, signed the apostolic constitution *Sapienti consilio*, which removed the American church from the jurisdiction of the Congregation de

Propaganda Fide, the agency of the church that nurtured development of the faith in lands where Catholics were neither strong in numbers nor ecclesiastically self-supporting. The move, in effect, certified the maturity of the American church and established it as a peer church alongside those of France, Italy, Germany, Ireland, and other historic centers of Catholic Christianity.

If the action was slow in coming, it was fast in paying dividends of multiple kinds. The American church flourished in numbers, vocations, apostolic industry— and in special generosity to the Mother Church. The Peter's Pence collection, the once-upon-a-time penny-a-house tax that originated in England in the eighth century to help fund the pope, and that was extended over time to the wider church, channeled millions of dollars from generous American Catholics to Rome for the maintenance of the Holy Father and the furtherance of his works of charity. Other more private gifts went as well from the United States to Rome, from wealthy laypersons, from affluent organizations like the Knights of Columbus, and from prosperous individual churchmen. John Cooney, Cardinal Francis J. Spellman's biographer, tells of a quiet $50,000 gift that Spellman made in 1957, a preinflationary year, to the Congregation for the Propagation of the Faith and its head, Cardinal Gregory Agagianian.[2]

So, of course, when the Vatican's fiscal operations began to show deficits in the 1970s—deficits so serious by 1979 as to necessitate an extraordinary convocation of the college of cardinals in search of solutions—it was to the American church (and a comparably comfortable

West German church) that Rome looked for special displays of financial magnanimity. Its hopes were not disappointed then, nor do they continue to be. American
Catholics have come to constitute the largest single
source of contributions to the Vatican,[3] so once again, in
1986, their generosity was counted upon to help offset
an estimated budgetary shortfall, this time of some $56
million—although at the same time worries were being
expressed that American donations might not have the
substantially positive effect they had had in previous
years because of the weakness of the American dollar in
the international money market.

The emphasis on the dollar notwithstanding, the
American church has historically been more than some
kind of magic money machine for Rome. Whatever the
situations of the Catholic church in other parts of the
world at any given time in recent centuries, Rome could
look to the American church and take consolation in its
loyalty, its obedience, and its remarkable orthodoxy. Ap-
prehensions were only occasional and likely as not misplaced, as at the turn of the century, when a conciliatory
but nonetheless concerned Pope Leo XIII issued an encyclical letter cautioning American Catholics against any
''among you who conceive of and desire a church in
America different from that which is in the rest of the
world.''[4]

Leo XIII was addressing a so-called heresy labeled
Americanism. If a heresy at all, it was less American than
it was European. Marveling at the rapid growth of the
church in the United States, elements of European
Catholics, in France particularly, seized upon a popular-
ized and imprecisely translated biography of Father Isaac

Hecker,[5] the American priest who came to Roman Catholicism partly by way of New England transcendentalism, to press for secular and ecumenical accommodations that theoretically would be as beneficial for the church in Europe as they had allegedly been for the church in America. Liberal European Catholics seemed especially impressed by the health that the church could enjoy and the success that a man like Hecker could have in a country where Catholicism was independent from state patronage. Hecker, founder of the Missionary Society of St. Paul the Apostle, known popularly as the Paulists, had acquired a wide reputation for winning converts, in part by emphasizing those things that Catholics and Protestants held in common, as distinct from those that separated them. That approach is the cornerstone of the modern ecumenical movement, but in the late nineteenth century, it smacked of compromise, of dilution of doctrine, of a waiving of prerogatives, and Leo XIII acted to combat any such development. The American hierarchy did have individuals who were known as *Americanizers*, prelates who would cultivate within the church policies and programs deemed advantageous to the wider American society. Nonetheless, Leo XIII was still addressing the wrong audience, though the name given the incidents would stick, as would some of their implied meanings. The reality remains that the issues that troubled Leo XIII did not exist in any threatening way in the United States. The American Catholic church was not in ferment—not before, not then.

But it is now and has been since the mid-1960s. The church that was once the very model of ecclesiastical decorum and propriety is very much in ferment. In a definite sense, the American church is still a muscular arm of worldwide Catholicism. It is large in numbers—indeed, huge. Despite certain financial problems of its own, it continues to be a prosperous church and a generous one. And latter-day controversies notwithstanding, it remains a church that is extremely deferential to Rome. A pope visiting the United States is subject, inevitably, to tight security arrangements; the United States, alas, has its full share of assassins, although so, too, has Rome, as the deplorable attempt on the life of Pope John Paul II in St. Peter's Square on 13 May 1981 unmistakably demonstrated. Nonetheless, a pope can travel in the United States and expect to be respected. Even the demurrer on women's place in the church which was entered by Sister Theresa Kane of the Sisters of Mercy during John Paul II's 1978 visit to Washington was so polite and refined that the implications at first escaped many hearing it, perhaps even the pope himself. Or was the pope too surprised, too taken aback, too circumspect himself, to react? In any instance, he gave Sister Kane his blessing, not a finger wagging, as in the case of a dissident Latin American priest he encountered in a reception line.

By the same token, a pope can travel in the United States without certain other worries that he might encounter elsewhere—like eggs being launched at the popemobile, his specially secured limousine, by disgruntled Catholics, or without being subjected, as happened in the Netherlands in 1985, to insulting exhibitions, like balloons in the shape of condoms being floated along the routes of his motorcade by people protesting the church's positions and his on artificial birth control, premarital sex, and other matters of sexual morality. The latter assurance threatens, however, to come to an end with the promise of San Francisco's homosexual community to greet John Paul II with angry demonstrations during his 1987 visit to that city.

But whatever happens (or does not happen) in San Francisco, the American church is generally a very proper church. At the same time, it is not a church without many complexities and its full share of perplexities.

To begin with, there are the widely publicized problems of orthodoxy and discipline, which have made celebrities and cult heroes out of many unlikely candidates for notoriety. These include many who are ordained, from archbishops to campus theologians. They include, too, a number of nuns who might have entered the convent expecting to lead lives of virtual anonymity, but who suddenly find themselves media personalities as they assert an independence of role and thought, plunging into ghetto apostolates and challenging church positions that strike them as sexist, all the way to abortion itself. Of course, to many in the church, these people are villainous rather than admirable. But however one views them, there is no escaping that they present difficult and challenging problems for the church, for in their own ways, they and the issues they personify reflect in the larger spectrum a church and a people in an intense, sometimes fierce struggle with their separate but also connected identities.

The paradox is that all this may still be only the tip of the proverbial iceberg, because on another level of the American church's existence is another type of problem—subtle, silent, largely unpublicized, but with implications that extend well beyond the precincts of the local church and that involve Rome as well. This is the erosion that is changing the face of American Catholicism before eyes that seem to be unseeing or unbelieving. It is the erosion of orthodoxy, of practice, and of interest in the institutional church. American Catholics are drifting, not away from the church, but certainly a distance from their old moorings.

The reflex impulse has been to lay a veneer of optimism over the most startling of developments. Several years ago, when the drift of young Catholics from regular or traditional religious practice was first becoming pronounced, Philadelphia's Cardinal John Krol advised against being overly alarmed, predicting that these young people would return to the pews once they were settled into marriage and had begun to raise families. Some have. Many more have not. Even professional religious sociologists are not exempt from the instinct to discount the bad news. Father Andrew M. Greeley and a colleague, Dr. William C. McCready of the National Opinion Research Center in Chicago, have been studying Catholic trends in the United States since 1963 and documenting almost unrelieved declines in official Catholic life in the form of school closings, fewer worshipers in the pews, and priests and nuns leaving the active ministry. There has also been a weakening of financial support, a point not invalidated by the fact that revenues may be up in some areas of giving; the significant detail is that the giving base keeps narrowing. But curiously, no matter how dark the picture, there are those—including on occasion Greeley and McCready themselves—who will see in the statistics some bright, positive development. Nothing, it appears, is ever so bad that it isn't partially good, or at least redeemable.

There are fewer Catholic schools—ah, but this is a wonderful opportunity for parents to reassert their role as the primary religious educators of their children.

There is a dramatic decline in vocations to the priesthood—ah, but this is a wonderful opportunity to reinvigorate the concept of the priesthood of the laity and to involve laypersons in ministeries of the church, as permanent deacons, eucharistic ministers, and the like.

There are fewer worshipers—ah, but this is a wonderful opportunity to eliminate the assembly-line aspects of Sunday-morning worship, to reduce the surplus number of Sunday masses, and to return the liturgy to a more solemn state.

There are traces of validity in all such rationalizations, but at what point does one pause and ask if there is not a wholesale delusion at work? The American church may not be a church in deep crisis, but today, it is not exactly a church that is flourishing. The statistics tell the story, and it is not one easy to be optimistic about. The statistics that follow (p. 10) from the *Official Catholic Directory*[6] provide a sobering twenty-one-year comparison between 1965 and 1986.

The totals tell only part of the story. For instance, there are 76,803 fewer sisters now teaching in Catholic schools than the 104,441 recorded at their peak in 1964. This is a decline of 73.5 percent, and viewed only prag-

	1965	1986	Plus/minus
Priests	58,432	57,183	−1,249
Seminarians	48,992	10,440	−38,552
Permanent deacons	0	7,204	+7,204
Nuns/sisters	179,954	113,658	−66,296
Brothers	12,271	7,429	−4,842
Parishes	17,637	19,313	+1,676
Educational institutions	14,296	9,834	−4,462
Students	6,095,846	2,866,123	−3,229,723
Teachers			
Religious	123,653	34,526	−89,127
Laity	75,103	136,157	+61,054
Catholic population	45,640,619	52,654,908	+7,014,289

matically, it is an especially significant drop. Historically, religious sisters have comprised a low-cost, seemingly inexhaustible labor pool for the church—in the United States, for the parochial school system in particular. That situation has been reversed. Today, the 136,157 lay teachers represent 79.7 percent of all teachers in Catholic schools. Though invariably paid less than their counterparts in public education, they nonetheless have suddenly become a major item in strained ecclesiastical budgets. Paradoxically, as expenses, including salaries, skyrocket for these schools, the American church is educating fewer and fewer of its young people, Catholic school enrollments having dropped from a high of more than six million in the mid-1960s to fewer than three million now. Part of that decline can be accounted for in terms of demographics, like the so-called baby-boomers' finishing school and moving into a world where the birth rates are significantly lower than they were when their parents conceived them a generation before. Other factors are also involved in the decline, such as different perceptions about the advantages of public over sectarian education and simple geographics, like the migration to the suburbs of many Catholic families. Catholic schools just didn't exist in many of the suburbs to which Catholics moved, and but for rare exceptions, economics precluded even thought of their construction. Thus, the phenomenon that, as the church was spending more for education, it was educating fewer of its young people— one-third fewer, in fact. Between the years of 1963 and 1974 alone, Catholic schools went from educating 44 percent of Catholic children of primary- and secondary-school age to 29 percent.[7]

However, another even more ominous problem may be signaled in those *Official Catholic Directory* comparison figures, and specifically in that statistic that on the surface would seem to indicate the least change of all: the total number of priests. If one accepts the figures for 1965 and 1986 at face value, there was a decline over those twenty-one years of 1,249 priests—not an insignificant drop by any means but, on the surface, hardly alarming given the respective aggregates for the two years of close to sixty thousand priests. Certainly, the decline in the number of priests would appear to be nowhere near as disquieting as the decline in numbers of sisters and brothers, whose ranks have been virtually decimated.

On the other hand, how does one reconcile the relatively small statistical change for priests with events of the late 1960s and the early 1970s, when priests were departing from the active ministry in what seemed to be wholesale numbers? Andrew Greeley has estimated that, between 1966 and 1970, 8 percent of diocesan priests and 9 percent of religious-order priests—a significant number—resigned from the ministry.[8] Similarly, Richard A. Schoenherr and Annemette Sorensen, prominent analysts of data on the clergy, have estimated that 12.5 to 13.5 percent of all diocesan priests active in 1970 resigned over the next ten years. They placed the actual number at 4,852.[9] Their conclusions were based on the 37,272 diocesan priests reported in the 1970 *Official Catholic Directory*.

But if such studies are accurate, why are not the 1965–1986 comparison statistics for priests more pronounced in their difference? The answer is in the bookkeeping. The totals are misleading, because in 1975, it was decided to include in the clergy totals American missionary priests, that is, those on duty outside the United States. Not hitherto counted in as part of the total of American priests, they were now being listed according to their diocese of origin. Accor. 'ingly, the number of American priests, which stood at 56,712 in 1974, leaped wondrously in a year's time by 2,197—probably not a startling leap as most statistics go, but certainly remarkable in a category where movement upward or downward is normally measured in a few hundred. Nonetheless, the new accounting procedure did have the effect of boosting totals for priests back to less worrisome levels.

But of course, it was all delusion. Most of these missionary priests were members of religious orders and accordingly, in the Catholic administrative scheme of things, beyond diocesan controls. A Boston Jesuit on a teaching assignment for his order in Baghdad or Cairo is of no particular use to a Boston archbishop looking for a body fill a pastorate in Roxbury. The numerical recovery in the category of priests, in a word, was no recovery at all.

Not only is the situation serious with respect to priests, it is near desperate, for the now-inflated totals do not reflect priests who are on sick leave, priests who are absent for higher studies or for other reasons, or priests who have retired because of age, a number that, in composite, averaged around 14 percent of the clergy in the late 1970s and that grows as retirement becomes a more common option for older clergy. Time was when there was no retirement program at all for priests. Ordained a priest forever, a priest served forever, or at least until he dropped. Nowadays, many priests go off at age sixty-five or so to spend their last years on Golden Pond. There are solid institutional reasons to commend this practice, one being that it gives younger priests a leadership chance at an earlier age, while moving pastorates and other ecclesiastical posts into more youthful and presumably more vibrant and energetic hands. On the operational level, however, it means that there are fewer priests to do the work that needs doing.

The implications are very real. In 1965, for instance, a Catholic parish without a resident priest was virtually unheard of, except for remote rural areas or mountain districts, where Catholics were not very numerous anyway. In 1986, however, no fewer than 1,183 of the 19,313 Catholic parishes in the United States had no resident pastor, a 12.5 percent increase over the previous year, and a 20 percent increase over two years before. There just plain are not enough priests to go around. When one factors in the astonishing fall-off in the number of seminarians—38,552 in two decades—it is apparent that the American church is plunging headlong toward a clergy crisis.

The reinstitution of the office of permanent deacon after Vatican Council II has blunted some of the urgency of the situation. Permanent deacons—and there are 7,204 of them now, whereas a few years ago there were none—can assume many of the time-consuming duties of the priest, and they can perform minor ministries historically reserved for priests. But their role is still limited. A permanent deacon may witness weddings, perform baptisms, counsel, and discharge certain other ministerial tasks, but he is precluded from exercising the most solemn sacramental functions of a priest. Most notably, he cannot celebrate Mass, and the Mass is the very center of the sacramental life of the Catholic church. For Catholics, the Mass is the reenactment of the Last Supper, the celebration of Catholic community, the source of the Eucharist, "the summit toward which the activity of the church is directed...the fountain from which all her power flows."[10] To be able to celebrate

Mass, in the Catholic understanding of things, is to be able to participate in the extension of the priestly office of Jesus Christ. A duly ordained priest may celebrate Mass; a permanent deacon may not. A permanent deacon is as impotent in this respect as the ordinary layperson in the pews. This subject will be discussed in other contexts in the book, but it is broached here to underscore how much the church is imperiled ministerially, and to suggest further that the problems of the past decade or two, real as they are, could pale alongside those that will accompany a truly severe clergy shortage.

Still, difficult as the problems of numbers are, they admit of resolution. A church short of priests, for instance, can promote vocations in new and imaginative ways and can expect a measure of return. Several years ago, the archdiocese of New York turned to Madison Avenue with $100,000 for an advertising campaign to recruit priests. If the campaign did not result in a rush on Dunwoodie, the archdiocesan seminary in Yonkers, it at least brought Catholic focus in a public way to a problem that church leaders regard as the people's as much as their own. For Catholic parents are expected to encourage vocations among their offspring, or at least not to place roadblocks in the way of one. The same expectation exists with respect to other Catholics in a position to influence those who might be receptive to the idea of a life in religion.

The New York archdiocese's was one approach. More daring was that of the Trinitarian Fathers. They once advertised for vocations in *Playboy* magazine and claimed to receive back seven hundred bona-fide in-

quiries. Very probably, they did, though their experiment did not exactly become practice in the field of
vocations' recruitment. The Missionary Oblates of Mary
Immaculate tried another tack. Recently, they used ac-
tor Don Novello, Father Guido Sarducci of ''Saturday
Night Live,'' in a print-media advertisement that
promised would-be priests first crack at parish rummage
sales, long mornings in bed, meals on the house in Italian restaurants, and a chance to help ''your fellow man.''
The pitch was a combination of spoof and seriousness.
Now, people may legitimately debate approaches such
as these. Was the medium wrong (because inappropri-
ate) for the Trinitarians? Was the message wrong (because overly frivolous) for the Oblates of Mary
Immaculate? But those questions stray into another issue. The point is that one way or another, new priests
can be recruited.

By the same token, a church short of funds can
harden the sell and look for income to rise. It has always
been this way, and no doubt will continue to be so, new
tax laws governing charitable donations notwithstanding. Religion dwarfs all other philanthropic fields as the
beneficiary of individual and corporate generosity. Neither injudicious use of these funds nor scandal—hardly
an exclusively Catholic problem, by the way—blunts
more than momentarily the American instinct to give to
religion.

By the same token, again, a church short of teaching sisters for its schools can go out into the marketplace
and hire lay teachers, as, indeed, the American church
has been increasingly forced to do in recent years. It is

a great expense, to be sure, but educational quality doesn't necessarily suffer as a consequence. Now, as for many years in the past, parochial-school students more than hold their own in national evaluation ratings.

All of which is to say that shortages of priests, sisters, brothers, schools, and funds are, of course, difficult problems, but by and large, they are manageable one way or another. More pertinent, there are other problems alongside which those of numbers and resources markedly diminish in significance. These are the problems of orthodoxy and of authority. A church short of personnel or of funds can always cope. It may not know when the next young recruit will knock at the door or how next month's heating bill will be paid, but as long as its believing community remains cohesive and in agreement on the articles of faith, it knows that its identity is intact, that the church that was still is, and will continue to be, world without end, as the Lord promised. For a church whose cornerstone is orthodoxy, this is an absolutely vital condition. It is insurance that the momentum of two thousand years has not been lost—indeed, is being carried forward; it is the consolation that, however bad the times, its believing community can be precisely defined. Nothing institutionally is more important in Catholicism than being able to define oneself in, by, and of the church's membership.

But what if the Catholic believing community begins to disintegrate? It has in the past, of course. Vast areas of middle and eastern Europe peeled off around the turn of the first millennium, when believing communities in the eastern division of the old Roman Empire split from the Church of Rome and formed what to this day is known as the Eastern Orthodox Church. Then again, in the sixteenth century, the Protestant Reformation and King Henry VIII's English "reformation" claimed whole nations of Catholics, as loyalties shifted and theologies were reshaped. And forever, there have been "defections" (if the word may still be used in an ecumenical age) of individuals—some for reasons as weighty as genuine loss of belief, some as petty as a minor hurt. The large difference between the past and the present, however, is that very many Catholics in disagreement or rebellion against tenets of the church no longer feel the compulsion to leave and take their belief elsewhere. They stay. They adjust, peacefully or otherwise. And they worship according to the dictates of their individual consciences. For them, *authority* is a nine-letter noun, not an ecclesiastical prerogative belonging to the leadership and forever to be heeded.

For instance, it was not many years ago that, when a Catholic married irregularly according to church law— say, in another church or before a civil official—that person often disappeared from the Catholic scene or quietly moved to the perimeter of the church. It was understood of the person and was pretty much accepted that an irregular marriage set the person apart from the rest of Catholics. That same situation does not exist today. Catholic divorce rates are not appreciably different from those for the rest of Americans: 445 divorces for every 1,000 new marriages, with the rate climbing year by year. Projected to the Catholic community, this means that there are more than five million American Catholics who are divorced or who are in so-called invalid marital unions. They are welcome in church, of course, but officially they are not supposed to be at the communion rail. Many are there anyway, and in good conscience.

There is also contraception. If 80 percent of American Catholic women of childbearing age and their spouses are indeed practicing artificial birth control, as the survey polls say, it appears not to have discouraged the full participation of those who attend liturgical worship, at least judging from communion lines. If some in the church hold artificial birth control to be a serious or grave sin barring the efficacious reception of communion, that precept seems not to trouble young Catholic women and men. Those still worshiping on whatever basis are at the communion rail along with the rest of the congregation. (Since the easing of fasting regulations, communion attracts virtually the entire congregation at Catholic masses.) Admittedly, one could be in the presence of the observant 20 percent of Catholic women of childbearing age who do not practice birth control, or who use only such natural birth control methods (e.g., rhythm) as the church approves. Still, the polls are not wrong. If lower Catholic birth rates do not confirm the widespread use of contraception, there is other documentation, including, in a more forthright, less inhibited age, the self-testimony of Catholics themselves.

Catholic couples nowadays commonly discuss their family-planning practices as unabashedly almost as they discuss, say, their toothpastes. Older Catholics with children of childbearing age are told when to expect to become grandparents: a year from now, two years, five years, never. Similarly, when Catholic writers sit down at their typewriters or word processors and reflect on the intimacies of their lives as Catholics, there is little hesitancy about acknowledging the use of contraceptives. It happens even in so decorous a medium as the daily newspaper that arrives at the front door, including the *New York Times*. The *Times* Living Section columnist Anna Quindlen not long ago confessed in the very second paragraph of a warm and moving appreciation of her Catholicism that ''Since the issue became material to me, I have not followed the church's teaching on birth control.''[11] It's a familiar acknowledgment. Even if 80 percent overstates the number of Catholics who practice artificial birth control, it can't overstate the number by much. A huge percentage of American Catholics have settled the issue of birth control on the basis of their individual consciences, as opposed to the official teaching of their church. Furthermore, birth control is just one issue to be so settled. Divorce and remarriage, as mentioned, are another. There are others, including abortion itself, where for a smaller percentage of Catholics conscience and personal moral preference have superseded the letter of church law. By the same token, it is likely that Catholics will make up their own minds on those issues of human procreation and the biomedical technologies of which the Vatican, according to its instruction of 20 May 1987 is so thoroughly disapproving, such as most forms of embryo transfer and artificial fertilization.

This is a startling new development within Catholicism, and the paradox—indeed, the supreme paradox—is that the phenomenon has roots of an ecclesiastical kind, for if the phenomenon can be traced to any rationalizing source, it is Vatican Council II and specifically that document which one German prelate, Bishop Walter Kampe, identified as the "American contribution to the Council."[12] This is the document *Dignitatis humanae*, the Declaration on Religious Freedom, which embodied the theological genius of the native New York City Jesuit, Father John Courtney Murray. *Dignitatis humanae* enunciated the ethical doctrine of religious freedom as a human right, personal and collective, and in so doing, it caught the church up with much of the modern world. But at the same time, the document opened something of a Pandora's box so far as the internal life of the church is concerned because, as the secular society itself demonstrates, a certain indivisibility invariably attaches to the notion of freedom. It can't be subdivided or fractioned.

That some Catholics would seize on the Declaration on Religious Freedom to justify departures from official teaching and established norms was recognized as a possibility by opponents of the declaration, and they stressed that likelihood in their unsuccessful fight against the document's adoption by the fathers of Vatican II. Murray recognized the likelihood, too, but regarded it as a necessary and not altogether negative risk in clearing up a long-standing ambiguity between the ancient church and the modern world, if not also between the church and its own people. If nothing more, Murray felt that the declaration would eliminate the double standard, which translated to "freedom for the church when Catholics are a minority, privilege for the church and intolerance for others when Catholics are a majority."[13]

But beyond the questions of church and state—the church and the civil polity—loomed the implications of the document for the church internally. Murray saw them with special clarity. "The conciliar affirmation of the principle of freedom was narrowly limited—in the text," Murray wrote immediately after the council. "But the text itself was flung into a pool whose shores are wide as the universal church. The ripples will run far." How far? "Inevitably, a second great argument will be set afoot—now on the theological meaning of Christian freedom. The children of God, who receive this freedom as a gift from their Father through Christ in the Holy Spirit, assert it *within the church* as well as within the world, always for the sake of the world and the church."[14]

The emphasis is added to "within the church" to dramatize Murray's perceptiveness. He sensed what was going to happen. Unfortunately, he was not around to help resolve the questions that would be spawned, dying in 1967 of a heart attack at the premature age of sixty-three, while a passenger in a taxicab. The assertion of Christian freedom was just beginning within the Catholic church, but Father John Courtney Murray would not be around to assist the church and its people through a future he saw quite clearly. Murray had not attempted to forecast the precise issues of Christian freedom that would engage the church, but they turned out to be roughly what he had predicted they would be: "the dignity of the Christian, the foundations of Christian freedom, its object or content, its limits and their criterion, the measure of its responsible use, its relation to the legitimate reaches of authority and to the saving counsels of prudence, the perils that lurk in it, and the forms of corruption to which it is prone."[15]

As for the issues themselves, they would take form in numerous ways and in numerous moral areas, ranging from noisy public dissent to *Humanae vitae*, Pope Paul VI's encyclical of 1968 that reaffirmed the church's traditional opposition to artificial birth control, to quiet departures from church teaching on everything from regular attendance at mass to, once again, that matter currently of ultimate moral concern to the church, abortion. With respect to the latter, a *New York Times*/CBS News Poll in 1985 found 36 percent of American Catholics expressing support for the legal status of abortion in the country and 55 percent favoring abortion in cases of rape and incest, or if the procedure were necessary to save a woman's life. By contrast, only 15 percent of the Catholics sampled subscribed to the church's position that abortion was wrong in all instances.[16]

But the most dramatic departure from tradition, certainly in terms of numbers, has occurred in the area of worship, specifically in the fall-off of American Catholics' attendance at weekly mass. Admittedly, church attendance is not a particularly useful yardstick for measuring the piety or the religious sincerity of a people. Some of society's biggest hypocrites can be found in the front pews of almost any church. On the other hand, Catholics are expected to attend mass on Sunday, or what is known as a mass "of anticipation" on Saturday evening. If not precisely a commandment of God (there are many other ways of keeping holy the Sabbath day, as directed

by the third of the Ten Commandments), it is a law of
the church—the very first, in fact, of the six commandments of the church learned by American Catholics. And
American Catholics, for their part, have historically been
remarkable churchgoers. By the standards of other countries with large Catholic populations, they are still
remarkable. The Brazilian Catholic church, for instance,
has some 105 million members in a national population
of some 130 million, the largest Catholic population of
any country in the world, but only 12 percent of them
attend Sunday mass.[17] Of France's 54.8 million people,
80 percent profess Catholicism as their religion, but only
10 percent are regular weekly worshipers at mass.[18] In
the United States, 51 percent of the country's 52 million
Catholics attended mass weekly in 1984.[19]

The U.S. statistics are imposing, even awesome by
comparison to those of other countries. Still, though the
same obligation to attend weekly mass obtains now as
then, the percentage of those doing so is not nearly large
as it was, say, a generation ago. In 1958, an estimated
74 percent of American Catholics could be found in the
pews of a Sunday morning. (There was no such thing
then as a mass of anticipation on Saturdays.) The drop
from 74 percent to 51 percent in twenty-six years' time
is precipitous, the more so because the decline was not
gradual but began suddenly and dramatically only about
fifteen years ago. And though 51 percent may be a large
figure, it is not exactly one to glory in or to be compla-
cent about, for it is an average figure. In some places,
the drop in church attendance has been so sharp as to
be nearly calamitous. A recent survey in the diocese of

Brooklyn, for example, estimated that only about 28 percent of those who call themselves Catholics attend mass regularly[20]—a figure that is not markedly inconsistent with a finding of my own. I recently asked three Catholic pastors to estimate what percentage of their parishioners were regulars at weekly worship. Two said 25 percent; one said 40 percent.

In contrast to the Catholic statistics, Protestant church attendance eased between 1958 and 1985 from 44 percent to 39 percent, and weekly synagogue attendance remained more-or-less steady, standing at 22 percent in 1985, with 58 percent of American Jews claiming membership in a synagogue.[21]

Excusing oneself from attendance at Sunday mass may not be a remarkable expression of religious freedom on the part of Catholics; indeed, it is a far less consequential exercise of conscience and personal decision making than others current in the Catholic community, notably in areas of sexual morality. But the significance of the development is not to be discounted too much on that account, for Sunday mass long enjoyed a place of enormous respect and importance in American Catholic life, far more than was to be found in recent times in other Catholic countries, excepting perhaps Ireland. A bishop friend of mine used to tell of a prominent Catholic layman, an absolute rogue, who would cheat all weekend on his wife, but who would hop off the train in the middle of a prairie in order to fulfill a Sunday mass obligation. Maybe my friend exaggerated a bit, but the story dramatizes the centrality of the mass obligation in the mind-set of American Catholics in days of yore. The

perceived importance of the mass obligation may have
been totally out of proportion to what really matters in
religion, what counts in belief, but that's beside the
point. The thing is that it existed, and respect for the obligation came to symbolize the very vitality of the American church. That a change has occurred in the perception
of that obligation speaks worlds about the new pattern
of self-liberation within the institutional church, accompanied by an assertion of personal responsibility and self-
control over conscience.

The factors contributing to this change are conceivably as many as the individuals involved, and not all of
them are religious factors by any means. American
Catholics do not exist, after all, in some kind of social
vacuum. They are not impervious to the forces of the
wider society, and if self-expression enjoys a preeminence in that society over dictated behavioral modes,
then something of this phenomenon is going to carry
over to Catholics and their religious habits as believers
and worshipers. But whatever the sum of the factors,
there remains the influence of Vatican II's Declaration on
Religious Freedom. That influence is real, however little it may be credited the further one gets from the declaration's adoption over two decades ago, or for that
matter, however little the declaration's influence may be
consciously realized as the assertions of religious freedom and conscience pass in the postconciliar church
from the isolated instance to the commonplace. Obviously, the church is caught in something of a bind in all
of this, for the church could not exalt the notion of
responsible freedom and proclaim further that, as far as

religious freedom is concerned, everyone should be "immune from coercion on the part of individuals or of social groups and of any human power,"[22] then turn around and tell Catholics that none of this pertains to them in their intramural situation. It had to be expected that Catholics would apply some of those notions to their own religious lives.

Stated another way, the church could not proclaim supremacy of conscience for people in the world at large and, at the same time, expect to keep the consciences of Catholics narrowly bound to the dictates of ecclesiastical authority and the letter of rule and regulation. It could not logically expect to, at least—and perhaps, least of all—in a country like the United States, where freedom of conscience is enshrined as an inalienable right and where some overspilling of the concept could be looked for from the secular to the religious.

In sum, however much ecclesiastical authorities might be anxious to preserve the old order with its obedient reflexes, they remain at a disadvantage. Vatican II's Declaration on Religious Freedom has provided not only a rationale, but also, for many, a justification, for the assertion of freedoms within the church. The declaration may not be explicitly invoked or, once again, consciously felt, but it doesn't have to be. Its influence is now pervasive.

Further, there is little that the church's leadership can do about changing this situation. The declaration is on the books. It has been pontifically promulgated. It can be reviewed and clarified. Theoretically, it could be superseded, I suppose, by another council or by a pope invoking the infallibility of office. But that is more easily said than done, and until then, there can be no substantive retreat from its contents. There cannot be from any conciliar document. That was underscored at 1985's Extraordinary Synod of Bishops in Rome. If a purpose of that synod was to roll back some of the progressive reforms of Vatican II, as not a few believed it was, then the effort was fruitless. For there was no going back. Pope John Paul II, as the synod's presiding officer, could only warn against ''any false interpretations'' of the council's documents. The documents themselves remained in place, including that declaration which ennobles the individual conscience. There should be no surprise about this. A council is the mind of the church in action, the *sensus ecclesiae* taking shape and form through prayer, discussion, and deliberation. Its dogmatic definitions and authoritative decrees, once officially promulgated, are binding on the church universal, including the church's leadership and the pope himself. As history cannot be rewritten, neither can a council—especially not by a synod, which is a deliberative body of a lesser sort, and not even by a pope, however strong the temptation might be for him.

Yet, if order and conformity are what a church wants, it can run a tighter ship, and a tighter ship is obviously what John Paul II is running these days. The Dutch church discovered this when John Paul II convoked a special synod of the Dutch bishops in Rome in 1980 and then, as the opportunities presented themselves, began moving into Dutch bishoprics confirmed conservatives for the purpose of returning the church there to a stricter enforcement of ecclesiastical discipline in matters of the liturgy, the sacraments, the priestly life, and religious vows. The Brazilian church's turn came when pressures built on it from Rome over the issue of liberation theology, a concept originating in Latin America that emphasizes commitment to the poor, while sometimes borrowing ideas from Marxism. In 1985, one of Brazil's most prominent theologians, Franciscan Father Leonardo Boff, was silenced, being summarily ordered by Rome to maintain ''a period of respectful silence'' on this and other matters of potential controversy. The order was kept in effect for eleven months, being lifted in 1986 after twenty-one senior Brazilian bishops traveled to Rome for meetings with John Paul II on matters of politics and church structure, during the course of which the pope admonished them not to try to ''substitute for politicans.''[23] The American church—vastly less liberal than the Dutch church and considerably less outspoken vis-à-vis Rome than the Brazilian church (a group of Brazilian bishops publicly protested Boff's disciplining as an action contrary to ''Christian liberty and charity'')—is feeling pressures akin to those of the churches in the Netherlands and Brazil; what was initially billed as a simple exercise of prerogatives over time has become a major assertion of Rome's authority and a concomitant suppression of elements of the American church.

The names of Archbishop Raymond G. Hunthausen of Seattle and Father Charles E. Curran of the Catholic University of American have dominated the news involving Rome and the American church in the past two years. On reflection, however, it is apparent that a closer watch and a firmer Roman hand on the American church began back in 1980, when from the desk of John Paul II, down through the Jesuit chain of command, came a directive ordering Jesuit Father Robert Drinan not to seek a sixth two-year term as the representative to Congress from Massachusetts' Fourth Congressional District. To some, the directive seemed an imperious intrusion on Rome's part into the American political process, a charge that church spokesmen countered, saying the action had been taken within ecclesiastical prerogatives and according to the letter of canon law (specifically Canon 139, paragraph 4, of the code then on the books), which could be construed as limiting priestly election to political office. There was a second priest involved in the 1980 controversy, a Norbertine priest in Wisconsin who had served in Congress, had lost his seat, and was seeking to regain it. But it was clear that it was Drinan whom the Vatican was primarily after and, as the preoccupations of the Vatican with questions of sexual morality would subsequently tend to confirm, not so much for Drinan's involvement as a priest in electoral politics, but for his political positions on the public funding of abortion. Though maintaining that he was personally opposed to abortion, Drinan had voted consistently for public funding of abortion; he drew a line in the process between his conscience as a Catholic and what he saw as his responsibility as a legislator concerned with everyone's human and civil rights, rather than the exclusive moral preferences of the Catholic church. That distinction between conscience and one's reading of his public responsibility as an elected official was not acceptable in Rome then. It is not now. Curiously enough, at the time, there were many priests in Latin America as fully involved in politics there as Drinan was in the United States. Their turn would come later, notably in Nicaragua in the instances of priests' holding high ministerial posts in the Sandinista government. But it was Drinan whom Rome would have first, undoubtedly because the abortion issue was involved.

What made the Drinan case especially startling at the time was that it followed many years of tension-free coexistence between the church of Rome and the church in the United States, an essentially trouble-free relationship that had weathered even the extraordinary public dissent from *Humanae vitae* by huge numbers of American Catholics, most notably in the Archdiocese of Washington, D.C., and on the campus of Catholic University, where opposition to the birth-control encyclical coalesced in and around the person of Father Charles Curran of the university's theology department. The Vatican would one day even the score with Curran, but that would be two papacies and several years later.

In looking back to *Humanae vitae* and its immediate aftermath in the United States, it is remarkable how much dissent from the encyclical remained an American issue. Unquestionably, Rome was shocked and scandalized by events in the United States. Public demonstrations against a papal encyclical and explicit repudiation of its teaching in confessionals and classrooms, from lecture platforms, and in the media were not the sorts of thing expected by Rome of American Catholics in any

historical context. Yet it happened, and pained as Pope
Paul VI was, and angry as the Roman Curia had to be,
no thunderbolts issued from the papal apartments, nor
fiats from the Curia. To be sure, dissent from *Humanae
vitae* was not peculiar to the United States. It existed
worldwide, to such a point, in fact, that national hierarchies were eventually invited to express their loyalty
to the pope on the issue. Nonetheless, dissent against
the encyclical was nowhere more intense than in the
United States. That Rome left it to the American bishops
to settle the unrest themselves is testimony to the restraint and the trust, if not also the wisdom, of Paul VI.
The same restraint, to say no more, could not be expected today, as was made abundantly clear by the
resurrection of grievances against Curran in 1985 through
the Vatican's Congregation for the Doctrine of the Faith
under Cardinal Joseph Ratzinger.

Of course, there is a different pontificate in place
now, and reigning popes largely set the ideological tones
of the curias. Ratzinger is a creature of John Paul II, but
he is hardly unique. His counterparts exist throughout
the whole of John Paul II's Curia. Accordingly, it is not
just Charles Curran of the Catholic University faculty
who has been called on the carpet of responsibility. He
has considerable company.

Consider, for example, the four male religious and
the twenty-four female religious who, in 1985, were
called to accountability by Cardinal Jean Jerome Hamer
of the Congregation for Religious and Secular Institutes
for lending their names to a paid advertisement in the
New York Times that declared that Catholics held a

"diversity of opinions" on abortion and asked for open discussion of the issue.[24] The male religious figures, two priests and two brothers, quickly issued clarifications that the Vatican found acceptable. The nuns, less intimidated by the pressures exerted on them, held back, even at the risk of expulsion from their religious orders if they did not recant. Eventually, all but two did accommodate the Vatican demand, but the episode has left strains of embitterment—as has the case of Archbishop Hunthausen, recent compromises notwithstanding.

The Hunthausen case is particularly interesting and perhaps especially significant because it dramatizes how pervasive Rome's close new watch is: not even a person extremely highly placed in the hierarchy is exempt from its overview.

Archbishop Hunthausen came under official review in 1983 when, in response to allegations by "reactionary elements" within the archdiocese,[25] the Vatican dispatched an apostolic visitor—in ecclesiastical parlance, a kind of modern inquisitor, and in American political parlance, a special investigator—to examine his ministry. Hunthausen had come under criticism by conservatives for his opposition to nuclear weapons and for his decision in 1982 to begin withholding 50 percent of his income tax in protest against U.S. arms policies. But the "reactionary elements" of his ecclesiastical jurisdiction had a whole second agenda of complaints based on what they claimed were Hunthausen's policies relating to sexual morality and other concerns of an ecclesiastical kind. The investigation proceeded under Archbishop James A. Hickey of Washington, D.C., Rome's apostolic visitor,

and the findings were forwarded to Rome. Rome subsequently produced a report that actually commended
many areas of Hunthausen's leadership, but that also admonished him to exercise "greater vigilance in uphold-
ing the church's teaching, especially with regard to
contraceptive sterilization and homosexuality."[26]

The story could have ended there, but of course it
didn't. The admonishing of Hunthausen was made public 29 November 1985 by the papal pronuncio to the
United States, Archbishop Pio Laghi. Six days later, on
3 December 1985, the Vatican announced the assignment
of an auxiliary bishop to Hunthausen, the Reverend
Donald W. Wuerl, a priest of the diocese of Pittsburgh.
Wuerl was a stranger to Seattle, but not to the pope making the appointment, John Paul II. They were acquaintances from Wuerl's days in Rome as secretary to the late
Cardinal John Wright, a one-time bishop of Pittsburgh
who became head of the Vatican's Congregation for the
Clergy. John Paul II was a regular at Wright's apartment
when, as Karol Wojtyla, the cardinal-archbishop of
Krakow in Poland, he would come to Rome for synods
and other meetings. He knew and respected Wuerl and
obviously handpicked Wuerl for the auxiliary's post in
Seattle. Wuerl disputed, however, that he was going to
Seattle as a kind of watchdog, maintaining that he would
be keeping his eyes on the road map of the archdiocese,
not the archbishop.[27] Not everyone was so sure, and it
was not long before their skepticism was confirmed.
Within nine months of Wuerl's going to Seattle, it was
announced that Archbishop Hunthausen had been
stripped of decision-making power in five areas of

responsibility traditionally belonging to the head of a diocese: the diocesan tribunal, which deals with annulments; liturgy and worship; moral issues relating to health-care institutions and ministry to homosexuals; clergy formation, seminaries, and instruction for priests; and supervision of former priests or priests departing the active ministry.[28] Authority in all those areas was delegated to Wuerl, and so was set the stage for an issue that eventually engaged the entire American hierarchy at its 1986 annual meeting. In May 1987, Rome reversed itself on many of its positions, but in the meantime Seattle Catholics had raised a question that many Catholics across the country had begun to ask themselves in contexts other than the Hunthausen affair alone: "What kind of church are we becoming?"[29]

Much else was happening between the Drinan and the Hunthausen cases besides the incidents involving Curran and the religious who signed the abortion ad in the *New York Times*. In December 1982, a Sister of Mercy, Agnes Mary Mansour, was named director of the state of Michigan's Department of Social Services. At the time, Detroit's Archbishop Edmund Szoka indicated that he saw "no problem" in the appointment and after Mansour's acceptance of the post, made affirmative comments in the local media on the subject.[30] What followed, however, was a mail "blitz" and an advertising campaign by antiabortion groups directed at the archbishop and the Vatican with the object of "getting" Mansour. (One ad urged people to write to the pope to express their opinions.) At issue was the department's administration of a state-funded abortion program. Soon Szoka was reversing himself, and finally, on 23 February 1983 he called on Mansour to resign her post. Mansour refused, declaring that though personally opposed to abortion, she could tolerate government funding of abortion out of consideration for American pluralism. It was a rationale not essentially different from Drinan's, but like Drinan's, it was unacceptable. The Vatican hurried Auxiliary Bishop Anthony J. Bevilacqua of Brooklyn to Detroit as its troubleshooter. Mansour kept her job, but she was forced to resign as a nun. Bevilacqua returned to Brooklyn and was soon promoted to head the diocese of Pittsburgh.

But the Vatican's watch hasn't been just on specific individuals. The mechanics of the American church have also come in for examination, as was attested to by Rome's naming of a special commission to look into religious orders and religious formation in the United States, with special attention being paid to the large losses in membership. The examination would extend from one end of the country to the other and would take commission members into seminaries and houses of formation—centers for spiritual renewal and theological study with links to larger divinity schools and institutes, usually Catholic, although not exclusively so. The commission was named in June 1983, and a preliminary report on the thirty-eight postcollege seminaries was made in 1986, which said that a majority offered balanced and faithful programs, but that some of them showed confusion about authoritative church teachings in moral theology. The work of the commission is yet to be completed, and the end result could be a strong affirmation of the manner in which religious men and women are taught and trained in the United States. But a common fear, one not allayed by elements of the interim report, is that the commission's report will eventually be used to reverse many innovations born of the postconciliar period.

We could go on, as we will later in the book, to cite other cases of disciplining and suppression. But these are enough for now. The conclusion is inescapable that a crackdown is in effect on the American church. Of note—indeed, the salient detail, at least through the early years of this crackdown—is that the instances of disciplining and suppression originated virtually without exception outside the American hierarchy and from Rome itself. Inevitably, the point of origin would begin to change to one degree or another as Rome moved a different type of bishop to the leadership of American dioceses, and also as Rome's predispositions and its will began to impress themselves on some bishops already in place. But, once again, it was not the American bishops who initiated the crackdown. It was Rome—indeed, the Rome of John Paul II—a circumstance that, given the way the church is run, would place John Paul II at the center of what has happened and continues to happen in the reordering of the American church. Unquestionably, he is concerned about the directions of the American church, and he has made a determination to do something about them. There is more than mere surmise about this. The crackdown became a subject of large media focus in 1986, but as far back as 1983, reports were circulating that the church in the United States was coming under intense Roman scrutiny. At the time, Milwaukee's Archbishop Rembert Weakland conceded after a trip to Rome that there was "tension between Rome and the United States right now." "I'm sure the Pope sees the American church as extremely vital," Weakland added, "but also like a plant that hasn't sunk its roots very deep. He believes it needs a lot of pruning."[31] Another bishop, speaking anonymously—and one wonders why, considering the innocence of the comment—remarked, "What bothers us most is the unspoken implication that we are somehow disloyal to the Pope. And that is simply not true."[32]

No one in Rome has leveled charges of disloyalty against the American bishops, least of all Pope John Paul II. However, it does seem certain in the light of the episcopal appointments of recent years—to Seattle, obviously; to Pittsburgh, very likely; and to other archdioceses and dioceses, New York, Boston, and Portland, Oregon, among them—that John Paul II prefers a more traditionalist type of bishop, one who is firmer and more rigorously orthodox than many of those who were raised up in the decade past.

That a different type of bishop had come to occupy many American archdioceses and dioceses in the several years before the ascendancy of John Paul II is impossible to dispute. He was not the archetypical Chancery bureaucrat, nor the one-time bishop's secretary, a type that once achieved the episcopacy with astonishing regularity, nor the former diocesan secretary for education, a favorite choice when the priorities of the American church were heavily weighted on the side of parochial schools.

Rather, he was a pastoral type, a person of broad social orientation, one whose young priesthood had been shaped by Vatican Council II, and who had won his miter when the enthusiasms of Vatican II were still strong in the American church, and who had incorporated into his ministry and witness specific concerns of the council, notably those addressed in *Gaudium et spes*, the Pastoral Consititution on the Church in the Modern World. This man had not voted at the council, of course, not yet having been a bishop, but better than many of those who did the actual voting, he had assimilated the council's teachings. One of the paradoxes of the council, it will be recalled, is that very many of the American bishops who voted for reform at the council were slow—foot draggers, as it were—when it came to implementing conciliar reforms in their home dioceses. Not so their successors, as with deaths and retirements the younger men began to occupy bishoprics.

That this new type of bishop made an immediate difference is indisputable. The American bishops of the council could boldly condemn the arms race in a conciliar document and call for the complete outlawing of war by international consent,[33] but it was not until the very last phase of the war in Vietnam that they could bring themselves as a body to a concrete condemnation of the fighting there. Yet, just a few short years after those long years of vacillation, the American bishops, thanks to the infusion of new members into the hierarchy, were grappling with a pastoral letter on nuclear weapons and world peace so revolutionary that the White House, fearful of what it perceived as the letter's pacifist options, would hurry a representative to Rome, urging the application of restraints on the bishops. The letter got written, but not before being placed under Vatican oversight, a precaution not taken by Rome in the instance of peace statements being issued around the same time by other national hierarchies.

The American bishops issued their arms pastoral, 45,000 words long, in 1983 under the title "The Challenge of Peace: God's Promise and Our Response," and then turned their collective attention to an examination of the American economic system. Hitherto, American bishops had lived quite comfortably with the American economic system, but not the new bishops of the 1980s. They found poverty and unemployment levels in the United States morally unacceptable, and they wondered about the equity of the nation's trade policies when the United States could be so rich and those with whom they were trading, notably in the Third World, could be so desperately poor. The economics pastoral, at 54,000 words even longer than the nuclear-arms pastoral, was issued in 1986 under the title "Economic Justice for All: Catholic Social Teaching and the U.S. Economy." Economics being less dynamic an issue than nuclear weapons, the economics pastoral did not generate as much attention nor elicit the same kind of public response as the earlier arms pastoral. The economics pastoral was also the victim of unfortunate but unavoidable timing. The final debate, ratification, and release of the pastoral coincided with the meeting of the hierarchy following soon after Rome's disciplining of Archbishop Hunthausen. The Hunthausen issue so dominated the meeting that the pastoral was handled almost as an afterthought. Nonetheless, the economics pastoral further demonstrated the scope and the solid practical dimension of the social concerns of this newly constituted hierarchy.

Coincidentally, many of these bishops of strong social orientation and maybe also greater open-mindedness had been raised up during the tenure of Archbishop Jean Jadot as apostolic delegate in the United States, 1973–1980. With the reestablishment of formal diplomatic relations between the Vatican and the United States, the office of apostolic delegate has been upgraded and the title of the delegate changed to pronuncio. But as far as function and influence are concerned, not a whole lot is different. Now, as before, the man holding the post as the pope's top representative in the country is the conduit through which, in the normal course of events, nominations to the episcopacy routinely pass. A pope may name anyone he wishes to any archdiocese or diocese anywhere in the world, but unquestionably, an apostolic delegate, or in the instance of the United States a pronuncio, is in a position to give shape to a national hierarchy through the names that are forwarded to Rome for confirmation there. In the course of his seven years' tenure in the United States, Archbishop Jadot unquestionably gave a strongly pastoral, progressive shape to the American hierarchy. The present American hierarchy retains the stamp of Jadot to a marked degree, as votes at the hierarchy's annual fall meeting as recently as 1986 have tended to confirm. At that meeting, centrist candidates for U.S. Catholic Conference positions, including the presidency itself, won easily and consistently over men who were post-Jadot appointees to the hierarchy. But the situation is changing with each new appointment to the hierarchy. The so-called Jadot bishops might control the votes in the U.S. Catholic Conference, but it is only for the time being. The ascendancy belongs to the "post-Jadot bishops."

Jadot, incidentally, was recalled to Rome in 1980 by Pope John Paul II and was placed in charge of the Vatican's Secretariat for Non-Christians—not the most important nor most prestigious of Curia departments, but not an unimportant one either in an age of heightened ecumenical sensitivities. The secretariat's head is ordinarily a cardinal. Jadot's predecessor was Sergio Pignedoli, a cardinal; the present head of the office is Francis Arinze, a cardinal. In any instance, as the grip of John Paul II firmed over the church and his concern about the American church quickened, Jadot is reliably reported to have been called in for consultation about developments in the American church and the bishops who lead it. He is said to have offered an assessment that departed from the prevailing Roman mind-set, whereupon he was promoted out of the Vatican and back to his native Belgium. When elevations to the cardinalate were last announced in 1985, Jadot's name was nowhere to be found. Arinze's was.

2

THE KNOWN AMERICAN QUANTITY

The Bishops

IN CONTRAST TO recent years—and, indeed, the present—one may find surprising how independent the American church once was and how forthright and self-possessed its leaders were when it came to dealing with Rome. As an example, when the growth of the American church in the eighteenth century dictated the establishment of an American diocese with its own resident bishop—a conclusion cautiously arrived at because of suspicion in many American quarters about Catholic political and evangelical objectives (Was this the vanguard of the Vatican?)—the priests of the American church asked that they, not Rome, choose the setting of the diocese and the man to head it. Neither was a *pro forma* request, given Rome's historic and zealously guarded prerogatives. Nonetheless, Rome acceded. The choices were Baltimore as the seat of the first American diocese, and Father John Carroll as the first American bishop. Pope Pius VI (1775–1799) ratified the choices in the brief *Ex hac apostolicae* of 6 November 1789 and the American Catholic Church was now a formal ecclesiastical entity.

Initially, the church's great growth was long the eastern seaboard, but the church moved rapidly inland with its immigrant members, and soon, in the burgeoning cities of the Midwest and across to California, new dioceses were being established and new bishops enthroned.

One tends to think of those early American bishops as rigid types out of an old seminary mold, formed as Rome would have them formed in the manner of the Old World, and responsive in turn to Rome. To be sure, these bishops were men of their day, but they were not exactly the conditioned, programmed prelates one might expect them to have been. They dramatized that fact when Rome moved, in the latter nineteenth century, to establish an official papal presence in the United States through the establishment of a tribunal or apostolic delegation in the country. The head of the mission would be the pope's personal representative. If the office were that of apostolic delegation—as fate decreed it would be—the prelate's title would be that of apostolic delegate.

Many in the American hierarchy strenuously opposed the whole idea.

Rome's objective was to bring the American church and its oversight into conformity with practice elsewhere, most notably in Europe. It believed that a delegate's office would unite the American hierarchy by helping to end disputes between the bishops; it believed, too, that a delegate's office would solidify American Catholic loyalty to Rome and the Holy Father. Some bishops, on the other hand, saw Rome's move as vitiating such autonomy as the American church enjoyed, and they resisted mightily. Others, perhaps seeing the handwriting on the wall—in other words, sensing that the appointment of an apostolic delegate was inevitable—argued that the American church should be represented by one of its own. It seemed a reasonable suggestion, but Rome rejected it out of hand on the grounds that an American prelate would not be in a position to deal impartially with conflicting factions within the American church. Of these, there were several at the time.

Practically speaking, the autonomy that some bishops were so anxious to protect was only an autonomy of "relative degree."[1] Limited though it was, however, it existed, and many bishops prized it as a bulwark of their episcopal authority.

One would expect American resistance to an apostolic delegate to have been a liberal cause. But it was liberals, notably the famous Archbishop John Ireland of St. Paul, who effectively promoted the idea of a delegate, partly to advance their own agenda, but also because some of them conceived of the action as helping to effect rapprochement between the Vatican and republican governments, including that of the United States. The notion was a kind of naive nineteenth-century religiopolitical idealism. But it existed, and it bolstered the logic of the liberals. In any instance, the issue of an apostolic delegate to the United States was settled on the side of the liberals. It was they who prevailed after intense intraepiscopal debate and ''lengthy and sometimes heated negotiations between the Holy See and the American hierarchy.''[2]

Unquestionably, the matter of an apostolic delegate would have been resolved sooner or later on Rome's terms. The point, however, is how difficult it once was for Rome to bring its will to bear on the American church, and how much pressure it was forced to exert to secure the cooperation of the American bishops. At one point, in fact, Pope Leo XIII (1887–1903) was so annoyed over American resistance to the appointment of a papal representative in the country that he was quoted as exclaiming in exasperation, ''Why don't they want the Pope there? If Christ were to return to earth, you would all rejoice to give him a welcome. Why not then receive his Vicar?''[3]

A papal vicar was at last named on 24 January 1893—Archbishop Francesco Satolli, later to become a cardinal, an honor that virtually all apostolic delegates to the United States could look forward to (though not Jadot, at least not yet). Satolli would be the first in an unbroken string of exalted apostolic representatives to the United States, but the significance of his appointment would outlast popular recognition of his name. For Satolli's appointment spelled not only the end of that measured bit of ecclesiastical autonomy that the American church had had, but an end as well to an incipient collegiality among the American bishops, however rough and unvarnished that collegiality. The collegiality component would be recovered in more sophisticated and potentially more effective form as a result of Vatican Council II, but not autonomy. Rome's authority would long since have consolidated itself over the American church.

With an apostolic delegate in place, Roman influence did not merely enjoy an ascendancy; it was near absolute. The delegate, in turn, was an official of paramount importance—not a surrogate pope exactly, but a long extension, at the least, of the arm of the Vatican Curia. This is not to say that certain American prelates would not occasionally be able to influence the delegate to remarkable degree, or to say either that some prelates would not be able successfully to circumvent both the delegate and his office. Cleveland's Archbishop Edward F. Hoban, for one, was able to advance an astonishing number of protégés to episcopal posts around the country, despite selection procedures for new bishops that favored (although not exclusively) the raising up of area priests to head the dioceses of their own geographical areas.[4] Hoban, Cleveland's coadjutor or assistant bishop, with right of succession from 1942 to 1945 and head of the diocese from 1945 to 1966, won his reputation of being a bishop maker through a close personal friendship with Archbishop Amleto Cicognani, apostolic delegate to the United States from 1933 to 1958. On the other hand, there was New York's Cardinal Spellman. He was able to bypass the apostolic delegate's office in

Washington through the long years of the reign of Pope
Pius XII (1939–1958) because of a personal friendship
with Pius dating back to Spellman's days as a young
priest in Rome. Obviously, despite all the canons and
codifications, the Catholic church is a place where, as in
almost any other, friendships and loyalties can shred red
tape and achieve unusual goals. Spellman, too, was a
bishop maker, spinning off auxiliaries and priest favorites
to ecclesiastical seats as near as Philadelphia (John F.
O'Hara) and as distant as Los Angeles (James F. McIntyre). Whereas Hoban's influence was circumscribed by
Cicognani's, Spellman's was virtually unlimited. He
could wheel and deal pretty much as he willed, even on
the Curia's own turf. He was so well connected in Rome
that there was no necessity for any business of his to
pass through an apostolic delegate's office anywhere, except by personal choice.

But Spellman's was a privileged case of extraordinary dimension. Other American bishops could not bypass, much less ignore, the existence of the apostolic
delegate, the pope's representative in Washington. Of
course, not all American prelates were docile and
deferential to the delegate. Andrew Greeley remarked
in his autobiography that, up to his death in 1965,
Chicago's Cardinal Albert Meyer "loved to do battle with
the apostolic delegate and with the authorities in
Rome."[5] But it is fair to presume that the vast majority
of bisops deferred, and continue to defer, to the apostolic
delegate and the authority that he represents.

The apostolic delegate's influence has reached, accordingly, into matters large and small and, as a rule, has
needed only to be indirect to be effective. The papal

delegate's mere presence in Washington was enough to establish that a broader set of principles took precedence over any that American bishops, singly or collectively, might wish to see in effect or might be inclined to implement on their own. The delegate dealt with the bishops. The bishops dealt with those under their supervision, including the laity. And until lately, at least, each on his or her respective rung of the ladder could be counted upon to respond obediently to the directive coming down from above. At one time, the response was so reflexive as not even to exempt a future president of the United States. In 1947, John F. Kennedy, then a member of Congress, was scheduled to appear at a banquet in Philadelphia's Bellevue Stratford Hotel marking the conclusion of a financial campaign for a chapel memorializing four chaplains—one Jewish, one Catholic, and two Protestant—who had died heroically in the sinking of the World War II transport ship *S.S. Dorchester* on 3 February 1943 ninety miles from its destination in Greenland. The banquet seemed an innocent enough event for a Catholic politician to be at—nay, the very place a Catholic politician who was himself a war hero should have been—except that, in 1947, the Catholic church was still in its ecumenical Dark Ages, and as one historian worded it, "the Holy See was not yet ready to embrace interdenominational cooperation in any form."[6] Accordingly, word went from the chancery office of the archdiocese of Philadelphia to the chancery office of the archdiocese of Boston counseling intervention to have Kennedy's appearance canceled. Kennedy did cancel, a decision that would return to embarrass him when he was running for the presidency in 1960 and was anxious to assure voters that he was his own man, not Rome's, not the American bishops'. Theoretically, the pressure on Kennedy was essentially a pas de deux involving two chancery offices and a couple of officials in each: the Reverend Cletus Benjamin in Philadelphia and Auxiliary Bishop John J. Wright in Boston. But the policy was Rome's, or was so interpreted, and it can be presumed that the pope's official representative in Washington was not uninterested in how the issue was handled.

The duties of the apostolic delegate—pronuncio, now that the office has been upgraded diplomatically—inevitably involve much that is ceremonial, such as traveling about for episcopal consecrations and diocesan anniversaries, and much that is routinely administrative, like the flow of papers between American chanceries and departments of the Vatican Curia. But it is pure delusion to believe that the pope's delegate does not function as a Big Brother keeping a Roman eye on things. Father Andrew Greeley can attest to this. A few years ago, when Greeley's syndicated column in the Catholic press raised one hackle too many for the apostolic delegate, Archbishop Pio Laghi, the delegate sent out what Greeley in his autobiography called "secret letters" to bishops warning them of their responsibility for what appeared in publications under their aegis. The delegate, in a word, had decided that the Greeley column was a cause of scandal for the faithful. His so-called secret letters did not mention Greeley by name, but it was clear who was in mind. Greeley folded the column on his own initiative in January 1983, its fate being evident. The column would eventually be killed by fiat, and Greeley thought it better to end it himself, while the column was still the most popular one in the Catholic press.[7]

By such means as "secret letters," confidential communications, private words, and, no doubt, discrete telephone conversations, most apostolic delegates have managed to project a graceful aura and to keep a low profile. The notable exception was Archbishop Egidio Vagnozzi, who held the delegate's post from 1958 to 1967. Vagnozzi was a blunt, tactless man who charged about heedless of diplomatic or ecclesiastical protocols. In 1961, for instance, when feelings were at fever heat on the issue of federal aid to education and the Catholic bishops believed that their schools were being given short shrift by Washington's bureaucrats, Vagnozzi went before a conference of twelve hundred Catholic laypersons and exhorted them to support the bishops against the president (John F. Kennedy, as coincidence would have it), because "the bishops know what they are doing."[8] The president, more committed to the quality of public education, apparently didn't know what he was doing.

The same year, Vagnozzi brought into question the integrity of American Catholic intellectuals generally in a baccalaureate talk at Marquette University, which stands to this day as a classic instance of clerical intrusion into academe and Roman suspicion of freedom of inquiry on the Catholic campus. This was Vagnozzi speaking at Marquette 3 June 1961:

> The complaint has been voiced more than once that in high ecclesiastical circles the intellectual is often

underestimated and also mistrusted. The question is whether we are confronted with true and genuine intellectuals, who are inspired by a sincere love of truth, humbly disposed to submit to God's Revelation and the authority of His Church, or whether we are confronted with intellectuals who believe, first of all, in the absolute supremacy and unlimited freedom of human reason, a reason which has shown itself so often fallacious and subject to error.[9]

If Archbishop Vagnozzi underwent chastening by the ensuing outcry in the Catholic intellectual community, it was such as not to be noticed. Two years later, in the spring of 1963, he acted through the rector of Catholic University, Father William J. McDonald, to have four progressive Catholic theologians banned as possible choices in a student-sponsored lecture series: Fathers Godfrey Diekmann, O.S.B.; Hans Küng; John Courtney Murray, S.J.; and Gustave Weigel, S.J. At first, Vagnozzi's involvement in the banning incident was circumstantial, but it quickly became accepted public knowledge as the principals began to speak out. Murray's biographer, now Bishop Donald E. Pelotte, S.S.S., accepted Vagnozzi's involvement at full face-value in the 1976 book *John Courtney Murray: Theologian in Conflict* and so did Gerald P. Fogarty in his scholarly history, *The Vatican and the American Hierarchy from 1870 to 1965*. So, in fact, does almost everyone.

It would be another four years before Vagnozzi would be recalled to Rome, where he would be elevated to the cardinalate and placed in charge of the Vatican's

Prefecture for Economic Affairs. He would not be missed by many in the United States, although to say that is to make a presumption about the dispositions of the bishops as a body. During Vagnozzi's years in Washington, it was not the bishops but the laity who, along with a few courageous priests, protested his controversial intrusions into American Catholic life. In an earlier time, it might have been different. However, by the mid-twentieth century the American bishops were a deferential group, certainly publicly. Vagnozzi might have made many bishops bristle—in fact, unquestionably did. But collectively, the bishops maintained a discreet silence.

Discretion is still the name of the game, although occasionally a dissenting episcopal voice is heard, and when it is, it is so remarkable as to make front-page news. A recent instance was Archbishop Daniel W. Kucera's public questioning of the "competence" of Cardinal Edouard Gagnon and the Pontifical Council for the Family in condemning a widely used series of texts on human sexuality approved for publication by Kucera.[10] Gagnon, allegedly speaking on behalf of the pope, John Paul II, had sent out private letters in 1986 condemning the texts, published as the "New Creation" series. In departing from the established norm and publicly defending his authority in the matter, Kucera, the archbishop of Dubuque, braved Roman displeasure. But there was no great rallying around the Dubuque prelate. Very likely, some bishops quietly continued to allow use of the texts, but for others, Rome's expression of disapproval was enough to settle matters as far as they were concerned. Bishop Leo T. Maher of San Diego, for one,

sent a letter to several parents and school officials saying that the series had been condemned by the Holy See,
and he ordered a halt to the use of the series in the sex-
education programs of his diocese.[11]

To understand more fully the role of an apostolic
delegate—or as is the case now in the United States, a
pronuncio—we should perhaps delve into the background of the office. The arrangement between Rome
and the American church is not unusual. The Vatican
maintains contact with Catholics everywhere in the
world through a diplomacy as intricate and a diplomatic
corps as sophisticated as any to be found in any country or national capital. The Vatican's representatives are
almost invariably ordained prelates, and the corps is a
bona fide one in the strictest of diplomatic senses. For
the Vatican is not only the headquarters of a church; it
is the seat of an internationally recognized city-state.
Some one hundred countries of the world exchange
representatives with the Vatican—indeed, most of the
noncommunist world. Vatican emissaries of ambassadorial rank are designated either apostolic nuncios or
apostolic pronuncios, depending upon the Catholic composition of the country receiving the papal representative. The rank of apostolic nuncio is equivalent to that
of ambassador extraordinary and plenipotentiary, and a
delegate so named and accepted is considered the dean
of the diplomatic corps in the country to which he is ac-
credited. To avoid diplomatic complications, an apostolic
nuncio is assigned only to predominantly or officially
Catholic countries. Other countries are assigned a

pronuncio. Of course, there are lesser diplomatic ranks, such as minister or first secretary, when the diplomatic agreement between the Vatican and the country concerned is for representation at a lower level.

Countries that have no official diplomatic relations with the Vatican are generally assigned an apostolic delegate. Though a papal representative, this delegate has no diplomatic status of a formal kind in the country of his assignment. He is a papal representative to Catholics as a people, not a representative to a government. Nonetheless, an apostolic delegate's presence in a country is contingent upon his acceptance by that country's government. The USSR, for instance, does not exchange diplomats with the Vatican and does not welcome an apostolic delegate within its borders. The situation involving the United States has varied over the years.

From 1797 to 1848, the United States and the Vatican maintained diplomatic contact at the consular level. In 1848, the American post was upgraded to that of resident minister, and this arrangement continued into 1867, when the American mission to the Vatican was abruptly terminated by the failure of Congress to appropriate funds for the office. The withholding of funds followed reports that the papal government had ordered the American Protestant church in Rome to move outside the walls of the city of Rome. The reports proved false, but the decision of Congress stood, and official diplomatic contacts between the United States and the Vatican came to an end. Satolli would arrive as apostolic delegate in 1893, but again, an apostolic delegate's role is, strictly speaking, that of intermediary between the pope as spiritual head of the Catholic church and the Catholics of a given country as members of that church. Several presidents, beginning with Franklin D. Roosevelt, circumvented oppostion, political and religious, to official American diplomatic contact with the Vatican by assigning personal representatives to the Holy See. But formal diplomatic ties were not reestablished until 10 January 1984 when President Ronald Reagan and Pope John Paul II agreed to ties on the ambassadorial level.

Conceivably, that agreement has large implications for the world of international politics, but as far as the American Catholic church is concerned, very little has changed. The office of the apostolic delegation is now a nunciature; the address is the same as before. The apostolic delegate is now a pronuncio; he is the same man who has been serving in Washington since 1980. Archbishop Pio Laghi, apostolic delegate, is now Archbishop Pio Laghi, pronuncio. If there are marked differences in his duties, they are such as not to be noticed. Undoubtedly, he is putting in the same work day; obviously, he is making the usual ceremonial appearances around the country.

What has changed—and it is a change not at all predicated on the renewal of diplomatic relations between the United States and the Vatican—is the role of the pope in the affairs of the American church. It is far more direct and sustained than a pope's role seems ever to have been in the past. The papal representative in the country may now be—indeed, is—a person of more exalted rank, but his personal power and authority take on a different quality with the pope's decision to involve himself so immediately in what is happening in American Catholicism. If the papal representative to the United States was once an alter-pope, an official who possessed a certain independence of action, and who could be appealed to, cajoled, persuaded, praised, and blamed for trends and happenings in the American church, he is less so at the moment. The pronuncio remains a man of large influence and authority, to be sure. But with the pope himself now personally involved in so much that affects the American church, it is the pope himself who becomes the focus of attention, not a representative who is suddenly more than ever an instrument of policy.

Nothing dramatizes more clearly the presence of the pope's hand in matters of moment in the American church than the appointments a few years ago of the men to head the archdioceses of Boston and New York, after those jurisdictions became vacant because of two deaths within a few weeks' time, Boston's Cardinal Humberto Medeiros dying 17 September 1983, and New York's Cardinal Terence Cooke dying 6 October 1983. The new year was still new when Pope John Paul II named Bernard F. Law to the Boston vacancy on 24 January 1984, and John J. O'Connor to the New York vacancy just a week later, 31 January 1984.

That Law and O'Connor were not advanced to the strategic sees of Boston and New York by the normal nomination and screening processes for the advancement of American bishops goes almost without saying.

Law, at fifty-two, was at the right age to move on from the rural, sparsely populated diocese of Springfield–Cape Giradeau in Missouri to something big-

ger. But it was like lightning striking twice in the same out-
of-the-way place for him to leap from a diocese of fifty
thousand Catholics to an archdiocese of more than two
million. Law's predecessor in Springfield–Cape
Giradeau, William Baum, had gone on to Washington, a red hat, and a spot in the Roman Curia. Still,
Springfield–Cape Giradeau could hardly be regarded as
a promising stepping-stone to the top of the heap. Earlier
Springfield–Cape Giradeau had advanced others to the
diocese of Kansas City–St. Joseph (Charles H. Helmsing)
and the archdiocese of Kansas City in Kansas (Ignatius
J. Strecker), but neither of those sees is comparable in
size or importance to Boston. In going to Boston, Law
was moving to an archdiocese some of whose parishes
would have memberships comparable in number to the
whole of the diocese he was leaving.

Even more of a surprise, however, was the advancement of O'Connor to New York. At age sixty-four,
O'Connor would have seemed beyond the age for an assignment as demanding as the archdiocese of New York.
Besides, he had been only seven months in his position
as bishop of Scranton, something of a dead-end diocese
for those named to it. The diocese of Scranton was
founded in 1868, but no Scranton bishop was ever
promoted out of it until O'Connor. Adding to the surprise
of his selection for New York was his own background
as a priest. O'Connor had spent twenty-seven years of his
priesthood as a naval chaplain. He had risen to the rank
of rear admiral and, for five years before going to Scranton, had held the post of military vicar to the two million
Catholics in the American armed forces. That is not an

unimpressive background by any means. Still, it is fair to presume that O'Connor was better known in military quarters than he was in ecclesiastical precincts.

But Law and O'Connor each had recently been active in ways that would commend them to a pope like John Paul II.

Law, as a bishop prominently involved in ecumenical affairs, was named by Rome in 1981 to take charge of petitions from a number of Episcopal clergy to join the Catholic church and its priesthood in the United States. The Episcopal priests were leaving the church of their ordination in protest against certain modernizing trends, particularly the admission of women to the hitherto all-male priesthood. In a certain sense, Law's activities could be interpreted as a progressive involvement, for the episode reflected a potentially important new openness on the church's part because many of the Episcopal priests coming to Roman Catholicism were married. They would thus be moving into the priesthood of a church that had historically insisted that its clergy be celibate. In some Protestant ecumenical circles, however, the whole episode was viewed as a blatant kind of poaching—one church capitalizing on the problems of another. Predictably, relations between the Catholic church and the Episcopal church came under a strain. John Paul II's involvement in events was at no time crass. He wasn't piping messages to Episcopal priests to lay down their loyalties and join Rome. Nonetheless, his role had to be central to the process directed by Law because as pope he would have had to approve the necessary dispensations for married Episcopal priests to become Roman

Catholic priests. The Catholic church in the United States has a severe clergy shortage, but it is unlikely that considerations relating to that fact influenced the pope's decision. If anything, the considerations were more personal and, likely as not, ideological. As one who is convinced that women should not be priests, John Paul II could be expected to sympathize instinctively with priests who left Episcopalianism because components of that church had decided to ordain women.

In any instance, in their new clerical situations as Roman Catholics, it was not likely that the former Episcopal priests would have roles of high visibility, and they would not be free to remarry and continue as Catholic priests if marital status changed for any of them. So the entry into the Roman Catholicism priesthood of married men who had been Episcopal priests, in fact, signaled little by way of change—at least, in the short run—as far as a married Catholic priesthood was concerned; the Roman Catholic priesthood will remain a celibate priesthood for the foreseeable future. If anything, the process overseen in this country by Law probably said more about women than about married priests. For in opening its sanctuaries to Episcopal priests who had left their church primarily over the issue of women priests, Rome, in effect, underscored its own objections to the idea of women priests. Those objections were made clearer again in the 1986 exchange of letters between John Paul II, Cardinal Joannes Willebrands of the Vatican's Secretariat for Promoting Christian Unity, and Anglican Archbishop Robert Runcie of Canterbury, in which John Paul reiterated opposition to the ordination of women and indicated that the ordination of women by some Anglican/Episcopal communities presented an "increasingly serious obstacle"[12] to any eventual Anglican–Roman Catholic reunion. Whatever the underlying meaning of events, however, it is apparent that Bernard Law won high marks with the pope for his performance on a matter of great interest to the pope.

O'Connor could be said to have won similarly high marks with the pope on a matter of intense interest to the pontiff. It was quite a different matter from the one that involved Law. Thus, O'Connor came to attention by another route altogether. As a member of the five-man bishops' committee that drafted the American hierarchy's pastoral letter on nuclear arms and peace, O'Connor came to attention as the person who was the counterbalance to the liberals, who conceivably would render the pastoral overly pacifist and would write into the document propositions that would undercut American military policy at home and around the world. O'Connor was the military pragmatist, not a hawk exactly, like one or two in the hierarchy, but nonetheless a proponent of the political and military "realism" that one commonly associates with the U.S. Department of Defense. Perhaps in recognition of New York City's strong peace constituencies, from the United Nations in midtown to the Catholic Worker and the Catholic Peace Fellowship downtown, O'Connor would soften Pentagon-like positions once he was named to New York. Nevertheless, there is little doubt that, at a time of nervousness in Washington and Rome about the bishops' pastoral evolving into an essentially pacifist statement with serious international implications, O'Connor's sober assessments of communist programs and goals kept the pastoral letter centrist in certain key passages. Inevitably, an unvarnished assessment of certain communist realities would impress a man like John Paul II, who had seen his native Poland come under atheistic communism's domination when he was still a young man, and who entertained no illusions about what this domination spelled.

Unquestionably, there were numerous other factors entering into the choices of Law for Boston and O'Connor for New York, but with those two appointments, within days of one another, Pope John Paul II was able to give the American hierarchy an orientation far more ideologically congenial to him as supreme pontiff than the one he had inherited. New York and Boston are not by any means the sum of the American church, but they are archdioceses of crucial importance by reason of sheer size and because of their location in primary informational and educational centers of the country. Their potential for influence is thus enormous. To be able to fill both archdioceses with men of one's own choice at virtually one time is a stroke of good fortune that might be prayed for to a favorite saint by any pope, but particularly a pope with strong convictions about how a church should be run in a country like the United States. In both instances, John Paul II opted for strongly conservative types, and he could hardly be disappointed with his choices, particularly with that of Law for Boston.

Law has been the very epitome of the model prelate of the papacy of John Paul II: devout, affable, able, and firmly Roman—especially the latter, as events were quick to demonstrate. Law barred women from preaching any longer at the Paulist Center in downtown Boston, and when it came time to fill the editorship of the archdiocesan newspaper the *Pilot*, at 157 years the oldest Catholic paper in the United States and one with a proud progressive history, he selected a "journalist and activist," who had made his mark, in the words of the *Boston Globe*, as a worker "for several conservative advocacy groups."[13] The appointment of Philip F. Lawler, thirty-six, would return the *Pilot*'s editorship to a layperson after decades of its being in the hands of priests, who, though highly competent in several instances, were still priests first and professional journalists second. Many viewed the appointment of a lay editor as a necessary precondition in the *Pilot*'s eventual reclaiming of the prestige that it enjoyed years ago under prestigious lay editors like John Boyle O'Reilly, James Jeffrey Roche, and Patrick Donahoe. But these same persons had to wonder, when the choice for editor turned out to be the person who, in the year the American bishops were issuing their nuclear-weapons pastoral, was founding an organization called the American Catholic Conference, one of whose objectives was to provide "a forum whereby Catholic laymen can develop and express their concerns about the misinterpretation of Catholic teachings, especially on political and social issues."[14] Lawler, in other words, was policing the liberals and progressives of the American church, including its bishops. But at least his group was providing a "forum." There would be less of a "forum" in New York, where pastors of the 410 parishes in the archdiocese were instructed in August 1986 to bar as speakers at parish events individuals who disagree with Catholic teaching. That directive came from the archdiocese's vicar general, Auxiliary Bishop Joseph T. O'Keefe, but it was strongly supported by Cardinal O'Connor after it became a topic of heated discussion in the news media and was challenged by Govenor Mario J. Cuomo of New York, among many others, as a restraint on intellectual activity. "Common sense dictates that you try to keep the fox out of the chicken coop," O'Connor wrote in his column in *Catholic New York*, the archdiocesan newspaper.[15]

The Law and O'Connor choices were not accidents. They established the pattern for the episcopal appointments of John Paul II to the American church, a pattern that has continued to be so pronouncedly conservative in character as to prompt Father Richard McBrien, head of the theology department at the University of Notre Dame, to describe the appointments in his syndicated column as "the sort a Pope Edwin Meese III would have made," a not entirely whimsical allusion to President Ronald Reagan's attorney general.[16] The center and the progressive wing of the American church's hierarchy gradually began to thin out and lose influence as more strictly traditionalist bishops were moved to the fore, prelates such as William J. Levada, a Los Angeles auxiliary bishop who was named 3 July 1986 to head the archdiocese of Portland, Oregon. Levada served at the Vatican from 1976 to 1982 as a staff member of the Congregation for the Doctrine of the Faith. If that were not enough to certify anyone's conservative credentials, there is the public record. In the controversy following the 1984 abortion advertisement in the *New York Times*, Levada entered print in the *Los Angeles Times* with an ''op-ed'' piece charging that ''public dissent from church teaching'' is in effect ''a deliberate decision to substitute one's own conclusions for the faith of the church.''[17] In similar vein, he declared in an address to Catholic educators that a Catholic theologian or teacher may legitimately engage in some forms of private dissent from church teaching, but that one who dissents publicly ''proposes [to others] a personal opinion or conclusion which directly contradicts some teaching.'' The person who does that, Levada added, puts his or her ''own judgment on a par with that of the magisterium,''[18] the church's teaching authority, an action that he obviously regards as presumptuous and unacceptable. If there were something akin in the church to labor's closed shop, this was it.

But even as one speaks in terms of ideological castes, and uses such words as *centrists*, *liberals* and *conservatives*, *progressives* and *reactionaries*, one has to concede that terminology is a problem, that it is the rare bishop—or any individual, for that matter—who fits neatly and completely into one clearly defined ideological category. Cardinal O'Connor may be an ecclesiastical hard hat, yet he has forcefully defended the rights of workers to unionize in Catholic hospitals. Cardinal Law may project as sexist to some for not going out of his way to make women part of certain rituals, like that of the symbolic washing of feet in the Holy Week rituals, but he has instituted an extraordinarily compassionate program for women who are in problem pregnancies and who have personal difficulties of other kinds.

Yet there is nothing new about this. Bishops, like the rest of us, do not come neatly packaged. Some of the great liberal bishops of the American church of a generation ago proved to be ideologists of quite a different stripe when Vatican Council II came along and the issues were different. Suddenly, the yardstick for measuring the ideology of the church's leaders, in the United States at least, switched from the political and social to the ecclesial and theological. With that development, a lot of images were tarnished. For instance, a bishop who might have been a darling of the liberal laity for his positions on world government, the United Nations, unionized labor, socialized medicine, public housing, and all kinds of enlightened government programs could lose his ideological reputation overnight when the new yardsticks were church reform and renewal, liturgical innovation, collegiality, and structural change in the administration of the church. Many did lose such reputations. By the same token, John Paul II escapes simple ideological classification. He may be an ecclesiastical conservative, a confirmed anticommunist, and a battler against Marxist influences on Catholic theology, but as the *New York Times* has noted, he "can sound like a revolutionary advocate of the disinherited," a crusader of the most liberal sort, when he talks about the plight of peoples of the Third World and the obligations of the First World to correct the injustices of an economic relationship that leaves so many millions without the most basic necessities, including drinkable water.[19] But however progressive and liberal any of the church's leaders may look on some issues, the true litmus test as far as life in the church is concerned is the one taken on their theology and their ecclesiastical politics. Here, the insistence nowadays is that the indicators be uniformly traditional, especially in the instances of bishops, because bishops, as successors of the Apostles, are the embodiment of the magisterium, the custodians of the orthodox, the church's teachers.

The irony is that Pope John Paul II could clone an entire hierarchy of Laws, O'Connors, and Levadas, and though the cloning most assuredly would produce a hierarchial caste preferred by John Paul II, it is not at all certain that it would rehabilitate the standing of the bishops in the eyes of American Catholics and, in turn, bring about a return of their authority over Catholics. American Catholics are unquestionably interested in what bishops do, especially members of their national hierarchy; for instance, they have watched the unfolding of the Hunthausen drama with a combination of fascination and wonder. But most Catholics are not particularly interested in what the bishops have to say to them as laypersons in the context of their individual Catholic lives. It's an old story—well, a story ten or fifteen years old, in any case. Dan Herr, then president and now chairing the board of the Thomas More Association of Chicago, was among the first to size up the situation more than a dozen years ago: "It is all too clear...that the bishops have lost their credibility and their power. They speak and few listen; they command and even fewer obey."[20] The comment might have seemed tendentious at the time, but it is pretty much recognized now as a fact of American Catholic life.

Even bishops seem willing to concede the point, for over time, the general, though not exclusive, disposition among many of them has been to do less commanding, at least of a blatant kind. But if anyone thinks that a scenario such as that involving John F. Kennedy in 1947 would be impossible today, that person is wrong. Archbishop O'Connor's public and unapologetic pressuring of Democratic vice-presidential nominee Geraldine Ferraro during the 1984 presidential election campaign, because of her position on abortion, was a clear sign that old authoritative impulses are not completely dead. Some bishops might indeed be inclined to command less and on a narrower range of topics, but others are quite capable still of exerting intense pressure on those of whom they expect obedience. O'Connor, for one, is not in the least bit timid about pressuring. The big difference, even in the instance of O'Connor, is that the response is not guaranteed the way it once was. Under discreet episcopal prodding, John F. Kennedy, then a member of Congress, quietly bowed out of an ecumenical fund-raising event and later finessed the reason, alleging a possible misconstruing of his presence as that of an official representative of his church rather than as that of a mere politician who happened to be Catholic—a tortured rationale even then. Ms. Ferraro was not so docile when she came under episcopal bullying. Politically, it cost her dearly, but she stood her ground and told her archbishop, in effect, that her life was her own and so was her conscience. Her stance epitomized one of the clearest new realities of American Catholicism.

As for Herr's comment, it was made in the context of an observation by Father John Tracy Ellis, the scholarly church historian, about a "virtual lack of leadership" in the American church, a condition that Ellis speculated could result in the failure of the church as a viable, believing community.[21] To be sure, there was a marked leadership void in the American church in 1973. New York and Boston were headed by holy but not particularly dynamic archbishops: Cardinals Cooke and Medeiros, respectively. Chicago was in the hands of a man waiting for the world to collapse around him, Cardinal John Cody. Los Angeles was still working its way out from under the legacy of a reactionary, Cardinal James Francis McIntyre, three years retired but still casting an indirect shadow over the wreckage he had left behind. All of those archdioceses are headed today by different men, different types—men who could be said, if we place ideological preferences aside, to possess qualities of leadership. Certainly, they are strong and assertive, even beyond their immediate ecclesiastical jurisdictions. In a few other sees, notably Milwaukee, men of leadership quality have also emerged. The situation is not the same as it was in 1973, and coincidentally, there has been a recovery of a certain sense of confidence in the episcopal leadership. It has come, however, not so much as a result of the involvements of any one or several of these individuals—some of whose leadership many Catholics could do without—but more because of their collective presence, and its epitomization in recent pastoral letters, particularly their letter on nuclear weapons and world peace. How long had it been—indeed, had American bishops ever heard themselves applauded, literally applauded, as a hierarchial group for a particular action? But they were applauded, loudly and warmly, by Catholics who kept a vigil outside Chicago's Palmer House, where the bishops met in May 1983 to cross the *t*'s and dot the *i*'s on the peace pastoral. Were these people peace extremists? Hardly. By and large, they were concerned Catholics happy to see their bishops engaged in a concerted effort, one body, one voice, speaking out of the most urgent topic of the day: peace. One bishop, voice cracking and eyes misty, exclaimed what a "great day" it was for the church in the United States. Whether or not the pastoral letter has had any large practical impact since (it probably hasn't), most American Catholics, no doubt, remain grateful for it.

Yet, though the image of the bishops as a collective body has been rehabilitated to a degree on one or more subjects of common concern, it does not follow that the office has. With few exceptions, a man becoming a bishop just isn't the decisive influence in the United States that he once was—and even in the cases of the exceptions, the bishop's influence goes only so far. Were O'Connor to force the issue of abandoning contraception, for instance, could many Catholics be expected to respond as he would program them? Hardly. Andrew Greeley, the religious sociologist who has evolved into a best-selling novelist, drove home the point of lost influence not long ago when, in a symposium on American Catholic literature, he asked, "Who takes bishops seriously anymore? Or the constraints of ecclesiastical institutions? Who worries about 'tutorism'? Not the average lay person or even the average parish priest. Why then should the potential Catholic writer be inhibited by them? Who cares if a book is denounced by a bishop, save the publisher who licks his chops at the thought that sales will soar?"[22]

In coupling "the average Catholic priest" with "the average lay person," Greeley radically broadened the implications of his questions: "Who takes bishops seriously anymore? Or the constraints of ecclesiastical institutions?" In effect, he made many priests as indifferent as the laity generally when he came to the matter of a bishop's authority. Greeley may be regarded in some circles as a bishop baiter, but he's been a priest long enough to know his colleagues of the cloth. To the extent that he is right—and my guess is that, on this, as on so many questions, he is far more right than wrong— Greeley has pinpointed both the challenge and the dilemma not only of the American bishops but also of the leadership in Rome. American bishops are not heeded as before, nor are ecclesiastical constraints what they were. Sin is a much more subjective concept, and so is that of obedience. Automatic acquiescence to command or directive, for instance, is no longer considered a responsible Christian response in conflict situations, nor is it regarded as an act of loyalty to the church. In sum, most of the old rules and regulations, whether written or just plain understood, are not held in anything like the respect they once were. Certainly, they are not being conscientiously observed. There is hardly an

American Catholic family anymore that does not have a son or a daughter, a niece or a nephew, an aunt or an uncle, a cousin or several of them, who are not in an irregular situation as far as Catholicism is concerned, or who is not alienated from it. In fact, it is not hard to find families all of whose children are "turned off"—alienated or nonpracticing, many out of sheer indifference. Most of these people, and certainly most of the indifferent, are not hostile in the least. They just aren't interested or don't particularly regard religion as a necessary element in their lives. It is uncertain who constitute the larger problem for the church—the alienated or the indifferent. Alienation can be dealt with because it has roots in something concrete—a grievance, a hurt, a skepticism, a rejection, a doubt, or an irregular personal situation of a religious nature. Alienation can be addressed. Indifference is far more difficult to counter, as its roots are nowhere. A hurt person can be appeased, his or her feelings assuaged. A doubter can be persuaded. A disbeliever can be reconverted. An irregularity can be corrected. But where does one start when the condition is apathy, a general lack of interest and concern?

That a large number of American Catholics exist in some kind of twilight zone of religion is confirmed by that 1985 *Our Sunday Visitor*/Gallup Poll survey cited in Chapter 1.[23] The survey found that 25 percent of those identifying themselves as Catholics considered religion "largely old-fashioned and out of date"—a statistic that the *Our Sunday Visitor* staff itself described as surprising. On the same point, another 27 percent indicated that they had "no opinion" whether religion was old-fashioned and out of date, an extraordinarily high percentage, it would seem, on so basic a question. Incidentally, the question in its entirety was: "Do you believe that religion can answer all or most of today's problems, or that religion is largely old-fashioned and out of date?" Only 48 percent of American Catholics were able to state categorically that religion was relevant and did supply answers in their lives. This was a finding statistically well behind that for Protestants and behind the national sample as well. Fully 66 percent of Protestants felt that religion could answer today's problems, and only 15 percent of Protestants believed religion to be old-fashioned and out of date. Nineteen percent had no opinion. In the national sample, 56 percent believed that religion supplied answers to current problems, 23 percent thought religion out of date, and 23 percent had no opinion on the matter.

Admittedly, polls can be made to say things by the mere framing of the question, and moreover, they are subject to sampling errors. But there is no more reputable polling organization in the United States than Gallup, and sampling errors in any well-conducted poll are going to be limited to a few percentage points, plus or minus. So the conclusion would seem inescapable from this poll that large numbers of those who call themselves Catholic in fact consider their faith to be unimportant or peripheral to their lives. But this can hardly be considered a large revelation to anyone who has been in a ministerial or parental situation over the past ten or fifteen years. The church in America is suddenly pervaded with people, particularly of the younger generations,

who conform out of some lingering instinct from the
past, or who observe the conventions of faith for reasons
of convenience or family peace. Many are the marriages
that take place in a Catholic church, and many the baptisms that are scheduled at the old parish church, less
out of a deep, personal religious conviction than out of
convenience, or a certain nostalgia, or a regard for the
religious sensibilities of parents and relatives.

I suppose that these are what one would call the
church's cultural Catholics, individuals for whom
Catholicism is not so much a compelling spiritual experience as it is a social circumstance, a shared history,
an accident of birth rather than an actual spiritual and
intellectual choice. There are many cultural Catholics out
there, and though very many of them may belong to the
younger generations, it would be a mistake to believe
cultural Catholicism is confined solely to those generations. Not a few older Catholics have moved into categories of belief where the orthodoxies and formalisms
of faith mean less than keeping in touch with their roots,
or maybe protecting their spiritual flanks—the Pascal's-
wager bit, hedging on the side of belief, just in case the
church's story is true after all. I have told elsewhere the
story of a luncheon in New York City with a prominent
Catholic politician of yesterday, a man who had unseated
a seated American president through a maverick, albeit
ultimately unsuccessful, presidential bid of his own. It
was a time when the upheaval in the American church
seemed at its height—priests leaving, convents emptying, pews emptying, and so on. Conversation drifted to
changes in our own religious existences, and our guest

was asked, half whimsically, whether he still made it to church on Sunday. "I've come this far," he responded, countering half whimsy with his own typical whimsy. "I'm not going to be shot down by a legalism."

Protecting one's spiritual flanks does not necessarily define one as a cynic, much less as a cultural Catholic. Pascal may have been protecting his spiritual flanks back in the 1600s, when he wagered on the existence of God on the proposition that if God existed he had everything to gain, and if God didn't exist—well, what had he lost for his trouble? Nothing. However, Blaise Pascal was anything but a cultural Catholic. Our luncheon guest wasn't one either—and still isn't, though like the rest of us, he certainly belongs to its current context. The cultural Catholic is a relatively recent phenomenon, certainly as far as numbers are concerned. This Catholic differs in kind from those lapsed or irregular Catholics of yesterday, who probably could be thought of as precursors of sorts to this new breed of Catholic. The times are different, and certainly, the irregular Catholic is treated differently—indeed, far more Christianly. One can be grateful for this, for the irregulars of days not too long ago had a hard time of it. Just to enter a so-called mixed marriage—one with a non-Catholic—could be traumatic for a Catholic. Almost any senior Catholic can remember when a "mixed marriage" took place on a weekday, in the rectory or at a church's side altar, and with the priest's nuptial blessing withheld. And of course, it wasn't long ago that Catholic cemeteries were operated as some sort of private preserve for the elect of God as determined by rule and regulation. There was consecrated ground and unconsecrated ground, and unless a Catholic died within the bosom of Abraham, so to speak, that person was denied consecrated ground. This was F. Scott Fitzgerald's lot. When he died in 1940, he was denied a Catholic burial on the grounds that "he was not a practical Catholic and...his books were not suitable reading material."[24] It took thirty-five years, a new outlook born of an ecumenical council in Rome, and the persistence of Frances Scott Smith, Fitzgerald's daughter, before F. Scott Fitzgerald's remains would finally repose among those of his Catholic family, according to his wishes.

The church can still be ironfisted, as people like Geraldine Ferraro and Charles Curran know only too well. It can also be cruel on occasion, as was demonstrated not long ago when a church official reversed a couple's plans to marry in New York's St. Patrick's Cathedral, because the man suffered from acquired immune deficiency syndrome (AIDS), the deadly disease transmitted by the exchange of semen or blood, which is often contracted by homosexual men. The couple fully informed the cathedral priest who had initially screened their application about the man's condition. The priest, Father John Clermont, seeing no impediments to the marriage, proceeded to set a date and time for the ceremony. However, the cathedral's rector, Monsignor James F. Rigney, voided the arrangements, saying that he felt people in a "life-threatening situation," such as AIDS, would receive better premarriage counseling in their local parish church than at the cathedral,[25] a curious sort of reasoning given a cathedral's status as the principal church of an archdiocese and therefore the one church before all others where one would expect to find both competence and the embodiment of an archdiocese's pastoral concerns. Heightening the strangeness of Rigney's decision was that it appeared to be in conflict with the attitude of the cathedral's chief priest, Cardinal O'Connor. Though O'Connor had often been at odds with New York's homosexual community, strenuously opposing, for instance, New York's Gay Rights Bill voted in 1986, he had often expressed compassion for people with AIDS and was instrumental in the archdiocese's establishment of an AIDS hospice in Greenwich Village, called "The Gift of Love." O'Connor eventually rescued the day when, through an aide, he reversed Rigney's reversal and opened the cathedral doors to the couple to marry in St. Patrick's if they met normal church requirements. They did, and they were married on Valentine's Day, 14 February 1987, at the main altar of St. Patrick's. But by then, the damage had been done.

So the cathedral incident occurred, and though undone in part, it inevitably brought on the church publicity that an organization proclaiming the love of Christ for the outcasts and the rejected of society, without exception, would be better off without. One would prefer to think that the St. Patrick's incident was an aberration, an embarrassment resulting from a hasty decision. One would like to think, too, that those people were wrong who traced initial motivations in the scenario to the Vatican letter of 30 October 1986 to the world's bishops warning against the prohomosexual movement. The letter charged, among other things, that advocates of homosexual rights "seriously threaten the lives and well-being of a large number of people."[26] It was a letter, in sum, that some, especially rights advocates, could interpret as condoning discrimination against those with AIDS. The unhappy fact, however, is that the decision very likely was not an aberration. In recent years, the church has made accommodations for the indifferent, the casuals of religious practice, the irregulars of belief, and those in unorthodox dogmatic and theological straits. But there are issues—and at the moment, homosexuality is one of them; abortion is another—that can regenerate old impulses of animus and that can be directed against anyone, including, as the St. Patrick's incident came close to proving, the pathetically sick. No one is spared—not the priest, and not the member of the so-called club. It seems hardly coincidental that Rome's briefs in the cases against Archbishop Hunthausen and Father Curran included complaints on both the abortion and homosexual issues.

The paradox in all of this is that the church's authority is often exercised the most severely against those who love and respect the church deeply enough to be motivated and engaged on its behalf—individuals, in a word, who value their faith and think it important to back that faith with a certain activism. With so many Catholics opting out or moving to the sidelines, one would expect these persons to be held in regard, not just for hanging in, but for being involved. To be sure, some of them may have an ax to grind, a cause to promote, a territory to protect. But at least, they care enough about the church to be anxious about working to improve it and its image. So often, however, their interest is dismissed, or worse, discounted as a vanity of mind, a quirk of personality—innocent or mischievous. Missing is the allowance that a deep religious sincerity can infuse that interest, along with a love and respect for truth, justice, and the church's very welfare.

The point is that altruism, devotion, and dedication of purpose are not qualities found exclusively in those who act and make determinations in the church from one side of the bar of judgment and authority. Dissidents can also be altruistic, dedicated, and devoted. Fernando Cardenal, the Nicaraguan priest, underscored the point in refusing Rome's demand that he resign his post of minister of justice in the Sandinista government. "To leave the revolution now," he said in opting instead for expulsion from the Jesuit order, "would be a desertion of my pact with the poor, and I can't but think it would not only be treason against the poor, but treason against my country."[27] Admittedly, not everyone is cut out like Cardenal to be a rebel, with or without a cause. Father Leonardo Boff, the Brazilian theologian, responded docilely to Vatican criticism of his work in the field of liberation theology. He took his disciplining, declaring, "I prefer to walk with the church rather than walk alone with my theology."[28]

Obviously, Boff's is the kind of attitude that authority, Rome's or any other, favors, but that can hardly be presumed anymore, perhaps especially by Rome. Catholics don't respond to orders the way they used to, not even priests. Curran's is a perfect instance. Pressured by Rome in 1986 to retract certain views on sexual morality or else lose the church's authorization to teach as a Catholic theologian on a Catholic campus, Curran reacted much as did Cardenal. He was altruistic and individualistic. Curran expressed respect for the Catholic tradition, but it was a respect combined with a sense of spiritual confidence and intellectual self-worth that in the new Catholic makes automatic acquiesence impossible to just any order from an authority figure. This combination of loyalty and defiance presents authority with a different kind of problem, an exasperating one, really, for the loyalty element defuses easy suggestions of treachery and deceitfulness. In many ways, the Catholic tradition "is the only one that makes sense to me, because it's a tradition which always said that faith and reason can never contradict one another," Curran remarked in answer to a reporter's question about why he didn't just leave the priesthood and the church to ensure his freedom to teach and write as he would: "It's a faith tradition that has always accepted the goodness of the human and the goodness of the human search for truth. And therefore, because of my own faith and because of my theology, I find myself very much at home in that church."[29] Nonetheless, as Curran made clear from the beginning, he would fight to the end for his principles, even going to the civil courts, if necessary, to retain his post of professor of moral theology at Catholic University. He made good on that court threat 27 February 1987.

The concession that Catholics like Cardenal and Curran—and millions of others on more anonymous levels—refuse to make these days is that a preeminent wisdom necessarily resides in Rome, one that automatically takes precedence when questions arise. They learn—indeed, see every day in the scene around them—that the church is a human institution. They know that human institutions are run by human beings, as capable as not of error, misjudgment, and intolerance. They know that not even popes fully escape their humanity. They know that popes are infallible by conciliar decree,[30] but they know, too, that the conditions governing the invocation of infallibility are specifically defined. They are not broad. Nor can infallibility be delegated or extended to others beyond the papal office.

The tradition of the church is that, for a pope to speak infallibly, he must meet several conditions. He must be addressing himself to matters of faith or morals; he must speak as the Vicar of Christ, in his office as pope, and to the church universal; and he must make clear his invocation of infallibility. Infallibility has been a dogma of the church since 1870, but in fact, it has been explicitly used only once—by Pope Pius XII in 1950 in defining the dogma of Mary's assumption into heaven.

The introducing of infallibility into the discussion is not so irrelevant as at first it might seem. Ordinarily one would not expect the infallibility issue to enter into an effort to return a conformity of word and response to the wider church. And indeed it didn't until Cardinal Ratzinger held in the Curran controversy that formal invocation of infallibility was not necessary to establish the errorlessness of the church's official position on a particular subject, when this was brought into question by a dissident or dissenting faction. Ratzinger's comment opened the flood gates of interpretation. For more than a century, Rome had been satisfied with a defintion of infallibility that narrowed its application to solemn declaration. If nothing more, the narrower application blunted charges of Catholic moral arrogance and allayed fears that the church would be pronouncing pontifically on everything under the sun, and claiming inerrancy for its word. Whatever the impression, that hasn't been the church's style, at least of recent years; Pope Paul VI did not even claim infallibility for *Humanae vitae*. The Ratzinger position, however, has so enlarged the concept of infallibility as to fuel a debate that could be around for years—or at least as long as Ratzinger is.

Until the Ratzinger fallback on infallibility, the tools of conformity had been authority and the expectation of obedience once the magisterium had spoke its mind. These lost impact because authority and obedience ceased to be the one-dimensional elements that they had once been in the church. Nothing is deader than the old maxim *Roma locuta est, causa finita* ("Rome has spoken; the case is closed"). Nowadays, authority is often questioned and obedience often withheld, because Catholics are aware that wisdom and good judgment are not the automatic Roman qualities they had thought them to be in a more innocent, less informed time. Rome speaks, and instantly, from many of the faithful comes the question, "But are you sure?"

Historically, there is fair reason for Catholics to ask such a question. The Catholic record for infallibility of judgment and decree—to take advantage of an opening provided by Ratzinger—is spotty to say the least. The

Galileo story is all too familiar. He suffered for Rome's ignorance about which was the center of the universe, the earth or the sun. It is no excuse to plead that astronomy isn't the church's forte. The church didn't do too well on some humanitarian and social issues either. The Crusades were scandals, and so was the Spanish Inquisition. Also, for centuries, the church lived at spiritual and political peace with slavery, and as late as 1745, a pope— Benedict XIV (1740-1758)—was reconfirming an ancient church proscription against interest charged on loans and instructing that any interest exacted be returned as something unjustly claimed.[31] There wouldn't be a Vatican Bank, a Catholic credit union, or a diocesan chancery office lending money to parishes even at discount rates if the old logic had persisted. Similarly, there wouldn't be an ecumenical movement if the old Catholic premise *extra ecclesiam nulla salus* (''outside the church, no salvation'') were still in place. That premise endured from the third-century teaching of St. Cyprian; through *Unam sanctam*, the 1302 bull on papal supremacy by Pope Boniface VIII (1294-1303); through the profession of faith sworn in 1869 by the Fathers of Vatican Council I (''This true Catholic faith, outside of which no one can be saved...''); and into the 1940s, when the rigorist interpretation of the premise by a Boston Jesuit, Father Leonard Feeney, caused embarrassment so acute in the United States and in Rome as to force suppression of the idea through the suppression of Feeney.[32] Twenty years later, in *Lumen gentium*, the Dogmatic Constitution on the Church, the fathers of Vatican Council II finally allowed that the divine ''plan of salvation'' included others than just Catholics—in fact, the unbaptized as well as the baptized. Vatican II, of course, also reversed popes like Gregory XVI (1831–1846) and Pius IX (1846–1878), who had held freedom of conscience to be beyond the pale of acceptability; in 1834, Gregory had even used the word *insanity (deliramentum)* to describe the notion that "freedom of conscience is to be asserted and vindicated for everybody."[33] Today, freedom of conscience is solemnly spelled out in conciliar decree.

One could go on, citing, for instance, the reversal that has taken place in the church's official outlook on the separation of church and state. The proposition was anathema until Father John Courtney Murray, S.J., at last had the opportunity to persuade the fathers of Vatican II not only that church and state could be separate, but that in separateness resided potentially greater freedom and fuller theological health for the church itself, particularly in a pluralistic state that guaranteed freedom of religion. He had earlier been silenced for suggesting such a thing.

The purpose of all this is not to belabor Catholic history, but to point up in defense of those who take maverick positions in the church that, just possibly, they could be proved right by time. Galileo was. John Courtney Murray was. More bluntly, a church that in its official teaching could err on such fundamental matters of faith and morals as the salvation of humankind and the basis of moral law, to say nothing about slavery, interest-income, and the nature of the modern state, could conceivably also be in error on many of the things on which it today demands assent of intellect and will from those it considers its dissidents.

As a human institution, the church has its fallible side. The paradox is that the clearer this becomes to Catholics on the cutting edge of new thought, the more adamant is the church's leadership about the preeminence of its own thought. Not long ago, John Paul II told an Italian lay group that only the official church "authentically interprets and transmits the Bible,"[34] a claim hardly calculated to advance ecumenical relations—or private Catholic reading and meditation on the Bible, for that matter. If the statement smacks of mind control, so also does the planned doctrinal compendium, initiated following the 1985 Synod of Bishops and slated for completion in the time for the 1990 synod.[35] The compendium is conceived of as a kind of universal catechism spelling out the church's traditional and fundamental teachings, but for a number of Catholics, it looms as a modern syllabus of errors, and the two previous syllabuses in church history, the 1864 syllabus of Pius IX, *Quanta cura,* and the 1907 syllabus of Pius X, *Lamentabili sane exitu,* have unhappy histories. Syllabuses are impossible, not only because people resent their attempt at mind control, but also because the rigidities they would enforce are generally beyond achievement. The church is not frozen in some kind of time capsule. Times change. The church changes. Any syllabuses come to read like parodies.

Rather than being forever fixed, the church's very doctrine evolves. Cardinal John Henry Newman, the famed nineteenth-century English prelate, spoke of the development of doctrine. Father Avery Dulles, the contemporary Jesuit theologian, uses the term *reconceptualization*. Whatever the more accurate word, the most cursory scanning of the church's history reveals what Father Francis X. Murphy, the Redemptorist, calls "a definite pattern of change discernible in the doctrinal, moral, disciplinary, and structural aspects of the church."[36] Murphy, a historian of Vatican II and perhaps the ranking American Vaticanologist, spoofs notions of the church's changelessness, claiming to have decoded the elaborate process that comes into play when, "due to the reflection of its theologians or the attitude of its faithful..., the church is about to accept a mutation in doctrinal explanation or disciplinary directive": the whole edifice of tradition seems to draw itself up and refuses to acknowledge the possibility of change; then, with the publication of a papal or hierarchial document that expresses a refusal to budge on the issue, an unwitting acknowledgment is made that a turnabout is already in process.[37]

Not only does the church budge, but as Murphy noted, its leaders often bungle, so that, in composite, the picture becomes one of shame as well as glory. In the ninth century, Pope Nicholas I (858–867) declared the use of torture to be unconscionably un-Christian; in the thirteenth century, however, Pope Gregory IX (1227–1241) went beyond torture and tolerated the death penalty for heresy. Pope Innocent III convened Lateran Council IV in 1215 to deal with such dogmatic matters as transubstantiation, or Catholic understanding of the conversion of bread and wine of the Eucharist into the body and blood of Christ. But by providing for the confiscation of goods and the banishment of heretics, the council set the stage for the Inquisition launched by Gregory IX. Popes championed the rise of the medieval universities and supported the Renaissance in its early stages; yet popes also sanctioned the burning of religious reformers and opposed the pursuit of human liberties promoted by the Enlightenment. Pope Leo XIII (1878–1903) sought to heal the breach between the church and the modern state and, in the process, gave new impetus to the church's social and political thought, but he was succeeded by a pope, Pius X (1903–1914), who condemned as grave error moves to accommodate the church's spiritual message to the consciousness of contemporary humanity.[38]

Murphy cited many of these instances of papal fallibility. He might also have added that, despite papal preachments over many centuries on the dignity of the individual and the sacredness of life, the papacy defaulted on both accounts when it was put to its greatest test in all history during the Nazi period. The pope at the time was Pius XII (1939–1958). His "silence" in the face of the Holocaust and the systematic extermination of the Jewish people initiated by Adolph Hitler is a subject of intense debate to this day, Pius's loyalists contending that his course was the only practical one and that he personally has been horribly maligned by history. Maybe he has been. On the other hand, Hitler died in his Berlin bunker on 1 May 1945, and three weeks later, the Third Reich had come to an end. Pius XII reigned as pope for another thirteen years, a generously long time, it would appear, to clarify his position and the logic of his "silence." He never did and thus left behind one of the most ambiguous chapters in papal history.

Obviously, episodes such as these take their toll on the church's credibility, including within its own community. A more sophisticated, better educated membership is a less credulous one, although the implications of that fact seem not to be grasped. On 15 April 1986, at St. Michael's College in Toronto, Cardinal Ratzinger was proclaiming that "the church's main job is the care of the faith of the simple."[39] The remark is embarrassingly paternalistic and terribly self-delusionary, for a "simple" faithful just plain does not exist anymore, certainly not in a country like Canada—or anywhere, for that matter, except maybe for Third World regions where educational opportunities are not the same as in the developed world. By and large, the Catholic church, as a religion of the developed world, is dealing with people who, as a body, are among the most literate, best educated in history. The Ratzinger comment would suggest that the church does not recognize this; so inevitably, it has problems.

Andrew Greeley would agree. Many of the church's internal problems, he remarked in his autobiography, exist because the church "was unprepared to be faced with a college-educated Catholic population"[40] Greeley was writing of the American church, and to be sure, nowhere is the observation truer than in the United States. The notion of a "simple" faithful is delusion—and insult as well. Today, the average American Catholic priest stands in front of a congregation very many of whom have educational credentials and life experiences surpassing his own. This would not have been as true a generation or two ago, and it would have been virtually inconceivable before that, when the priest comprised the church's educational elite. But it is true now, and the implications are enormous. Among other things, it means that, in communicating its message, the church can make no presumptions based on the credulousness of people. In a more querulous age, there will be those who will question persistently. But they do not constitute the essential challenge. Rather, it is the educated and informed believer. The church has to make sense as never before.

This is to say that the game is the same but that the rules are altogether different. Time was when the response to authority was so automatic in the church that it was necessary merely to control the decision-making apparatus. People responded to authority. With the decison-making apparatus firmly in the hands of Rome, the church took on the characteristic of a giant monolith. That it was never the massive, uniform entity it gave the appearance of being is beside the point. So many Catholics responded as expected that the church was a people united in a sense as close as possible to the literal.

That is what is missing in today's church—and is probably lost forever. The divergences in the church are so deep, convictions are so strongly anchored, and the forces of change are so strong—social, political, economic, *and* religious—that, in the words of Jean-Guy Vaillancourt of the University of Montreal, "It is unlikely that Catholicism will ever return to a state of stability and consensus."[41]

Stability and consensus are obviously the goals of Pope John Paul II, and a starting point for their return to the American church is probably less the taming of dissidents, however dramatic those cases might be, than it is the reconstitution of a more traditionalist hierarchy—because, presumably, bishops set the tone for the local church, as the church in the United States.

The pope has to start somewhere, admittedly. But in starting in the United States with the bishops, he is starting (has started) with the most stable and predictable element of the American church. During the tumultuous upheavals of the late 1960s and the early 1970s, for instance, when priests by the hundreds were quitting the active ministry for other careers and many of them for marriage, the American hierarchy lost only two of its members to the forces of change: an auxiliary bishop in St. Paul–Minneapolis and another in Providence, Rhode Island.

American bishops, chosen with special care, have always been predictable—and loyal to Rome. Even in the agony of his public humiliation in September 1986, Seattle's Archbishop Hunthausen voiced respect for the higher authority that had diminished him personally and professionally. Asked if he should not view as a demotion the directive from Rome that had stripped him of much of his authority in his own archdiocese, he said, "I'm only human; of course, I wonder. But we are challenged now to find a way to make this work."[42]

By the same token, Hunthausen's brother bishops, when forced to take a public stand on his unprecedented and questionable demotion, sympathized with him but nonetheless affirmed "unreservedly their loyalty to and unity with the Holy Father"[43]—a choice of words that priest-columnist Richard McBrien protested on the grounds that "no earthly agency or person commands 'unreserved' loyalty. God alone merits that."[44] Kevin H. Gunning, a Washington, D.C. writer on religious affairs, was also critical. "To reject out of hand the authority of the Roman bishop is bad theology and bad politics," Gunning declared. "This every bishop knows. He would not be a bishop if he didn't." Nonetheless, Gunning continued, the bishops had missed an opportunity: "In not injecting themselves into or commenting on the Hunthausen case beyond procedural remarks, the bishops appeared to have missed the chance to affirm the autonomy and authority of the local church, to uphold the rights of free and educated conscience, to communicate to the Vatican that the Catholic faith may impact Americans differently, and that there is a place for responsible dissent within the church."[45] The *Boston Globe* headlined his commentary, "Catholic Bishops Play It Safe." They did and are not absolved even now.

The bishops, in a word, are not in dissent or rebellion. Nor are they free-lancing. When Cardinal O'Connor's quasi-official visit to Israel at the end of 1986 disturbed Vatican officials because of O'Connor's plans to meet with Israeli political leaders in their Jerusalem offices, O'Connor hastily backed off, apologizing profusely as he stood embarrassed before the world. He may have placated the Vatican, but he upset Israelis and caused such distress in the American Jewish community that fifty-four Jewish organizations, virtually every major Jewish group in the United States, issued a statement faulting O'Connor and saying that his trip "did more harm than good."[46] O'Connor's New York archdiocese covers a geographical area that has more Jews than any city in the world, and it would be natural if he saw himself as something of a bridge builder between the Christian and Jewish communities. But when his initiatives came into conflict with Vatican diplomacy—the Vatican not recognizing Israel, not favoring Israeli sovereignty over Jerusalem, and not wishing to convey any impression that a change of policy toward Israel was imminent—there was no question whose will would dominate. O'Connor hastily reorganized his plans. The trip was salvaged to a degree by O'Connor's meeting with the Israeli officials at their residences rather than their offices, but by then, hardly anyone was happy— and O'Connor himself had eaten a lot of humble pie. Still, his was not an uncharacteristic response to an expression of Roman feelings. Any American bishop would have reacted as he did. They are remarkably responsive to Rome and the higher authority that resides there.

But bishops are one thing. The same deferential respect for authority, beginning with Rome's, does not exist on other levels of the American church. The laity have their own minds, and so, too, for that matter, do religious, and particularly priests. The nuns who stood their ground over the 7 October 1984 paid advertisement in the *New York Times* on the issue of Catholics and abortion indicated that deference to authority is no longer automatic. And nothing could make clearer the independent spirit of the modern Catholic than Father Charles Curran's determination to fight the church's action against him to the very limit of possibilities, ecclesial and civil. Priests are not in rebellion any more than bishops are. But if bishops are subservient, priests are anything but. If they were in the past, they are not now.

Whether Curran and others like him who are controversially involved across the spectrum of issues, from church policy, to matters of personal and social morality, to questions of peace, justice, and social welfare are being fairly or unfairly treated depends on the circumstances of the individual case. This much is certain, however: the heavy hand with which so many of those allegedly problem cases are being handled is certain to take a toll on the religious vocational outlook of young Catholic men and women. Clerical vocations will most assuredly be affected, for many young men are going to be hesitant about entering a profession—answering a call, if one prefers—where so much of one's life work can be abruptly withdrawn, stripped away, trimmed, or terminated by fiat, to say nothing of petulance, whim, or bias of a sexist or ideological kind. "Who needs any of that?" the young Catholic asks of himself or herself.

The church, in sum, has enough problems without causing more for itself. Nowhere is this truer than in the matter of the priesthood and of priestly vocations. Even without such mangled incidents as those affecting Archbishop Hunthausen and Father Curran, an image problem exists as far as the priesthood is concerned. A machine needs cogs. A church needs ministers. The

Catholic church needs priests. But the American church is in short supply of priests—so short, in fact, that it is a very serious question whether the church has enough of them on hand and coming along in the seminaries to carry the institutional church confidently into the future.

3

THE UNKNOWN AMERICAN QUANTITY

The Priests

IT WAS ONE of those stories deep inside a newspaper, run as an announcement, but masking a problem greater than the news conveyed. The story appeared 19 June 1986 on page 10 of the *Church World*, official newspaper of the diocese of Portland, Maine, declaring that Dominican Father Roger G. Blain would be leaving as pastor of SS. Peter and Paul parish in Lewiston at the end of the summer for reasons of health. The Dominican order had administered SS. Peter and Paul since September 1881, a total of one hundred and five years. However, the story said that there would be no replacement from the Dominican order for Father Blain; his replacement would be a diocesan priest. The reason was simple but, from a ministerial viewpoint, alarming. The Dominicans, in the paper's words, were suffering "a lack of vocations." The problem for the American church is that the Dominicans are not an isolated case. The lack of vocations is widespread, for orders as well as dioceses, for religious sisters and brothers as well as for priests. The lack is especially acute as far as priests are concerned, for priests are central to the ministry of a sacramental church. The difficulty is that priests retire, priests die, priests leave the active ministry—and they are not easily replaced, in Maine or anywhere else. The Catholic-priest labor pool is at drought level in many parts of Catholic Christendom, and one of them is the church in the United States. The diocese of Portland would find a substitute for the departing Dominican, but it would be tapping an already strained clerical supply of its own.

To be sure, the parish situation in Lewiston was not a common one. In fact, for the diocese of Portland, it amounted to something of a luxury arrangement, an order priest fulfilling what is essentially a diocesan obligation. Religious-order priests administer American parishes as the exception rather than the rule. Order priests, by and large, are the specialists—religious professionals in education, care of the sick, missionary work at home and in faraway lands. They are more likely to be found, therefore, on campuses, in hospitals, in the inner city involved with particular groups, in foreign lands, or in out-of-the-way places like an Indian reservation or an Eskimo community. The parish is overwhelmingly the preserve of the diocesan, so-called secular, priest. If the order priest is the ministerial specialist, the diocesan priest is the generalist. He is the one who encounters the masses of the faithful on the level of their everyday religious and spiritual needs. He is expected to have the comparable gifts of the old-time family doctor, the general practitioner—who made house calls to boot. The parish priest administers the Catholic parish. His territory may range from a few blocks to several square miles, and it may number anywhere from a few hundred to several thousand families. As of 1986, there were 19,313 parishes in the United States.

The complication for American Catholicism is that, as the number of parishes increases to accommodate Catholic demographic realities—population growth, suburban and exurban migration, and new emigration, notably from Hispanic countries, most of whose émigrés are Catholic—the number of priests available to serve these parishes decreases. Between 1968 and 1985, the decline was from 37,453 to 35,052, a loss of 2,401. Once again, to repeat an earlier point, the loss may not seem especially great in round numbers, except that the 1985 figure is deceptive, for it includes several thousand whose ministry is actually at an end because of retirement—priests, in a word, who are ministers on paper, mere statistics, not energetic, working bodies.

Actually this group is something new in Catholicism, evolving in the main from a 1966 policy decision of Pope Paul VI setting retirement for priests at age seventy-five. The effects of Paul VI's decision were dramatic and near-instantaneous, and nowhere more than in United States. In 1968, as dioceses were inaugurating retirement programs in response to the papal directive, there were in the United States only seven hundred or so diocesan priests who were listed as inactive because of retirement, ill health, or other forms of absences from the ministry. Just fifteen years later, in 1983, the number was 5,223, the majority of whom had reached the retirement age of seventy-five.[1] They were carried on the rolls as a statistic, but for all practical purposes, they were priests without assignment or regular function. Thus, to return to the comparative statistics, there were in the years between 1968 and 1985 not merely fewer priests in the United States, but *many fewer* when the retirement factor was entered into the equation. Further, the decline continues.

The disarming detail is the subtlety of this continuing decline, certainly by comparison with fifteen or twenty years ago. Priests retire; they go on sick leave; they take sabbaticals. But they have always done these things to one degree or another, so such departures, now as before, do not startle in the way that certain departures of the late 1960s and the 1970s did, specifically those abrupt and often sensational resignations from the active ministry. It was a time when one did not know what to expect to hear next from the pulpit or to read in the newspaper. A priest might announce from the altar that this was his last Sunday on the job, as he had his wife and children to take care of; it happened. Or a newspaper might disclose that a Jesuit provincial or some other prominent priest had gone off and married. There were so many instances of that sort that many wondered whether the priesthood was coming apart. It didn't. Rather, the abrupt, sensational resignations have leveled off, or they have seemed to. Maybe, on the other hand, the Catholic public is just so inured to priestly departures that it doesn't take notice as it once did, or maybe the media are sated with the story and no longer so interested as they were in what priests decide to do with their lives. Whatever the reasons—and there are surely many—we do not hear or read anywhere near so much as before about priests leaving to pursue a new career, to marry, to rediscover themselves. The priesthood actually seems serene and on course.

Nonetheless, unauthorized resignations still occur, and they thin the ranks as certainly as do deaths, sick leaves, and sabbaticals. The ordination of new priests each spring—that perennial source of replenishment of the clerical ranks in the past—takes place now as in the past, but the numbers are fewer. The decline in the numbers of new priests may seem slight from year to year as percentages go, but it is steady, and the effects are felt throughout the system. Between 1984 and 1985, for instance, there were 111 fewer diocesan priests, a manageable decline, it would seem, in the context of a total of 35,052 priests. But the decline goes on year after year, while at the same time the Catholic population (of nominal Catholics, at least) continues to grow. From 1984 to 1985, the Catholic population of the United States increased by 106,891, to 52,286,043 persons. The pattern seems set for the indefinite future, for studies see no turn around in the respective rates of decline for priests and of growth in the number of those who are counted as Catholics. Thus, by the year 2000, it is estimated that there will be 65 million Catholics in the United States, but 50 percent fewer active diocesan priests than the present number to minister to them.[2]

It is a decline–growth ratio that the American church can ignore only at the peril of its future. Obviously, the fact is not lost on many, for most American dioceses are planning for a tomorrow that will be quite different from their yesterdays.

The diocese of Worcester, Massachusetts, for instance, projects a 9 percent decrease in the number of priests for each decade over the next fifty years and thus has instituted a needs-assessment study to identify future problem areas of Catholic life in the context of the diminishing supply of priests.

In the archdiocese of Boston, where the number of active priests declined from 1,002 in 1984 to 943 in 1986, and by a total of 374 priests over a fifteen-year span, the future is now. Accordingly, on 15 December 1986, on the recommendation of the archdiocesan Presbyterial Council, Cardinal Law announced new guidelines for the assignment of priests within the archdiocese, based on what is known as a *sacramental index*, a formula that takes into account the number of baptisms, marriages, and funerals in a parish. The guidelines raised by 25 percent the statistical basis for assigning additional priests to a parish. At the same time, heads of archdiocesan agencies and other apostolates were asked to review their personnel needs, the objective being to make more priests available for sacramental duties.[3]

Meanwhile, in the diocese of Fall River, Massachusetts, the priest shortage is such that it has been "strongly recommended that priests begin to curtail the vast numbers of scheduled masses." The recommendation came in connection with the recognition that "there is a grave shortage of priests to serve the needs of the faithful." Among the considerations, no doubt, was the health of priests; a person can do only so much. There was also the stated reminder that priests "have to satisfy mass obligations within a reasonable time"; in other words, a priest accepting a stipend offering for a mass must be able to meet his commitment sooner rather than later. Where this is difficult or impossible, it is advised in the Fall River diocese that priests send the requests and offerings to priests serving in foreign missions.[4]

Across the United States, the multiple-priest parish (parishes in which a pastor has one, two, or three curates, or where a team ministry is operative) is already becoming a thing of the past, and the talk, even from the pulpits, is of a day when one priest will be in charge not of one parish, but of several in a geographical area—a return, in a way, to an earlier time when a parish priest commonly cared, too, for a mission chapel or two serving Catholics in the outlying communities of his district, generally rural or mountain. The return of that day is not far off in the United States. There could be a quick way out of the problem—several ways, in fact. But quick fixes are foreclosed by persistent Roman opposition to such ideas as women priests, a married clergy, or even a return to the active ministry of priests who left the active ministry and married, very many of whom would welcome the opportunity to return to full- or part-time ministerial service.

The situation, in sum, shapes up as being a historical rewrite, of sorts, of the one reported to Rome way back in 1785 by Father John Carroll, when Carroll was not yet a bishop, the country's first, and the American church was still the "American mission." Carroll wrote Rome on the matter of marriage between relatives, seeking waivers from certain impediments of consanguinity so that certain intrafamilial weddings might be made more possible, thus reducing the number of interdenominational marriages, where the Catholic party might be lost to the spouse's faith. Pertinent to this discussion is the condition described by Carroll, as well as its consequence—a state that could conceivably be duplicated. "As for their observance," Carroll declared, "in general [American Catholics] are rather faithful to the practices of their religion, and in frequenting the sacraments. All fervor, however, is lacking...since many congregations attend Mass and hear a sermon [only] once a month or every two weeks. To this extent we are overwhelmed by the scarcity of priests."[5]

Unless every sign is wrong, every trend misleading, the American church is headed for a comparable scarcity of priests in the not too distant future, though crisis will be forestalled for at least a while because of liturgical and ministerial alternatives that did not exist in Carroll's time. Permanent deacons, for instance, are becoming more and more a fact of life in the American church, although, as mentioned, permanent deacons, who must be male according to the present discipline, possess only limited sacramental powers. But at least they can perform baptisms and officiate at weddings; there probably wasn't a permanent deacon in all of Christendom in Carroll's day, the office having fallen into disuse after enjoying wide popularity in the early church. Similarily, there is the new office of eucharistic minister, one that functions under a 1973 authorization of Pope Paul VI.[6] Eucharistic ministers, who may be either male or female, serve as special assistants in the distribution of the Eucharist at mass and, outside the mass, as visitors carrying the Eucharist to the sick, the aged and the infirm, shut-ins generally. They, too, were unknown in Carroll's day. In the United States, many dioceses have used the office of eucharistic minister to involve the laity more intimately in the life of the church, its liturgy, and its ministry. In actuality, however, the office exists on the books as an emergency measure, for the supplying of appropriate pastoral service when there is an insufficient number of priests and deacons to meet pastoral needs. The Vatican provided a pointed reminder of that detail when it vetoed the use of eucharistic ministers at liturgies during John Paul II's 1979 visit to the United States, on the grounds that there would be sufficient numbers of priests on hand at the pope's masses to handle the distribution of communion. (Some viewed the ruling as a male-chauvinist tactic to shut women out of this privileged participation in the papal liturgies, which it may or may not have been. In any instance, it will be interesting to note what the policy is for eucharistic ministers during John Paul II's 1987 return visit, plans for which are proceeding at the time of this writing.)

Most parishes have several eucharistic ministers, and some parishes have them by the dozen. And everywhere that they exist, they multiply the hands of the priest in unique ways. Along with other functions, they can lead the worshiping community in nonsacramental ceremonies, such as Bible vigils and what is called the Extraordinary Rite of Communion. This rite is modeled on the structure of the Mass, but when it arrives at what in the regular Mass is known as the Liturgy of the Eucharist, it omits the consecration and uses preconsecrated communion hosts maintained in a reserve for occasions when a priest is absent or otherwise unavailable. The rite is becoming commonplace in one-priest parishes. On a priest's day off, and when he is sick or on vacation, a eucharistic minister will take over, delivering the readings, leading the prayers, perhaps preaching a homily, then distributing the preconsecrated communion hosts stored for the contingency.

The hands of the priest are likewise being multiplied on administrative levels, as many dioceses employ men and women—nuns, religious brothers, and laity—in roles once exclusively fulfilled by priests. Laypersons in increasing numbers head diocesan offices as school superintendents, financial directors, and the like. Nuns and brothers, who one day might have achieved their apostolic and professional plateaus as school principals, now may be found in exalted positions involving broad responsibilities. The diocese of Fargo, North Dakota, for instance, lists a nun as an assistant chancellor, and on 17 February 1987 the diocese of Portland, Maine, advanced a nun to the position of vice-chancellor—Sister

Rita-Mae Bissonnette, R.S.R., a Millinocket native who ten years earlier had become one of the first women in the United States to serve as an advocate in a diocesan marriage tribunal.[7] The diocese of New Ulm, Minnesota, had placed five parishes under the charge of nun-administrators by 1984. They may have been pioneers of a sort, but even then, they were hardly unique. The revised Code of Canon Law, which took effect in 1983, provided that parishes could be administered by others besides priests, even "a community of persons," when a "dearth of priests" existed. Among others, the dioceses of Richmond, Superior, and Tulsa today have nun-administrators of parishes, and in the Williamsburg section of Brooklyn, three nuns, not a priest, run All Saints parish. A priest already deployed as a prison chaplain acts as a part-time moderator of the Williamsburg parish to celebrate Mass and to handle sacramental duties, but otherwise, it is the sisters—members of the Dominican Sisters of Amityville, Long Island—who are in charge, among other things doing what they can to improve a neighborhood struggling against poverty, neglect, and a shortage of housing. Among other symbols of change, a permanent deacon can be found administering a parish in Denver.

But to some observers nothing has been more innovative or surprising, given the once-reactionary history of the place, than the election of a nun, Sacred Heart of Mary Sister Mary Milligan, to the presidency of the board of directors of St. John's Seminary, the major seminary of the archdiocese of Los Angeles,[8] long since a tightly secured bastion of orthodoxy. Her election was the more surprising because just a few years earlier, Catholic circles had been buzzing with rumors that Rome was close to a decision that would ban female spiritual directors in male seminaries, theorectically on the grounds that seminarians consulting a spiritual director should be able, should they so desire, to make a sacramental confession to that person, and nuns are not empowered to give absolution. The rumor did not prove true, but the possibility of its being proved true has not yet been dismissed.

These are all personnel breakthroughs of a positive sort, even though most of them may have been forced by extenuating circumstances, rather than being initiated by a generous impulse to broaden the roles of Catholics generally in the life of their church. But this, too, is an old story. Almost every innovation in the modern church has resulted from necessity rather than an acknowledgment that some people were being shut out from meaningful involvement in the church, and that it was this injustice that needed to be rectified. Parents of Catholic schoolchildren were not brought onto diocesan and parish school boards until the problems of costs, faculty, and enrollments began to overwhelm the clerical supervisors and it became apparent that nothing was going to be solved without the participation and cooperation of parents. Parish councils did not come into existence until it was clear that the old system of unilateral decision making was becoming increasingly unacceptable at the grass roots. (In some places, parish councils may be ineffective or a sop to those who wish to think they are participating in a meaningful way in the decisions of their parishes, but at the least, they represent an effort to involve the church's membership in decisions that were once unapologetically made for them entirely by someone else.) By the same token, it is likely that periodic public financial statements, now routine from the Vatican to the smallest parish, were born of a diminishing ability to manage escalating expenses on old levels of income. There may be fewer clerical salaries to pay, but any saving is more than offset by salaries for lay teachers in the schools, as well as for lay workers in the parishes and other church institutions. Then, too, there are the costs of maintenance and development. The church doesn't stand still. Nor is it impervious to inflation. It has to support and sustain itself financially. When the pinch is tight, and when the needs of people are great, it is often easier in the church, as in the public sector, to be forthright about what one needs than it is to proclaim one's profit and abundance.

The instigations for policy change in the church are often forgotten as change fixes itself in custom, which is probably just as well. The world moves ahead, not backward. What does not lose significance, however, is the problem at the root of change, particularly if the problem is chronic. Maybe the wider employment of nuns and religious brothers, and of the laity, in ministerial and administrative roles in the church would have come one day or another, but it is certain that it was hastened by a problem situation, specifically, the failure of the priesthood as a vocation and profession to attract candidates in numbers comparable to the past and sufficient for the church to meet its needs of the moment.

The implications for a church as large as the American one cannot be minimized. The church needs priests, but getting priests and holding them to a lifelong commitment becomes more difficult by the year. Nor is this a uniquely American problem. According to the Vatican's Central Office for Church Statistics, Asia is the only region of the world where the number of priests is increasing, the total rising from 25,981 to 28,266 between 1973 and 1984—the last year for which the comparison figures were available at this writing. Everywhere else the total is down, including in North America (Canada and the United States), the number having dropped from 72,749 to 69,337.[9] As the number of priests declines, the ratio of priests to Catholics as a body inevitably decreases. It stood at one priest per 1,586 Catholics in 1973; it was one priest per 2,069 Catholics in 1984. These statistics are consolation for no one at the church's leadership level.

The Vatican releases its statistical studies of vocations worldwide on a regular basis. In recent years, its statistics have shown a remarkable and at the same time sobering trend. They show that vocations are experiencing a notable rise where the church is beleaguered (in Poland, for example) and where the church is newly emerging (in Asia and Africa); on the other hand, vocations are suffering a marked decline where the church has been long established, in areas that are often thought of as strongholds of the faith: Western Europe, Canada, and the United States. In the United States alone, the number of seminarians plunged from 42,767 in the 1966–1967 academic year, to 18,029 in 1976–1977, and to

10,372 in 1986–1987, according to figures of the Washington-based Center for Applied Research in the Apostolate.[10] This represents a 43 percent decline over the past decade, and a 76 percent decline over the past twenty years. Nor has the decline been arrested. Between the 1985–1986 and the 1986–1987 school years, there was a 4 percent drop in starting enrollments, from 10,811 to the 10,372 figure cited above.[11] It would seem that, in some places, the priesthood may be a calling with a patriotic dimension to it and, in others, a ticket to an education, status, and maybe a better life. But to the extent that a vocation was ever either of these things in the United States (actually the American priesthood never had any of the former about it, but at times, it had considerable of the latter), that characteristic of a vocation has long ceased to exist. The priesthood in the United States must attract candidates on the pure and unqualified grounds of being a call from God to be of service to others.

Theoretically, that is what a vocation is and always was, except there were such emoluments of office as security and status, which throughout history have heightened the attractiveness of the calling. They still exist, to be sure, but not in such clear-cut fashion as before. The comforts of the middle class now make those of the clerical caste pale, and a priest's status can disappear the moment he steps beyond the church's sanctuary, and it often does. The guarantees of yesterday are gone, eroded by a changing society and the tides of postconciliar renewal. A better educated, more independent laity has offset the standing and lessened the preeminence that the priest once enjoyed as scholar and authority figure in the Catholic community. At the same time, the satisfactions of the priestly life are suddenly less, partly because values that the priesthood enshrined have been superseded by other values that often are precluded to those in the priesthood—marriage and parenthood, most notably. The marriage value cannot be realized under the current discipline, but canon law says nothing about priests not being parents, so a few priests—a pastor in Chicago, Father George H. Clements; an associate pastor in Vancouver, Washington, Father Jim Mitchell; and others, no doubt—have taken the step, novel for priests, of adopting children. Clements and Mitchell are each fathers of three adopted sons. Obviously, theirs is not the total solution, and maybe not even a desirable middle course in fulfilling the parenting instinct. Certainly, it is nothing that the church's leadership encourages, and it is doubtful that it will ever become a commonplace. But that clerical adoptions happen at all testifies to the void that some priests feel in their lives and the compulsion they are under to fill it.

Obviously, for some priests, the priesthood in its traditional contexts is not the idyllic state that Catholic mythology would have it be, nor, as the vocations' shortage attests, is it viewed any longer by those in search of a career as the Garden of Eden that some would identify with a "higher calling." The glamour is gone from the calling, and religious sociologists are studying the reasons. One such study, conducted in 1984 under the aegis of the United States Catholic Conference, came up with a set of "plausibles" to explain the phenomenon.

The "plausibles" included the requirements of celibacy, permanent commitment, and lack of encouragement from parents and priests, traditionally the primary promoters of vocations.[12]

The problems besetting the priesthood and the religious vocations generally are more multifarious than just those "plausibles," of course. And when all the sociological studies are completed, the findings will very likely support a variety of conclusions. Sociological studies frequently do. But if the least common denominator is what one is looking for, Eugene C. Kennedy, the Chicago psychologist and author who was himself once a Maryknoll father, has come up with one that helps explain the change that has overtaken the priesthood and, to some extent, all areas of religious life, both those in it and ultimately those contemplating it as a career. Observed Kennedy:

> The once dominant role of the priest in the Catholic culture has been modified considerably in the past two generations. The fact that priests are no longer protected people, excused for their misdeeds and amply rewarded for their good ones, is a sign of the restyled Catholic culture in which they function. Their vulnerability to evaluation and criticism means they also function in the manner of other professionals. In other words, priests are now more subject to the dynamics that govern professional life in the broader American culture.[13]

Paradoxically, as Kennedy noted, this is a circumstance that was long thought desirable for the clergy, including by priests themselves. However, being realized at a moment that the priesthood is in something of a major identity crisis, the achieving of the goal becomes something of a contretemps, an inopportune occurrence. "Priests feel unhappy, lonely, uncertain of their futures," remarked Kennedy,[14] and small wonder. Priests see classmates and colleagues of long standing quitting the active ministry, and they know that the easy rationalizations, most of them blaming the priest ("He shouldn't have been ordained in the first place," or "His hormones got the best of him"), don't provide the answers they once appeared to. In this context, it is academic whether this clergy drain is qualitative. Some hold that it is the best and the brightest who are leaving, but who's to say really? "There is no evidence that the resignees were better educated or scored any higher on measures of emotional maturity than those who remained," Andrew Greeley wrote at the high tide of clergy resignations in his 1977 social portrait of American Catholics.[15] But best or just good, the brightest or the merely competent, priests leave, and even though the departures now are many fewer than before, the phenomenon takes a toll on those who stay in place—as, indeed, so must the disinclination of the younger generation of Catholics to take up the priesthood as a life. One would expect that many priests cannot help but ask themselves if they are not quite literally God's fools.

The common presumption, arising perhaps out of the innate sexuality of all who breathe, is that priests leave the active ministry in order to marry. Some do, of course. For many, however, marriage is not so much the immediate reason for their leaving as it is a step that follows sequentially in the reordering of their lives. Actually, there is nothing unusual about an ex-priest wanting to marry. It was the Lord God, none other, who said in Genesis 2:18, "It is not good that man [Adam] should be alone," and accordingly God provided Adam a "suitable partner," whom Adam called "woman."

The fact remains, however, that priests leave the ministry for a variety of reasons, and marriage is only one and not necessarily the first of them. Andrew Greeley has cited other reasons, including personal loneliness, frustrations of the job, and loss of faith, and he concedes that there are probably more that his study, done in 1977, did not explore. "In summary," said Greeley, "those who leave the priesthood seem to be those who do not like being priests."[16] Which, in a way, is to say the obvious.

More provocative, even if more observational than sociologically scientific, is the conclusion of John Cogley, the respected reporter and commentator on religious trends for *Commonweal* and the *New York Times* from the 1940s into the 1970s. Cogley, who died in 1976, argued in a 1973 study of American Catholicism that many of the priests leaving the active ministry did so because the "professional priesthood no longer made much sense" to them.[17] Some priests "no longer knew what was required of them or what their role should be in a secularized society," Cogley remarked. Some felt "strangulated by a too-slow-to-change institutional apparatus." The more embittered, "a smaller number," joined those "who were alienated from institutional religion of all kinds."[18]

Interspersed, meanwhile, throughout all these types, Cogley's and Greeley's, were those who believed that, in an increasingly secularized society they could actually be of greater service to humankind in a secular rather than a clerical role. I once heard a priest speculate in complete seriousness that someone who sells insurance was in a position to contribute more to people's lives, to help people more, than was he as a priest, and at one point, he seemed ready to chuck the one profession for the other. In a more thoughtful moment, he decided to work in the inner city. He left the priesthood and joined a "head start" program in a mid-Atlantic state, where he has had a successful and totally satisfying career.

But whatever the reason or combination of reasons for a priest's leaving the active ministry, this much is certain: the decision is not fraught with the pain and agony it once was. Married or single, the ex-priest is not the pariah, the social leper in the Catholic community that he used to be. He is not stigmatized. Nor does he have to slink off and set himself up in some distant community where he is not likely to be recognized, rather like some ex-convict or informer in a governmental protective-custody program. Most former priests blend into communities of their own choosing with a minimum of scandal or tongue wagging following in their wake. Bernard M. Kelly, the former auxiliary bishop of Providence, who resigned from the active ministry in 1971, opened a law office in the state of Rhode Island. James P. Shannon, the former auxiliary bishop of St. Paul–Minneapolis, who resigned as bishop and married in 1969, has also pursued a legal career and moved into corporate America as a vice-president of General Mills and executive director of its foundation. Shannon's standing in the Catholic community was so thoroughly rehabilitated by 1986 that he received the centennial medal from the college he had headed as a priest, the College of St. Thomas in St. Paul.

Not only is it easier to leave the priesthood and to survive with dignity, it is also easier to express from within the priesthood one's complaints about clerical and church life in general. When the California priest Father James Kavanaugh, since resigned from the ministry, dared to express publicly in 1966 a wish to be able to marry, he had to do so under a pseudonym and in a publication beyond the control of the church, the *Saturday Evening Post*.[19] At the time, it was, purely and simply, a matter of survival. The church didn't suffer "troublemakers" or dissenters. It was a situation that priests were aware of and protected themselves against. The best reporting at Vatican Council II (1962–1965) was done in the *New Yorker* by a priest, now generally conceded to be Father Francis X. Murphy, C.SS.R. But precisely because Murphy was a priest—and still is—prudence dictated his use of a pseudonym. Today, Murphy moves back and forth between his real name and the pseudonym Xavier Rynne, with no particular effort to disguise who is who. But time was when he could easily have been silenced had he used his own name. If we think back to those reports in the *New Yorker*, the wonder of it now is that he was not silenced, at least in the beginning, for almost everyone seemed to be in on the Murphy/Rynne secret.

Pseudonyms are not the necessity for certain types of priest-writers that they once were, although they are still used—probably more for personal reasons of a psychological kind than for reasons of professional security. Some people no doubt find it easier to bare the soul and to register complaints and grievances under a pseudonym than to use their own names. But even in instances of this sort, it is not necessary to seek out a secular publisher, as Kavanaugh had to do in 1966. No formally or officially Catholic publication would have touched Kavanaugh's article in 1966, but today, far bolder statements appear in the Catholic press of the United States, in publications under impeccable auspices. Kavanaugh's article was entitled "I Am a Priest, I Want to Marry." When the pastor of a thousand-family parish in the Midwest sat down in 1986 and wrote his article "I'd Like to Say: 'If I Had a Son, I Wouldn't Want Him to Be a Priest!' " he did so under a pseudonym, Father William Wells, but his article appeared in about as formally Catholic a publication as one could hope to find anywhere: *St. Anthony Messenger*, a high-circulation monthly (421,782 copies) published under the auspices of the Franciscan Friars of Cincinnati.[20]

Articles appearing under a pseudonym immediately discount themselves, yet the "Wells" article in *St. Anthony Messenger* claims attention, for it testifies in a direct, personal way to so many of the points being made

by professional sociologists, as well as one or two beyond them. The article speaks, for instance, of work
overload, a complaint that will come as a surprise to
those who think of the parish priest's job as belonging
in a "cushy" category. It never was; it isn't now. In
what other profession is a person expected to be on call
at any hour of the day or night? Police and firefighters
work shifts, and there are those to take over when their
shift is done. People in industry work their eight-hour
days. Most doctors have office hours, and it is the rare
one indeed who makes house calls nowadays. But the
priest is expected to be forever at the other end of the
phone for sick calls, counsel, or advice. If he installs an
automatic message-recorder, he'll be criticized for tech-
nologizing the priesthood, substituting his presence with
that of a mechanical device.

However, demands of time and person are less the
focus of the "Wells" article than are certain problems
registered by sociologists of religion, including many
priest-sociologists. These fix on "loneliness, isolation,"
and the feeling that somehow priests just can't "relax"
and be themselves; Wells unconvincingly adds a demurrer about salary, complaining that "the majority of
priests in the United States make less than $10,000 a
year." To be sure, $10,000 is not a grand sum, but it
would seem comfortable enough when so many basic expenses are taken care of and perquisites are figured in.
Priests have rectories, housekeepers, secretaries, living
expenses, car allowances, vacation time, and medical and
retirement plans. They are not exactly a hardship class
of people.

The "Wells" article is on firmer ground when it dwells on the stress factors that make the priesthood difficult for those in it and unattractive to those inclined to consider it as a vocation. Here again, celibacy emerges as a chief complaint.

Celibacy has been heralded by the church for centuries as a holier state, a "treasure," a sign of a priest's "undivided and liberated heart," a "gift of the Spirit," a life different from others in that it is lived "in intimacy with God."[21] The fact is, however, that for half of the church's life, holiness was not bound up with celibacy, certainly not in the unqualified way that it is now in the Roman Catholic or Western church. (It still isn't in the Eastern Uniate church.) For centuries, priests married and raised families. It is true that, as early as the fourth century, the church sought to restrict the freedom of clerics to marry, and of those who married anyway, it sought to require celibacy, a measure it enforced by denying promotion to priests with children. However, it was not until the eleventh century, when Pope Gregory VII (1073–1085) achieved a widespread reform of the clergy, that celibacy actually became mandatory for priests of the Roman or Western church,[22] and marriage became impossible. To this day, the discipline remains different in the Eastern church, where candidates for Holy Orders may marry before becoming deacons, although not after ordination. In any case, so many individual exceptions have been made to the rule, mostly for married Protestant clergy moving to Roman Catholicism, that celibacy is hardly the *sine qua non* it is held to be. Pope Pius XII (1939–1958) extended at least one exemption to the celibacy requirement in the instance of a Scandinavian Lutheran minister who converted to Catholicism, and of course, John Paul II opened the sanctuary gates to a dozen or more in the instances of Episcopal priests who left their church on the issue of female ordination.

The case against mandatory celibacy and for an open priesthood, where priests may marry or not, has been argued from almost every conceivable angle. The tack of the "Wells" article is to condemn celibacy as the denial of a basic human right to marry, a line of argument being increasingly used by those on the side of change. "Every person has the basic right to marry, the church teaches, yet," says the "Wells" article, "if you want to become a priest you must surrender that right forever." The church would counter that the vow of celibacy is one made freely "for the more perfect observance of chastity."[23] This is a logic that has prevailed for years in the church's thinking, and that has withstood contentions that mandatory celibacy is psychologically unsound, asocial, and even antisocial. Mandatory celibacy may conceivably be any of these things or not. What is becoming increasingly probable, however, is that, in a sexually expressive age, when the church itself has conceded the importance of intimacy and of conjugal love (physical love between men and women in the spousal relationship),[24] the celibacy issue stands in danger of being settled on terms alien to the church's wishes and completely apart from its shaping by the simple expedient of some priests' taking the matter into their own hands. Clerical wives and clerical concubines have long been alleged to be common in Latin American countries, and not long ago, a North American priest, one who served in Montana, published an autobiography in which he maintained that he openly exercised a married priesthood for five years with permission from diocesan authorities[25]—an allegation, incidentally, that undoubtedly contributed to Archbishop Hunthausen's grief in Rome. Before going to Seattle, Hunthausen served in Montana, from 1962 to 1975 as bishop of Helena. The last two of those years as bishop of Helena coincided with two of the five years in which the author of the autobiography, Michael Miles, claimed to have practiced his married priesthood. When the ex-priest's book drew attention in the media for its startling claims, Hunthausen answered back in a statement issued 17 July 1986. He declared that he had allowed Miles—who was laicized by Rome and who married in 1973—to continued working as a lay minister in Resurrection parish, a campus ministry parish at Montana State University in Bozeman, a permission Hunthausen described as consistent with church teaching and discipline. But he categorically denied that he had ever given Miles permission to function as a priest. '' Whatever a reader might construe from the book, at no time,'' said Hunthausen, ''did I ever agree to, much less foster, any kind of experiment in married priesthood.'' In a statement that followed on 29 July 1986 Hunthausen's successor in Helena, Bishop Elden Curtiss, dismissed the ex-priest's claims as ''half-truths and distortions.'' Curtiss labeled the book ''fiction.''[26]

As for the anonymous ''Father Wells,'' he contended in the *St. Anthony Messenger* article that ''mandatory celibacy has become the millstone around the neck of the priesthood and is threatening to destroy it." The comment smacks of rhetorical overkill, particularly set as it is by "Wells" amid allegations of secret clerical marriages, of priests' "passing off their wives as live-in housekeepers," and of "heterosexual and homosexual priests" taking lovers, "some of whom cohabitate right within the rectory." The author described them as priests of his acquaintance. The implication of such talk as this is that a celibate clergy is something of a sham in the United States, and that the parish rectory is anything but the refined, decorous place parishioners think it to be. Admittedly, celibacy is a problem, and undoubtedly, cases exist of the kind described in the "Wells" article. But that they are as common as the article suggests is open to serious question. I would also be inclined to question the figures in *Newsweek's* issue of 23 February 1987 alleging that 20 percent of American priests are homosexual and that half of these sexually active, and further, that 20 percent of American priests are heterosexually active.

A licentious clergy is not the clergy of my experience as a born Catholic and an editor and writer who has spent thirty-five years as a specialist in Catholic religious news. I have known any number of priests who left the active ministry and married, either sooner or later. But those are cases apart. Apropos the "Wells" allegations, over all those years I have known personally of only one priest who turned out to be secretly married—a New York pastor, now deceased. An exceptional priest, he was forced to make a choice between family and priesthood when his children neared teenage and in effect became circulating notices of his private life. He resigned the priesthood. Every other case of a related kind of my experience requires a leap to judgment that, even now, I am not prepared to make. Those cases aren't many. There was the pastor who retired in the fullness of years and moved to Florida with his housekeeper of years, and there was the priest (from New Zealand) who arrived at an international press convention I was attending in Vienna with his "sister." One was tempted to be more judgmental in the second instance, as the "sister" was a handsome woman and, if the reader will excuse the oxymoron, she and the priest danced terribly well together. On the other hand, maybe they were siblings. Whether they were or not does not vitiate my point. The priests of my acquaintance have been a remarkably chaste group of men, and more faithful to their vows than many married men I know have been to theirs.

The *St. Anthony Messenger* article is on more tenable ground when it turns to young people and the resistance of so many of them to the very idea of a religious vocation. "Father Wells" contends that, in his fourteen years as a priest, he has not been able to persuade one young man to enter the seminary and undertake studies to be ordained. Each time he has broached the subject with a prospect, he claims to have been rebuffed, always, professedly, with more or less the same answer: "I don't want to spend my life alone. When the church allows priests to marry, I'll consider becoming a priest. But not until then."[27]

It is hard to believe that, in fourteen years on the job, this pastor in his early forties did not hear at least one other reason from someone for not wanting to be a priest. Still, in sociological study after study, including those under ecclesiastical auspices, the celibacy requirement looms large among the reasons for lack of interest in a priestly vocation. Certainly, this is true in the United States. The celibacy requirement discourages young prospects and also appears to take a toll on older men in clerical life, again in terms of loneliness, but also, it would seem, for certain smaller percentages by contributing to anxieties, frustrations, and other psychological and medical disorders. Priests by my contention are a chaste group, and by no serious account can they be said to be a behavioral time bomb waiting to explode. Yet, in 1986, more than one hundred priests and members of religious orders met in Morristown, New Jersey, for a regional conference of the Canon Law Society of America, at which a major topic of discussion was sexual abuse of children by priests. More than forty cases of child molestation had been reported in the previous two years, and as the *New York Times* stated in its report of the meeting, "church officials in this country are beginning to talk openly about the problem."[28] They would have little choice obviously, when shortly before and since the church has been confronted by such sensational cases as the Lafayette, Louisiana, priest who confessed to raping or sodomizing thirty-seven children and was sentenced to twenty years in prison for his misdeeds; the Rhode Island priest who was sentenced to a year in prison after pleading no contest to twenty-six charges of sexually assaulting boys; and the Alabama priest who committed suicide after being charged with sexually molesting an altar boy, and who left behind a note saying he would rather be a dead memory than a living disgrace to the church.

The Morristown meeting followed a similar session for bishops in Collegeville, Maryland, and one for priests in Arlington, Virginia. To recall them and the topic of focus is not to suggest that sexual dysfunction is a concomitant of clerical celibacy. Much less is it to suggest that a large percentage of priests are debased. As was declared by Father Thomas P. Doyle, a priest then assigned to the Apostolic Nunciature in Washington and a speaker at the Morristown meeting, the molestation cases involved a "miniscule" percentage of the nation's fifty-seven thousand priests.[29] That is no doubt so, although that circumstance doesn't help much. Cases of this sort hurt mightily. They're bad for the church's image, its moral leadership, and its credibility—even, as Doyle mentioned, its finances, because the withholding of donations is forever an effective way to register anger and upset. "It is the most serious problem we in the church have faced in centuries," Doyle said of molestation cases.[30] That may be hyperbole, but it is certainly true that incidents of that sort, with all the unhappy publicity they generate, translate into a very serious problem for priests, and prospective priests as well. They erode morale among those already in the priesthood, and they cause prospects, certainly a percentage at least, to look elsewhere in terms of career and vocation. Sexual deviation among some in the priesthood is not "the most serious problem" the church has had to face in centuries, Doyle's comment notwithstanding, but given all the difficulties that the church is having in holding its priests and attracting new ones, it is about as nasty a problem as the church could want to have at the moment.

There are problems. There are also perplexities, and two of the knottiest of the latter arise out of the postconciliar efforts to upgrade the professionalism of the priesthood and to involve the laity in the church's ministry. The efforts have had the desired results, to be sure. But they have not been without their complications.

Two innovations especially have proved something of a mixed blessing.

The first is the periodic evaluation and limited tenure of pastors, in most places six-year terms, renewable upon review for a second six years. The program was introduced to strengthen the priesthood pastorally as well as professionally, and it exists from diocese to diocese in varying degrees of strictness. In other words, the letter of the program is not etched in stone. Bishops can make exceptions in their individual dioceses, and they regularly do. Those who have watched the program evolve are convinced that it has helped to strengthen clerical performances. But although helping in this respect, the program has also injected a note of uncertainty into the life of a priest by rendering him subject to an ongoing analysis, as if he were some kind of cog in the corporate machine. This isn't all bad by any means. There were too many instances in the past of a parish's being turned into the fief of some untouchable pastor. Limited tenure and periodic evaluation are protections against incompetents and parish tyrants. Certainly, they strengthen the odds against them. On the other hand, this same program les-

sens much of the old security that went with the territory, because even with the best of performances, a
priest can be expected to pack up and move on when his
six or twelve years are up. A pastoral assignment, which
seemed an utter blessing at age fifty, can thus turn into
a cross when the priest reaches fifty-six or sixty-two and
is asked to step aside because of tenure limitations. As
Eugene Kennedy has commented, ''To ask men to start
again in new parishes even as they approach the normal
age of retirement is demanding more than we do of almost any other group of professional people.''[31]

The second innovation of mixed blessing is the ex-
pansion of the ministry to include laity—men and
women—in roles once reserved exclusively to priests.
Permanent deacons—men ordained in a major order and
called *Reverend* but still generally perceived by the Catholic in the pew as laymen—now counsel those preparing to receive a sacrament for the first time; they officiate
at weddings and baptize their grandchildren in solemn
church ceremonies. Men *and* women, individuals who
grew up in a church where no one except the priest ever
touched by hand the consecrated communion host, and
where even the handling of the sacred vessels was
limited to the specially designated, now take ciborium
in hand and distribute the Eucharist to communicants.
In emergencies and on days of special devotion, such as
First Fridays,[32] they carry the Eucharist to the sick and
the shut-ins. They teach Christian doctrine, and like permanent deacons, they help prepare young Catholics and
converts for initiation into the sacraments. All this is ex-

actly the direction in which Vatican Council II pointed the future in emphasizing the concept of "the common priesthood of the faithful" existing alongside "the ministerial or hierarchical priesthood," each in its own way being "a participation in the one priesthood of Christ."[33]

Thanks to the council, in two decades the concept of a priesthood of the faithful, or the laity, has passed from the abstract to the concrete, and, it would seem, at a moment of particular appropriateness given the shortage of priests. Priests realize this and most undoubtedly welcome it, although it must be disconcerting to a certain number of them, even those ordained as recently as fourteen years ago, that 50 percent of what was their unique ministry at ordination is now shared by laypersons. In a word, the ground is narrowed on which the priest's services are absolutely necessary. Priests are not rendered completely dispensable by the new developments involving the laity in some areas of ministry, but many cannot help but wonder when their role is virtually contracted to that of celebrant of the sacraments—and, indeed, of those sacraments that cannot be delegated to or assumed by a permanent deacon. Some may be able to rationalize that the situation actually exalts the priest more, placing him on a higher pedestal, as there are still sacramental functions that only a priest can perform. But rationalization does not come easily to all. For many priests, the exclusivity of the priestly role once again is lessened, and lessened with it is a bit more of the status of office. If a layperson can do so much that a priest can, what is the great point in being a priest? The narrow role of dispenser of certain sacraments inevitably has less and less appeal to priests.

Still, whatever the problems or the drawbacks to the job, the majority of priests are happy in their vocation, certainly happy enough to recommend it to and encourage it in others. This is a point worth noting, for it wasn't the case a few years ago. There has been a turnaround in attitudes.

All studies agree that personal encouragement of young men is vital in the development of vocations. A vocation may be a calling from God, but God needs help. In this context, the role of parents is of special importance, as the home has traditionally been the seedbed of vocations. But hardly less important is the role of priests. The priest is the role model. However, being a role model would not seem to be sufficient of itself at a time when so many parents have assumed different attitudes toward vocations in the family. So far as the priesthood is concerned, for many parents the prestige of having a priest-son has been replaced by the desire to have grandchildren, a prospect which a priest-son cannot be expected to advance, given the celibacy requirements of the church. The preference for grandchildren over a priest in the family may dominate even more if the parents, like those of the so-called baby-boom generation, continue to have fewer children and continue to invest in those fewer children their hopes for the continuity of their family line. Recent studies show parents to be more willing to encourage sons to become priests than was the case a decade ago, but it is doubtful that the old mystique of the priest-son will ever be in the future what for so long it was in the past.

In such a circumstance, the influence of the priest becomes more vital than ever for the perpetuation of his profession. The priest must be willing to promote the calling that is his. He must radiate the conviction and the joy of his experience. There's no arguing that. "If priests are not happy in their work, they are not going to be effective recruiters of future priests," Father Richard McBrien has observed. "On the contrary, they will dissuade others, directly or indirectly, from considering the same vocation."[34]

But priests are happier. Certainly they emerged as happier in a National Conference of Catholic Bishops study comparing the attitudes of American priests in 1970 with those of 1985.[35] In 1970, only 28 percent said they were "very happy" as priests, but in 1985, that percentage rose to 39. By the same token, 87 percent of priests in 1985 rated the "joy of administering the sacraments and presiding over the liturgy"—the very fundamentals of the priestly life—as satisfactions of "great importance" to them, an increase from 80 percent in 1970. These are strong, positive findings, although they are counterbalanced in part by some negatives. For instance, fewer priests thought that the life and work of a priest provided "opportunity to exercise intellectual and creative abilities," down five percentage points between 1970 and 1985 from 53 to 48 percent. And fewer priests found satisfying the "respect that comes to the office," down three percentage points from 23 to 20 percent. However, the negatives were not so strong as to

continue to depress the statistics in the area of willingness to encourage vocations. The level of encouragement
was highest in 1965–1966, when 60 percent of priests indicated that they "actively encourage" men to enter the
seminary or novitiate. That percentage figure dropped
sharply in 1970 to 30 percent, but by 1985, it had made
its way back to 48 percent. Interestingly enough, only 1
percent of those polled in the 1985 survey said that they
"tend to discourage men from entering [the priesthood
or religious life] now and advise them to wait until the
future is more certain." Twenty-seven percent in the
1985 poll said they "encourage men [to enter] but advise
them about the uncertainties surrounding the role of the
priest today,"and 22 percent said they "neither discourage nor encourage men, but allow them to make up
their own minds."

Some sociological studies have traced a correlation
between the clergy drain and the encouragement of vocations; specifically, as resignations from the priesthood
leveled off, encouragement of young men to enter the
priesthood rose again. A confidence factor would seem
to be at work here; individuals are obviously more disposed to recommend a life, a career, that is able to hold
its members than to recommend one in which a distress-
ingly large number quit and walk away as the years pass.
But to encourage vocations—even to advertise for vocations, as, it was noted earlier, religious groups are now
doing in unusual places—is not the same as getting
them. Religious groups can target young men in ads in
the Catholic press. They can target young adults in
men's magazines or, as the Benedictine Monks of New-

ark Abbey did on 20 January 1987, in the *New York Times* with an ad aimed smack at the yuppie generation and appealing to men of this group in terms of idealism over life-style: "Nice clothes. A nice car. The newest stereo system"—Is material success, in effect, all it takes to make one happy? The slickest approach, however, is not likely to turn things around, for resistance persists—to such a degree, in fact, that the priesthood more and more takes on the appearance of being a class of geriatrics.

In 1970, the median age of American priests was 47.6 years. In 1985, it was 53.4 years. The median age, in short, is climbing steadily toward the sixty-year mark, where "Father William Wells" saw it heading in his article.[36] Some dioceses are getting there faster than others. The diocese of Brooklyn, which is probably as typical as any in the country, saw its ordination class drop from thirty-two men in 1960 to four in 1984 and already has a median age of fifty-four.[37] In the diocese of Davenport, Iowa, a heartland area where presumably new trends would be slower to evidence themselves, the median age of priests has passed fifty-six.[38]

Only an infusion of young blood can reverse the aging levels of the American priesthood, but even such an infusion could create problems of its own if it continues to prove true that such vocations as the priesthood is now attracting are, in fact, coming mostly from the ideological right. National profiles are showing that young men choosing the priesthood are decidedly more conservative than their counterparts of fifteen years ago, and so rigidly orthodox an institution as Thomas Aquinas College in Santa Paula, California, is able to boast that 11 percent of its alumni have been attracted to a priestly or religious vocation, and that 8 percent of the college's alumni remain today in such orders as the Benedictines, the Dominicans, the Legionaries of Christ, the Oblates of the Virgin Mary, the Carmelites, and the Poor Clares.[39] Father Richard McBrien, the Notre Dame theologian and syndicated columnist, theorized in an interpretative commentary on a 1984 Catholic University study of male religious vocations in the United States that "the vocations crisis is as much qualitative as quantitative," and he added that current recruiting and training practices favor the ordination of men who are "more dependent, institutionally oriented, sexually indifferent and conservative."[40] This development may have the advantage of reducing generation-gap polarities in the priesthood. Older priests very likely do possess at least some of those qualities attributed by McBrien to the new generation of priests in stronger measure than the generation of priests coming in between. On the other hand, the departure from the priesthood of so many priests of the middle generation who were of liberal bent has undoubtedly also narrowed generational polarities somewhat in priestly communities. In any instance, apart from the dubious asset of a reducing of polarities, it is hard to see what possible advantage there could be in having a conservative, essentially right-wing priest taking his place in today's church. The development can only widen the gap between those at the altar and those in the pews, because if one thing is observationally clear before all else about the new generation of Catholics, it is that they are anything but clerically dependent, institutionally oriented, sexually indifferent, and theologically conservative. A more conservative priesthood may complement a more conservative hierarchy, but both could find themselves preaching to deaf ears or across seas of empty pews, as the distance grows between them and a membership that is increasingly independent and liberal across the ecclesiastical board.

4

THE UNPREDICTABLE AMERICAN QUANTITY

The Laity

THE RENAISSANCE OF religious belief and practice among young people is one of the hardy perennials of the print media. In 1984, for instance, the *New York Times Magazine* featured an article by Fran Schumer, vaguely identified as a writer living in New York, remarking that "it is not uncommon to see students wearing crosses and yarmulkes on campuses across the country, and few hide the fact that they go to church or synagogue."[1] Schumer quoted Harvard University's Harvey Cox, theologian and author of *The Secular City*, one of the seminal books of the 1960s, as testifying to the "tremendous resurgence of religious interest" on his campus. Peter Steinfels, editor of *Commonweal*, the Catholic-oriented lay journal of opinion, added that "there is the sympathetic entertainment of a religious belief in intellectual circles that you wouldn't have detected ten years ago." The very next year the *Times* was back to the same story with a Christmas Day article by reporter Dirk Johnson on the revival of interest in religion among college students in the New York metropolitan area, certified by students' "enrolling in religion courses and volunteering for charity work in numbers that many chaplains believe suggest a spiritual renaissance on campus."[2] Rabbi Ruth Sohn, assistant Jewish chaplain at Columbia University, was cited by Johnson as saying that "people are coming back to religion in a way that some of us once went to the counterculture." Religion, she added, "is being seen as an alternative to the values—or lack of values—in the mainstream."

Even the Catholic campus is pictured as experiencing something of a religious renaissance. Father Theodore M. Hesburgh, president of the University of Notre Dame from 1952 until his retirement in 1987, commented in an interview shortly before stepping down that religion was not only alive and well on the South Bend campus, but thriving. "I see things today that I didn't see when I was a student," he declared. "I think the students today are very much more spontaneous in the practice of their religion."[3]

Nor is the phenomenon that these people speak of apparently limited to campuses and the current generation of college students. The magazine *Boston Business* recently identified one of its authors, Dan Wakefield, as a person "now at work on a book for Doubleday that expands his *New York Times Magazine* article [of] a year ago on returning to the church."[4] Nonetheless, it is the campus generation, from which, incidentally, Wakefield graduated some years ago, that currently fascinates people across the age spectrum in the general society. Obviously so, for it is with that generation that so much of the future belongs, not excepting the future of belief and religion in the United States.

There is no reason to doubt the accuracy of these reports or the validity of the impressions conveyed by any of the commentators. On the other hand, there may be ample reason to wonder whether the "good news" of the stories translates to "good news" for institutional religion, institutional Catholicism most especially.

The religion of institutional Catholicism is rooted in a complex set of principles, adherence to which has traditionally been the measure of the orthodox Catholic, the Catholic in good standing. Far from being relaxed, these principles are today being vigorously reinforced in the name of orthodoxy and the papacy. Not that popes have not always been orthodox. Indeed, they have. But historically, some popes have been more tolerant about unorthodoxies and solicitous about the errant than others. John XXIII, for instance, throughout his papacy, projected attitudes that made love and human understanding elements of an importance that transcended the letter of official rule and regulation, and Paul VI, much as it might have gone against every instinctual preference of his own as a priest, accommodated the applications of priests to resign and return to the lay state with a magnanimity that has come only lately to be appreciated. John Paul II is a good and holy man, but he is a hard hat on the issue of laicization. On religious matters he is, to repeat, a man of orthodoxy.

The religion of orthodoxy is not, however, the religion that is said to be booming on campus, nor is it the religion that the generation of young adults generally is particularly interested in. Michael Norton, one of those quoted in the Johnson article in the *New York Times*, underscored the point. Norton, nineteen years old at the time he was interviewed, told of being educated in Catholic schools on Long Island, but being plagued by a sense of ennui when he enrolled at Yale. In his sophomore year at Yale, Norton joined what was described as a charismatic movement, and soon, he was participating in one of the dozens of Bible study groups that the article said were meeting virtually every night in the university's dormitories. "My entire life has changed," Norton, a violinist and a geophysics major, proclaimed to the *Times*. "Since I was saved, I sleep better at night. I confessed my sinful ways to God. Now the anxieties and pressures are gone."[5]

His, maybe. But not necessarily the anxieties and pressures that accrue to institutional Catholicism, the ecclesial church, because of dispositions of that sort. Norton's is not exactly the Catholic mode. "Sinful ways," for example, are not to be confessed just to God, but to God through a priest in the sacrament of reconciliation— the sacrament Norton's parents knew as confession, before the terminology was changed after Vatican II. Similarly, "Bible study groups" are fine in their place, but it is the Mass that matters in the Catholic scheme of

things, and it is very likely not without significance that
Norton mentioned nothing of the Mass. Indeed, strange
as it may seem, the emphasis on the Bible, in the Yale
encounter groups or anywhere else, may actually move
some Catholics—who knows, maybe even young Norton himself?—away from the Catholic mainstream. For
though the Bible is the fundamental source of Catholic
dogma, and central to Catholic thought and teaching, its
expression in a popular biblical spirituality is actually
more Protestant than it is Catholic. It shouldn't be this
way, but it the way Catholic Christianity has evolved.
The Bible is in virtually every Catholic home—collecting
dust. Catholics are expected to get to church and attend
mass. A dormitory encounter group may help a young
student like Norton sleep, but the Catholic church has
a different prescription for his being "saved."

The purpose of all this is neither to belittle encounter groups on campus nor to fault formal Catholicism for
its failure to nourish a biblical spirituality among its
members. It is rather to point up the likelihood that the
religion that young people like Norton are discovering
is not the religion of the institution, least of all of institutional Catholicism. More than that, it may be a religion
that, as suggested above, actually moves many in the
generation of young Catholics further from the reach of
the religious institution of their origin. Institutional
Catholicism has an important stake in this generation of
believers and, consequently, is hugely interested in the
directions that religion takes among those who constitute its membership. But it is not at all certain that that
interest is reciprocal. Though, as in a formal institution,
the one true God may be the object of the search, institu-

tional religion is nonetheless not a consuming concern for many of those seeking to return to religion or to add a religious dimension to their lives.

On the other hand, many of those young Catholics in a continuum of faith cannot logically be considered consolations of a reassuring kind, either, to the institution, at least not if—beyond the element of assent—faith is supposed to be supported by a working knowledge of what it is that the faith is all about, what it is that the faith encapsulates. To mean anything, a faith should be informed. But American Catholicism stands in danger of becoming a body of religious illiterates, certainly in comparison to what used to be the case. Not that past or even today's older generations of Catholics were or are exactly what might be called theological sophisticates. But at the least, these generations of Catholics knew their prayers, and they had a grasp of the rudiments of faith, having been drilled in the rudiments of faith and the catechism—the old *Baltimore Catechism*, to be precise. The *Baltimore Catechism* was long lampooned as an instrument of religion by rote and, for all practical purposes, is now dead and discarded. Such existence as it is able to claim, it owes to Catholic fundamentalists, Catholics of the far right. Yet that catechism produced generations of Catholics who carried throughout their lifetime a knowledge of the faith that in retrospect must be categorized as unique. "Why did God make you?" "God made me to know him, to love him, to serve him in this world and be forever happy with him in the next." Catholics almost without exception could tick off answers like that to all sorts of questions. Maybe the answers did not help much when faith met a crisis or came up against a serious intellectual or dogmatic challenge. But at least those generations of Catholics had a good idea of what they stood for as believers. Today, almost any Catholic of a senior age—say, from forty-five on up—can call up from memory banks religious information and statements of belief that must fairly astound those of today's younger generations, for many of whom religious literacy is pretty much limited to a few elementary prayers like the "Our Father" and "Hail Mary."

Is this exaggeration? A few years ago, I explored the subject of religious literacy on an assignment from *U.S. Catholic*, the national Catholic magazine published by the Claretian Fathers and Brothers out of Chicago.[6] In researching the article, I encountered a young Catholic mother who worked as a floral designer, and who was busy putting together colorful arrangements of flowers for families decorating their homes for the March 19 Feast of St. Joseph, a feast marked with devotion and festivity by the Italian community in the city where she worked, Gloucester, Massachusetts. "Who was St. Joseph, anyway?" the woman asked. On the same assignment, I encountered a middle-aged mother in a suburban Boston community whose high-school daughter had just been accepted for admission to one of the nation's leading Jesuit colleges. It was immediately before Easter. The mother told of a question put to her by the daughter as Holy Week drew to its close and the family readied itself for Easter Sunday. "Mother, what happened at Easter?" the daughter inquired. Similarly, a nun connected with a religious continuing-education institute outside Washington, D.C., told me of novices arriving in her religious order who didn't know all the names, nor even the number, of the sacraments, the very spiritual building blocks of Catholicism. And an ex-Jesuit, working then as an antiquarian bookdealer (he's since died), told of bumping into a young lad hurrying to church on a hot summer morning, his cassock and surplice flung over his shoulder and whipping in his wake. "What's the big rush?" asked the ex-Jesuit. "Gotta get to the church," responded the lad. "Something big's going on, but I don't know what." It was August 15, the Feast of the Assumption, a holy day of obligation for Catholics.

A certain lack of acquaintance with the refinements and details of faith can be found among members of any religious group, the fine points of any faith generally being matters for the creed's leaders, its theologians, its professionals. But the faithful, those subscribing to a particular creed, are logically expected to know something of their religion—in fact, they must, if that faith is to nourish and sustain itself and be able to survive any serious personal, group or institutional test. If membership in a church is merely an accident of birth, then faith does not always stand on the best of ground. Like the good seed in the Gospel of Matthew that fell on barren land, it could wither and die. Faith cannot be merely instinctual, or inherited and expect to flourish. It must also be informed. In an area where Catholicism must have strength—the religious literacy of its members—it is losing vigor.

Nor is the future particularly promising, in substantial part because Catholic parochial schools, the seedbeds of religious literacy for millions of American Catholics over many generations, are fewer in number and are educating fewer and fewer Catholic children. Fewer than one in four Catholic children of school age are enrolled in parochial schools, and that ratio shows no sign of turning itself around soon.

Not that parochial schools, even in their boom days, were expected to do the total job of educating Catholics in their religion. By the most idealized projections, it could never be realistically hoped that the Catholic school system would educate all Catholic children. The Catholic school system actually fell behind Catholic population growth when the system was growing at its fastest clips, including in the 1950s. From the beginning, the slack in educating Catholics in their religion was supposed to be picked up in other ways, including, of course, with the Sunday sermon—except the Sunday sermon seems never to have been a totally effective vehicle for instruction, and it certainly isn't these days. The quality of the Sunday sermon is a constant complaint of Catholics in the pews. Only one-fifth of Chicago Catholics in a 1977 study considered their priests' sermons fine, indeed excellent, according to religious sociologist Andrew Greeley, a percentage about the same as that for the national average in a 1974 study.[7] This compared to a two-fifths, or 40 percent, excellency rating in 1952. Are priests not preparing their sermons conscientiously enough, or do their congregations expect more? Or could it be that the modern average Catholic congregation is so disparate in composition—in terms of age, ethnicity, education, and therefore intellectual level—that preachers of sermons inevitably have difficulty achieving a focus that is going to reach and satisfy all segments of their congregations. That could very well be. It's not a uniquely Catholic problem, of course, but it may be a special problem in Roman Catholicism, given the church's emphasis on universality and a seeming presumption that it can forever reach across human divides with its messages framed in a single context. If once it did, it doesn't always work that way anymore. And it seems not to be working at all with the new generation of Catholics. In Greeley's late 1970s study, only 15 percent of Chicago Catholics under age thirty rated sermons as excellent, and across the nation, the percentage was even lower, standing at 12.[8]

Sermons aside, the common alternative to the religious education in parochial schools has traditionally been the instructional system that Catholics know as the Confraternity of Christian Doctrine and call the CCD program. Every Catholic parish in the United States is theoretically responsible for the religious or catechetical education of its girls and boys of school age, including those not attending parochial school. Over the years—in fact, even today—catechetical methods have varied from parish to parish. But generally they have involved one-hour weekly religious instruction classes, sometimes after a Sunday mass, sometimes on a weekday afternoon or evening of convenience to the parish as a whole. Many public-school districts have cooperated in the effort of religious groups, including Catholics, to educate their young members in their faiths. Many, for instance, have agreed to released-time arrangements, arrangements whereby pupils are released from their public-school schedule for an hour or so on a given day so that they may attend a class in religion at another site; the courts, of course, do not allow the use of public property for instructional purposes of a denominational kind out of legal considerations rooted in the clause of the Constitution concerning separation between church and state.

On paper, the Confraternity of Christian Doctrine program would seem from every possible vantage point the perfect vehicle for reaching those whom the diocesan school, for whatever reason, could or did not include in its process of religious education. But the most promising programs on paper have often flunked the test of implementation. The CCD didn't get the job done. It is not getting the job done now. It is a bust. It is, in Greeley's blunt words, "an abject failure."⁹

Inevitably, CCD or any religious-instruction program would have been in trouble once the shortage of nuns began to make itself felt. The parent is supposed to be the primary religious educator of the child, but in the United States, for years, the task of educating the Catholic child in his or her religion has pretty much been passed on to and assumed, in turn, by the sister. It was the religious sister who taught the Catholic child most of the prayers, and it was the religious sister who inculcated a knowledge of Catholicism in generations of American Catholics—first through the diocesan school system, and then additionally through the Confraternity of Christian Doctrine, sisters being called upon to double in brass, as it were, as the CCD program expanded to an apostolate of major dimensions. But all of a sudden, nuns came into short supply, and as soon as they did, religious education began to feel the effects, most immediately in the CCD program. The program was taken over by lay volunteers, by and large dedicated people of enormous goodwill, but without the pedagogic skills of the religious sister. Dioceses instituted hurry-up training courses for their CCD teachers, but the CCD operation nonetheless slipped gradually into something of an amateur effort. It remains one today, attempts to correct the situation notwithstanding. Priests have to plead from the altar and in parish bulletins for people to teach CCD classes, and those who respond are often totally untrained, not even having gone through the diocese's training course for CCD teachers. It might be added that many priests also have to plead with parents to send their children to CCD, and to threaten to delay the children's admission to the sacrament of confirmation—administered as a rule to Catholics during their teens—if they are not conscientious about seeing to their presence at CCD. It is a detail suggesting that the problem of religious education is complicated to one degree or another by parental indifference to it.

Apart from the ineffectiveness of CCD, it may also be wondered if parochial schools themselves are providing the same religious education to young Catholics that they once did. There is no doubt that parochial schools are not only good schools, but probably even better than when the senior generations of Catholics were flocking to them in such large numbers. For one thing, facilities have been upgraded. More important, teacher qualifications are of a higher standard. Teachers hold the necessary degrees and measure up to requirements set by the state. Even textbooks are improved. One would have a hard time finding a geography textbook, for instance, like the one a child of mine brought home from St. Mary's School in Glenshaw, Pennsylvania, in the mid-1960s. In the chapter dealing with Greece, the land and its people, the geography asked prayers for the people of Greece, for most of them were Greek Orthodox believers, and theirs was a so-called schismatic religion. Religion no longer intrudes into everything in the parochial school, from geography and history to mathematics and English. The parochial school is of a distinctly higher professional caliber.

Desirable, indeed necessary, as all these pedagogical improvements are, something has gone at the same time out of the parochial school, most notably the presence of nuns. Such nuns as are to be found in parochial schools nowadays are more often likely to be administrators than to be teachers. Even though a nun, probably the school's principal, may conduct the religion class, gone is the witness to religion and the committed religious life, which the sister in her garb provided by her very presence. The lay teacher may be better qualified than were many or most nun-teachers of the past, but this lay teacher is a different kind of authority figure and the conveyer of a different set of values—no less inferior in their own right to the values conveyed by the sister in religious vows, but different nonetheless, if only because of their more secular context.

Does the displacement of nuns by lay teachers mean that even those going to parochial schools are coming out of them with less of a knowledge or grasp of faith than those who went before? Not necessarily. Yet one might legitimately raise that question on the basis of the report that the editors at *U.S. Catholic* commissioned as a companion piece to my 1984 article on religious illiteracy. The report[10] was written by Matt Scheiber, a Chicago-based editor and free-lance writer, and focused on the knowledge of Catholicism which a presumably typical incoming group of young Catholics brought with them to the University of Notre Dame. Notre Dame, most everyone would agree, is a thoroughly Catholic institution; at the least very many of its students are graduates of parochial and Catholic high schools.

What did they know about their religion?

"They can name the primary sacraments of Baptism, Confirmation and Eucharist," the author reported.

> Most students can name the other four, or they at least recognize them. But their grasp of the sacraments' meanings tends towards the superficial. Students can name only a couple of holy days, but they participate in all. [By which the author presumably means they accept a free day from class on all holy days.] They recognize the books of the Bible, but can't divide most of them into the proper Testaments. Less than half know the Ten Commandments from memory, but most have learned them sometime in their upbringing. Notre Dame freshmen are familiar with gospel parables but not with their interpretation. They recognize such figures as Abraham and Moses but know little else about the Old Testament. They are unaware of any tradition of Catholic social teaching.

It should be said that, rather than being unrepresentative of the new generation of Catholics, the Catholics of Scheiber's report would actually have been the elite of that generation. They were individuals of superior intelligence, attested to by the mere fact of their having gained admission to the Catholic university that, in the United States, is thought by many to come closest to Ivy League status. Ninety percent of Notre Dame's student body is Catholic. Of the freshman class surveyed by Scheiber, 60 percent had some Catholic education, 44 percent had graduated from Catholic high schools, and more than 80 percent came from families considered by the freshmen to be "religious" or "very religious."

U.S. Catholic entitled Scheiber's article "Mass Confusion on a Catholic Campus," a headline with a nice pun and one whose application was not restricted just to the incoming freshmen. Scheiber sat in with 150 students on the first day of Father Richard McBrien's "Catholicism" class. All the students, the author said, had already completed at least one theology course.

"Which came first—Augustine or Trent?" Professor McBrien asked. No hands were raised. Individuals were called upon for answers. The first four hazarded no guess. Eventually, a couple of students came up with answer and dates, but the class's agony wasn't over. Nor its embarrassment. No one knew what the magisterium was. A few remembered when Vatican Council II was held. *Transubstantiation*, the word in Catholic understanding describing the eucharistic conversion of bread and wine into the body and blood of Christ, drew a blank. No one knew that the Canon of the Mass was the Eucharistic Prayer. The name Martin Luther struck a familiar chord, but the most concrete identification of him, said Scheiber, was that he was a reformer (which is fairly concrete, I'd say). Everyone, of course, knew Catholicism's "two great commandments—the sixth and the ninth, governing sexual behavior: "Thou shall not commit adultery" and "Thou shall not covet thy neighbor's wife."

Inevitably, much of this absence of religious knowledge could be expected to be rooted out during the students' time on campus, and Notre Dame could be expected to be returning to the society a more informed Catholic. It does. It also turns out a remarkably observant Catholic as far as religious practice and regular worship are concerned, and this has not gone unnoticed. Pope John Paul II himself not long ago is said to have greeted the bishop of Fort Wayne–South Bend, Indiana, then William M. McManus, with the comment, "You're the Bishop of South Bend, where 85 percent of the college students go to Mass."[11] South Bend, needless to say, is the home of the University of Notre Dame.

The pope's admiration—maybe the word is *awe*—may be surprising, but it is fully understandable in the light of another observation by Notre Dame's Father Theodore Hesburgh, this time in a 1986 article in the Jesuit journal *America* defending American Catholic higher education against articles and norms being drawn up by the Vatican's Congregation on Catholic Education, measures that Hesburgh felt forced the best American Catholic universities to choose between being real universities and being really Catholic, when, in fact, they were already both.[12] He argued in effect that, to the extent that religion was the criterion, the American university system was doing a better job than it was being credited with by Rome—a better job even than many of the great Catholic universities elsewhere in the world were doing.

As a member of educational commissions that had taken him to virtually every corner of the world, Hesburgh drew comparisons between the situation with respect to religion in American Catholic universities, chartered as they are by various states and many of them under the control of lay boards, and that which he found in pontifical universities[13] around the world. "In our state-chartered Catholic universities and colleges," wrote Hesburgh, "the students must study Catholic philosophy and theology. Not true elsewhere. The vast majority of our faculty are committed, practicing Catholics. Not true elsewhere. Most of our Catholic students practice their religion by daily or at least weekly participation in Mass and Holy Communion. In the best pontifical university I know in Europe, three percent of Catholic students attend Sunday Mass."

In other words, religious practice is the rule, not the exception, on the American Catholic campus, and not just at Notre Dame, where 85 percent of the student body is said to worship.

Obviously, in an enclosed, self-contained environment such as a residential Catholic campus, one would expect behavioral patterns, including those relating to religious observance, to be socially reinforced by the shared, commonly accepted values of the group. Participation in religious practice at Notre Dame, accordingly, does not differ markedly from that which may be found at, say, Holy Cross College in Worcester, Massachusetts, or Mount St. Mary College in Emmitsburg, Maryland.

However, as brilliant as may be the job that Catholic colleges and universities do in maintaining among their students the heritage of faith, the fact remains that these institutions are still reaching only a relatively small percentage of Catholics of college age. If with thousands of schools and almost two million students the parochial school system is educating fewer than 25 percent of Catholic children in the junior age categories, the 242 Catholic colleges and universities of the United States are handling a proportionately smaller percentage again with their much smaller enrollment of 550,000 students. Even so, nothing is to be presumed about the religious solidarity of these students as graduates, for they are being sent into a secular society where the cultural, social, and religious reinforcements of the Catholic campus are virtually nonexistent.

Social and religious reinforcing elements are virtually nonexistent for all of Catholic life in the United States, although this wasn't always the case. Once upon a time, there were Catholic enclaves, where there existed something of the religious homogeneity that survives on the Catholic campus. But Catholics do not cluster in communities or in tenement or apartment neighborhoods as they did in earlier days. There are cities and boroughs with large Catholic populations, but even there, the touchstones of identity are new and different. For one thing, they're not likely to be the neighborhood Catholic parishes. Middle-aged New Yorkers who grew up in heavily populated Catholic areas of the Bronx might still be inclined to identify themselves, in terms of their origin, with membership in a particular parish. I'm thinking of old Westchester County friends who, at gatherings bringing together others from the borough, connected with one another not so much in terms of a borough, a neighborhood, or a block, as of the Catholic parish—like St. Barnabas, or St. Helena, or Christ the King. The impulse carried over from their childhood. As teenagers gathering new acquaintances at a dance, for instance, it was the parish one lived in and belonged to that, along with one's school, helped establish one's identity. "Where are you from?" One didn't answer Soundview or the Taylor Avenue area. One said, "Holy Cross." The same was true in other cities. It is difficult to imagine anything like that being common today. The Catholic culture isn't parish-centered the way it used to be. Parishes themselves have changed. Yesterday's families have moved out, many of them making it to the suburbs, leaving the old neighborhoods and points of identity to others, among them the newer waves of immigrants. Very many of these people are Catholic, to be sure, but as will be seen in a later chapter, they are Catholics of a different tradition from the one that the American church has largely known until now.

In any case, the parish church—which was once the focus of community for so many Catholics, their social as well as their spiritual center—no longer enjoys the preeminence of place it once had. The parish church stands there, as solid and imposing as ever, but as often as not, it's been reduced to a kind of spiritual convenience store, a place people go to to fulfill an obligation of worship—and even then, in numbers smaller than before. Most of the time, the parish church is locked up, and so, too, is

the parish hall. The lock on the door is, from the viewpoint of the Catholic community, a woeful sign of the
times.

Compounding the woe is the fact that, if the parish
is the center of anything these days, it is too often likely
to be the weekly or biweekly parish bingo game. That
might seem preposterous to Catholics of the senior
generations, who remember when the parish church was
open all day for prayerful visitations (fear of vandalism
to church property hardly existed then), and when the
parish hall was the scene of a range of religious and cultural activities, from instruction courses to lecture and
entertainment programs of sundry kinds. All that is
pretty much past—except, as I said, for the bingo game.
Doubtful, you say? Alas, not. A recent Notre Dame
University study of Catholic parish life found that, after
the liturgy of the Mass, traditionally the central point of
Catholic worship, bingo attracted the highest percentage
of participation in American Catholic parishes. Pastors
or administrators of 1,099 parishes were surveyed as part
of the Notre Dame study, and bingo claimed a 60 percent popularity rating, far outdistancing all other aspects
of parish life.[14] A poor third to mass and to bingo was
adult religious education at 21 percent. Children's religious education stood at 20 percent and was followed by
lenten services or devotion to the Virgin Mary at 12 percent, parish social or fraternal organizations at 10 percent, and "other" at 10 percent. The "other" category
included parish councils, social services, justice activities,
liturgical preparation, and youth ministry—all mentioned
with some frequency in the study, but none of them of-

ten enough to rate specific identification by category and percentage.

Bingo, in the words of the Notre Dame report, is a curious social phenomenon among Catholics, a phenomenon that the report added "has a staying power among many parishioners that has outlasted the concern expressed by many bishops, pastors and fellow parishioners about bingo as part of the regular parish budget and stewardship program." There is no mistaking that concern. The diocese of Houma-Thibodaux, Louisiana, has ordered the phasing out of bingo by 1991, and prominent prelates like Chicago's Cardinal Joseph L. Bernardin and New York's Cardinal John O'Connor have expressed reservations about parishes' relying so heavily on funds derived from bingo. Yet bingo survives, and to the extent that it does so as a distinguishing sign of the community of the American Catholic people, the American church is embarrassed, and maybe in trouble, too. For though bingo may help pay the debts, it is not going to save anyone's soul, inspire anyone's commitment, redeem any person or thing. And despite all that is alleged for bingo as a game of fun and recreation, it will forge no bonds of loyalty; it will inspire no one's witness. Bingo is community at the level of the least common denominator—Reno and Atlantic City come to the parish hall; the return of pin-wheeling gambling in slightly masked form. But Catholics seem to love the game, and many parishes are hooked on it. The parish of my birth in central Massachusetts survives on bingo.

One can make too much out of the bingo finding of the Notre Dame study. The bingo bit is real, however.

For very many, bingo is a fact of American Catholic life. Still, in the final analysis, it is essentially the stuff of bad jokes. ("What's the eighth sacrament?"—jokes like that.) For all its visibility and popularity, bingo is not one of the marks of the American church, not one of its chief identifying characteristics. Having made those admissions, however, we have to say that bingo stands as a symbol of the sorry times on which the element of community has fallen in the American church. Admittedly, the church's essential mission is to preach the good news of salvation, not necessarily to promote community. Still, community is important for the elements it contains within itself for facilitating the witness to charity and human understanding that the Lord commended, and also for promoting salvation itself among members of the community.

Community, therefore, is a prized component of faith. But it is not the ultimate value of faith. If it is community one wants above all else, one has to look elsewhere so far as American Christianity is concerned. Religious community exists, but it often is more a Protestant value than a Catholic one. One glimpses this fact in churches such as those described in Grace Mojtabai's remarkable study on the people of Amarillo, Texas, a city where economic livelihood is linked to the assembly of nuclear weapons. Mojtabai's book[15] touched, among much else, on the place of religion in the lives of the people of Amarillo, a subject she returned to in a lively *Commonweal* interview.[16] The interview is especially pertinent for the contrast it provides between creed and community, between a creedal church and a church focused strongly on community, and by extension, between the church of Rome's vision and the Catholic church that could be evolving in the United States. Mojtabai's picture was of the South Baptist church and a Christian people existing within the parameters of a loose ideological conformity. "Second Baptist was formed as a mission church from First Baptist," she noted in the *Commonweal* interview. "But I'm not sure that at First Baptist they are familiar with what's being taught at Second Baptist. More, I'm not sure that the pastor of First Baptist knows what his five hundred and twenty-five Sunday school teachers are saying. These are not creedal faiths, so there's a certain freedom within limits."

Now, there might be all kinds of community in the Southern Baptist church in Amarillo and everywhere else that that church exists. There might have been all kinds of community back in the Catholic Bronx a generation or two ago. But community is not the essence of traditional Catholicism. Creed is, and it is the church of creedal conformity that Pope John Paul II is determined to preserve in the United States. The problem for Rome is that, at the same time the American Catholic church is suffering a loss of community, it is losing much of its creedal orthodoxy. It is becoming a counterpart of sorts to the Baptist parish churches of Mojtabai's Amarillo experience, and it is all happening in record time. In 1965, the American Catholic church was a remarkably orderly place, where Catholics streamed to church in astronomical numbers (nearly three-quarters of them on a regular weekly basis), and where Catholic minds and consciences were systematically bound by the church's law, its very word. But that blissful state ended. It showed signs that it might be ending in the mid-1960s, but there was no mistaking the end when it came in 1968. Pope Paul VI issued his birth-control encyclical, *Humanae vitae*, and suddenly there was a different American church. Catholics rebelled. They turned off. But surprisingly, they didn't leave their church. At least, very few did. They stayed, and the species known as the cultural Catholic came into being. With this event, Catholic creedal conformity was lost, very likely forever.

Nothing prepared the church for this eventuality. Everyone knew that a birth-control encyclical was coming, and everyone knew that its impact would be enormous, whichever way the pope went. But responses were read in the context of the past. The conservative or right-wing expectation, as Andrew Greeley has observed, was that Catholics, who had begun to drift out of line on the birth-control issue, would heed the pope's word and that those using birth-control pills or other forms of contraceptives would stop.[17] In a related context, the liberal or left-wing expectation was that Catholics would continue to use the birth-control pills and contraceptives and just leave the church. The latter Catholics were the surprise. They stayed. There was, as Greeley has noted, a notable decline in religious devotion, but there was no noticeable increase in "disidentification" from the church because of *Humanae vitae*. The proportion of those born Catholics but ceasing at some time in their lives to continue to be Catholic was 12 percent in 1963. In the early 1970s, in the wake of *Humanae vitae* and other unsettling developments that followed in the encyclical's wake, such as the clergy drain, the proportion had increased by only three points, to 15 percent, where it has remained since.[18] Catholics stayed; they continue to stay, but—and this is the key to the phenomenon—they stay on their own terms. Indeed, the unofficial perimeters of church are constantly pushed outward, as with applications of conscience, many Catholics pass beyond the "settled" issue of birth control and adopt avant-garde positions on questions ranging from homosexuality to abortion, divorce, and remarriage. Easiest of all are decisions relating to matters of religious practice and worship. The old expectations are meaningless. These Catholics practice and worship as they will. Gone is creedal conformity, and born is an entirely new species of Catholic.

At first, this new species was without a name. There was some early talk about a modern or "mod" Catholic, but the phrase did not achieve vogue. The phrase was used, among other places, in a book of mine.[19] Andrew Greeley advanced the term *"communal Catholic,"* writing a whole book on this new type Catholic[20] and staying with the term through at least two subsequent books.[21] It is not exactly clear to me whether Greeley was using the term *communal Catholic* interchangeably with *cultural Catholic.* Andrew Greeley is a man of keen distinctions. But at the very least, his description of the communal Catholic corresponds to what is generally characterized now as the cultural Catholic. In any instance, it was the term *cultural Catholic* that achieved currency.

Who are the cultural Catholics, and how many of them are there?

To answer the second question first, they exist by the millions, but precisely how many millions is anyone's guess. In 1978, the National Conference of Catholic Bishops estimated that some twelve million American Catholics were nonpracticing, and they announced plans aimed at evangelizing them, and maybe picking up other unchurched Americans in the process. Many of the twelve million were undoubtedly cultural Catholics. The bishops' program of evangelization never got off the ground in any noticeably concrete way, but the plan itself was implicit admission by the church's leadership that a new category of Catholic existed in the United States, a subgroup with its own identifying tag, and probably larger than the bishops' estimated figure of twelve million.

In his 1979 book *Crisis in the Church*, Greeley commented that there had been ''a substantial increase'' in the number of ''communal Catholics'' since the first National Opinion Research Center study in 1963, ''rising from 30 percent of the population to 50 percent.''[22] These seem, on quick impression, rather high percentages for both years. My instinct as a religious journalist, as distinct from Greeley's as a sociologist of religion, would be to place the figures much lower. For 1987, however, I am prepared to be told any amount, particularly as the Catholicism of so many in the new generations of Catholics—my own children among them—is observedly more cultural than it is informed and ecclesial. I would extend this observation from Catholics in their late teens,

the age when religious directions begin to express themselves independently of other parental or institutional influences, through to Catholics in their early to
mid-forties.

Not that every one in that group is a communal or
cultural Catholic. One continually comes across stories
of individuals whose Catholicism is a vibrant element not
just in their personal lives of worship, but in the witness
to faith that they bring into society, people like those the
National Catholic Reporter wrote about recently: the forty-
six-year-old president of a Chicago advertising agency,
who has moved between social activism on behalf of the
inner-city poor and promotion of business ethics as a
teacher in the classroom and as a discussion-group
leader; the thirty-two-year-old nurse who left the church,
returned, and is now working in an outreach center in
an impoverished area of Rochester, New York; the thirty-
one-year-old philosophy professor in California who
gave up his post to become an official with the Catholic
League for Religious and Civil Rights in Milwaukee, and
who now sports a lapel button reading "Catholic and
Proud."[23] Still, for every one of them, there are more,
one fears, of the type that John Cort, a one-time Catholic Worker and activist in the Association of Catholic
Trade Unionists, described in an *America* article comparing the social activism of Catholics of the 1950s and 1960s
with that of the mid-1980s. Cort, who was a part of the
Catholic scene as far back as the 1930s, conceded that
there is "a residue of idealism in young people," adding
with emphasis "thank God!" Still, he continued, "I am
afraid young people are not responding now as before.

Why? Prosperity mainly. The bitch goddess success is riding high. You see it in the whole yuppie phenomenon: Get it while you can get it; cultivate your own garden.''[24]

Cort's comment was not made in any specifically cultural-Catholic context. He was lamenting the passing of a certain type of social activist, not indicting a whole new generation. But it is likely, as he suggested, that the old-style social activists are fewer and that their presence is less pronounced than that of the cultural Catholic.

So, to get, therefore, to the question: Who are the cultural Catholics?

Cultural Catholics are those living, in Richard McBrien's apt phrase, at the margins of the church.[25] They believe, but in no systematic, much less programmed way. God exists. Christ was divine, and if not divine, then prophetic. We can see that there is obviously a momentous theological significance between being divine and being merely prophetic. But for cultural Catholics, the question is esoteric, a distinction for the preoccupation of theological specialists, not themselves. As for church, the notion has a validity, although not an exclusive one. The odds on salvation through the Catholic church are good, but not necessarily better than those that exist outside Catholicism. The sacraments—some of them, at least—retain an importance, but often primarily as rites of passage. Baptism initiates the baby into the Christian community; confirmation is a kind of Christian bar mitzvah, symbolizing one's coming of age; marriage formalizes one's place, and maybe also respectability, in the general society. Attendance at Sunday mass is not regarded as a particularly important item in the list of religious priorities.

Cultural Catholics are also just about completely uninterested in church structure. This is especially true among the young. The plea that John Paul II addressed to the young people of France during his visit to Taize in October 1986 could just as easily have been made to the young people of the United States, for the detachment that exists in France is also to be found in this country. The church "needs your presence and your participation," the pope pleaded to the French youths.[26] That may be true enough, but it is doubtful that, as a consequence, young people, there or anywhere, are likely to involve themselves en masse in the life of the church. Nor is it likely that they will subscribe to the pope's assurance that their ecclesial presence and participation will enable them to "perceive with more lucidity" the problems of the world and of their own lives. One hasn't read of the pope's plea reversing the situation in France; a similar plea—likely to come during John Paul II's 1987 trip to the United States—will also very likely be without impact here.

If the truth be told, cultural Catholics of the United States do not expect to receive lucidity, guidance, or instruction from their church's leaders—neither from the pope, the bishops, or the priests—on any issue pertaining to their individual lives. Their posture may be imperious. It may be presumptuous. But it exists. The cultural Catholic knows that there are standards, and that there are ultimate values and ultimate reasons for things. But the extent to which all or any of these apply to his or her life is a matter for subjective determination. The cultural Catholic will question the world out of the context of this culture called Catholic, but this person will look to conscience, not the leadership, when drawing conclusions about what to do or what to believe.

Surprising as it may seem to some, these Catholics are basically loyal to the Catholic tradition. The old mystiques surrounding Catholic authority may, for them, be effectively dead, but in them, much of the culture survives, and cultural Catholics will accordingly respond to situations in their everyday lives out of that culture. They may even belong to a parish, though it should be said immediately that this hardly makes them institutional insiders. Their expectations of the church are minimal. If they seem and are more in than out of the church, it is because the parameters of the church are so different. It is easy to be on what McBrien has called the "fringes" of the church when the fringes have been pushed by rank-and-file Catholics so far beyond what they were twenty years ago.

It should be made clear that this new type of Catholic is quite different from the "spectator Catholic" who has historically existed in the church—the Catholic, that is, who is more-or-less along for the ride; the Catholic who belongs, who gives, who worships, but who does this more-or-less perfunctorily while leaving to others the commitments to and the involvements in the church's apostolates and social apostolates. At times in the past, when apostolic initiatives were in high gear, as during the 1950s, the "spectator Catholic" was often held in scorn as an observing do-nothing. Today, the "spectator Catholic'' could be considered something of a god-send. At least, this type is present and troubleless. The ''spectator Catholic,'' caring or not, sees what is going on. The cultural Catholic does see and usually doesn't care. Interest and eyes are trained elsewhere. The cultural Catholic isn't angry or anything; the cultural Catholic just isn't concerned and can't be bothered about what is happening in the church.

Who holds the key to the future? Like it or not, the odds have to favor the cultural Catholic.

In his book on the communal (cultural) Catholic, Andrew Greeley looked ahead from 1976 and made three predictions for the ten years to follow. He predicted that ecclesial Catholicism would decline (''This is a bad thing, and I lament it,'' said Greeley); that communal Catholicism would grow, expand, and become more self-conscious (''This is a good thing, and I rejoice in it,'' he added); and that, over ''the very long range,'' the ecclesiastical institution would be reshaped by the cultural forces that produced the communal Catholic, and that communal Catholics, in turn, would ''articulate, reinforce, sharpen, and develop.''[27]

Greeley was focusing, of course, on the American experience—the communal or cultural Catholic committed to Catholicism as a community of Americans and to what Greeley called the Catholic symbol system, often clung to in an inarticulate and unexplicit way. As prognosticator, he was on the mark. In the ten, now eleven, years since the writing of his book, ecclesial Catholicism has indeed declined, and by the same token, communal or cultural Catholicism has grown and expanded.

Whether it has become more self-conscious, I'm not exactly sure. I'm not even sure of what *self-conscious* means in this usage. But this much is certain: Communal or cultural Catholicism has become firmly rooted. It is rooted and it is here to stay. Unquestionably, it has also begun to reshape the ecclesiastical institution, as Greeley predicted, though the signs may not yet be dramatically pronounced. Greeley himself evidently didn't expect they would be. He said he wasn't sure what a church reshaped by the cultural forces that had produced the cultural Catholic would look like, except that it would be "an interesting one." He commented that he didn't expect to be around to see it.[28]

But that was more than ten years ago. Maybe he is seeing it now. Maybe we are all seeing it and not recognizing precisely what we are seeing because of the subtleness of it all. Or maybe we are disbelieving, because once before we thought we saw a new church taking shape, then found it disappearing almost as quickly as it had appeared. That was the so-called underground church, which materialized in American Catholicism in the postconciliar period. The underground church was a loose conjoining of disaffected Catholics of the late 1960s and the early 1970s around progressive priests who shared their unhappiness over the rate and extent of church reform resulting from Vatican II. At one moment, the underground church seemed everywhere. There was hardly a Catholic community without its semiclandestine group, which met regularly for an avant-garde liturgy, as well as for camaraderie and dialogue self-reinforcing of the group on matters of moment to them—social, moral, doctrinal, ecclesial, behavioral, and sexual. If nothing more, the movement held forth the prospect of the development within Catholicism of a kind of high-church–low-church situation, such as exists in Anglicanism. But the movement petered out as many of the participants lost interest in the reforms that had once seemed so urgent, and also as they realized that, by the invocation of conscience, there was plenty of room for them within the official church. In other words, the rules of membership would be theirs, not those of the magisterium. The assertion of self and the application of conscience had suddenly rendered the underground church superfluous.

What is happening now is quite different and, as remarked, is infinitely more subtle than anything that has occurred in the past. The American church is indeed being reshaped by the cultural forces that produced the cultural Catholic. It is being reshaped if not by cultural Catholics themselves, then in response to them. One detects this most clearly on the birth-control issue. The American church for all practical purposes has conceded the case. Most Catholics who still avail themselves of the sacrament of reconciliation do not confess artificial birth control as a sin; priests do not make a big deal of its practice; and though the pope may expostulate regularly on the subject, such statements as issue from members of the American hierarchy have about them more a *pro forma* ring than one of consuming moral urgency. Once upon a time, they did, but that passion is now reserved for the abortion issue.

There are other instances of a church being reshaped—the blind eye, for instance, that most priests apply to the living arrangements of couples presenting themselves for marriage. Premarital sex is a Catholic taboo, but Catholic couples' living together before marriage is common nowadays in the United States. Many a diocese has a regulation requiring couples to live apart for a period of weeks or months before it will allow them a church marriage. But the regulations are observed more by way of exception than by way of practice. Similarly with baptism. Baptism is no longer in Catholicism the automatic sacrament, a sacrament just for the asking. Now, most dioceses are insisting that the parents of babies to be baptized be themselves observant Catholics, so that there will be a reasonable chance of the faith's being passed on to the child. Nonetheless, baptism is not refused—though, to be sure, there are instances where it is delayed until the parents demonstrate the seriousness of their Catholicism.

One could go on, citing, for instance, the acceptability of organizations and outreach programs, which were once viewed as mischievous or at least unnecessary in the life of the church—programs such as that for separated and divorced Catholics founded early in the postconciliar period by the late Paulist Father Jim Young. Young's ministry with divorced and separated Catholics was initially viewed with a jaundiced eye in many church quarters, but today, there are more than one thousand outreach programs across the country, and what began as a something of a suspect special ministry by an upstart young priest at the Paulist Center in Boston is now an established apostolate of the institutional church.[29]

But perhaps the most remarkable example of a church in the process of being reshaped is the open attitudes and open doors to individuals who not long ago would have been considered pariahs: the ex-priests. Ex-priests are now welcome participants in many church apostolates; scores, for example, serve on Catholic college and university campuses from one end of the country to the other. Similarly, prominent Catholics—ex-priests and laypersons alike—holding ambiguous relationships to the church of their origins are often invited to speak out their ambiguities and in the most sacrosanct of places. James Carroll, the ex-Paulist who is now a best-selling novelist, was invited not long ago into Quigley Seminary in Chicago to address a convention of priests, sisters, and lay ministers of the Archdiocese of Chicago. Carroll conceded that his life now was "marginal to the life of the church,"[30] but nonetheless he is a man of faith, who, by his own testimony hadn't left the Catholic church.[31] But his is a faith, a Catholicism that Rome would find hard to live with. In his Quigley Seminary talk, for instance, Carroll spoke of a church of disbelief and argued that to be born in the spirit is to believe with Jesus that "the spirit blows where it pleases." Rome would have no problem with that, but it would with his contention that to be born in the spirit is to embrace the *present* Kingdom (Carroll's emphasis) with all of its ambiguity and lack of clarity. "Ambiguity and lack of clarity are of the essence of this faith," he continued. "Doubt is of the essence of it. Disbelief is of the essence of it." Then within those hallowed seminary walls, which had probably never heard such talk before, Carroll offered his description of what the church has become in our generation. It is a church where "we see blasphemy disguised as orthodoxy, cruelty disguised as tradition, sadism disguised as authority, Manichaeism disguised as spirituality.'' He urged his audience— priests, sisters, teachers, evangelists, youth workers, and retreat leaders—to preach the gospel of Jesus Christ ''as you live it and as he did,'' specifically, ''Disillusionment, not holiness. Doubt, not certainty. Disgrace, not honor. Pilgrimage, not possession.'' In that context, he encouraged more nuanced ministerial and personal approaches on such questions as those relating to intercommunion, abortion, homosexuality, and feminism. ''Encourage the anger of Catholic women,'' he said with respect to the last category. ''And if priests and bishops continue to refuse to make the sacrament of orders available to them, support those women whose vocations take them into other Christian denominations where the priesthood is a possibility.''[32]

None of this is to hold up James Carroll as a living image, a model, of sorts, of the communal or cultural Catholic; that would be presumptuous on my part. It is only to say that communal or cultural Catholics think very much as does he, beginning with the basic premise that, like Carroll, they do not accept any definition of church membership that puts them ''outside or even on its margins.''[33]

Indeed, if one were to presume anything, it is that Carroll, given his generational fix as well as his educational training and early vocational background (a born Catholic now in middle age, trained for the priesthood and once a priest), is probably more religiously oriented in the formal sense than the average communal or cultural Catholic. This presumption is lent weight by the comment made to Dan Wakefield during the interview that was the basis of the *Boston Business* profile on Carroll. "I'm still very religious," said Carroll. "I worship as a Catholic regularly. I worship with my wife, who is an Episcopalian, and it's been my privilege to reconnect with the [Episcopal] Cathedral of St. John the Divine in New York City, where I was a guest preacher as a priest many years ago. I was invited back to the pulpit there and have preached three times at the cathedral in the last year and a half." Then, in the very next sentence, he introduced the note of ambiguity of status mentioned earlier. "I haven't left the Catholic Church," declared Carroll, "but I have an ambiguous relationship to it."[34]

But obviously, his ambiguity does not render him uninterested in or indifferent about passing the faith along to his children. In the Quigley Seminary talk, for example, he related a lovely exchange with his three-year-old son Patrick as they crossed the Boston Common one day "after Mass." The son announced that he knew what Jesus Christ meant. "You do?" said Carroll, admitting that he was "quite pleased" and ready to tousle the son's hair approvingly. "Yes," said the son. "It means 'god-damn-it.' "

Carroll used the story to emphasize that he was before his audience to speak for that large segment of the population, Catholics included, who use the name of Jesus Christ more in cursing than in blessing: the disenchanted, the angry, the alienated. But the story did more than help to launch Carroll into his talk. It opened a window on James Carroll and, in the process, obliquely raised a question about the generation coming along that

thinks so much like him. Will members of that generation be as interested in or conscientious about passing
on the faith element and its culture, which survive in
them?

There's no ready answer to that question. Much depends, of course, on the staying power of the culture
called Catholic in a pluralistic and highly secularized society. Will it be able to hold the communal/cultural
Catholic? Will it be able to grip the children and
grandchildren of today's cultural and communal Catholics? Also, as Andrew Greeley asked in his book
on the communal Catholic, how many of those in the
generations coming along will have drifted away from
the ecclesiastical institution and from the Catholic community before a church emerges that can effectively speak and appeal to the communal or cultural
Catholic?[35]

Today's cultural Catholic is drawing on a background strongly imbued still with the influences of the
traditional faith. He or she very likely came from what
would be called in the old parlance "a solidly Catholic
home," a place where the faith was accorded unqualified respect and where its influence was pervasive, from
the crucifix on the wall to the blessed candle kept for
times of emergency, such as storms or illnesses. Chances
are that this cultural Catholic had some formal Catholic
educational training, grew up a regular churchgoer, and
retains many of the ideals, motivations, and, yes, inhibitions of pre–Vatican II Catholicism. This Catholic may
not realize it, but she and he suddenly comprise a
unique species, one pivotal to the church's future. For

this species of Catholic—bridged between an orthodox past, out of which cultural Catholicism grew, and an un- orthodox future, in which cultural Catholicism is likely to dominate—holds the key to what the American church will become. For better or for worse, the welfare of this church is rapidly settling on the shoulders of the gener- ation of bridge Catholics, and what they do and don't do to preserve the past that gave them shape is crucial.

For those who want the past to carry forward, it is not exactly easy to be optimistic. In the old days, faith and culture were handed on from generation to gener- ation like a cloned unit of heredity. The faith is not be- ing handed on in the same way these days. Thus, the link to the church and its culture weakens. The child is the parents' creature, so inevitably Catholics of my so- called bridge generation carry with them much of what shaped their parents, whatever sorting out of ideas and ideals may have occurred in the meantime. How much of this religious heritage will be passed on by the new generations to the generations succeeding them is a mat- ter of conjecture. Chances are that it will be less than what was received—and far less than what would be needed to preserve the orthodoxy that a Pope John Paul II would insist on for the American church.

Perhaps the Fordham professor James R. Kelly was right when he wrote in *Commonweal* back in 1971 that maybe the most the church could hope for in the future as it was evolving then—and indeed, continues to evolve now—was an administrative cohesion. In such a cohe- sion, the external symbols of Catholicism as a minutely defined religious denomination would survive, but within that cohesion, the theological and doctrinal possibilities would be as multiple as they are within Protestantism. Kelly based his possibility on the altering perception that Catholics were developing with respect to themselves and their church, specifically, "the explicit realization that Christ's action is not to be identified (a) with Catholicism, (b) with all Christian churches, (c) or even with the sum of professed Christians"[36]—a point that Carroll echoed in Chicago when he said the spirit blows where it pleases, "even among atheists"; a point, in fact, that Vatican II itself broached by conceding that separated churches and communities—all non-Catholics, in other words—are "by no means...deprived of significance and importance in the mystery of salvation."[37]

Whether the Catholic church's future, in the United States or anywhere, will reduce to the kind of administrative cohesion envisioned by Kelly is a matter of speculation to go with points posed earlier. What is certain is that, with their increasing openness to other spiritual traditions, and with their "creative doubt" (Kelly's term) about the Catholic church in many of its present embodiments, cultural Catholics quicken the likelihood of an American church with a different kind of Catholicism taking its place in Christendom. The speed with which this will come about will be determined by cultural Catholics themselves and the interest they retain in their spiritual and cultural roots. They could make this "new" church an extraordinarily interesting one. But if the roots are allowed to wither, there could be left only a remnant church, a remnant culture.

5

THE AMERICAN
CHURCH AND THE
SECOND SEX

IN HIS BRIEF but very insightful contribution to Candida Lund's anthology *If I Were Pope*,[1] Robert E. Burns, the Catholic author and editor, wrote that if the papal tiara were placed on his head, one of his first acts would be to call an extraordinary synod of the world's bishops to respond to a "terrible scandal" prevailing in the Catholic church. That scandal, he declared, is the church's "disenfranchisement of women," a condition that effectively deprives Catholic women of the rights and status available to Catholic men merely by reason of their gender. Burns wasn't the only writer in Lund's book to make the observation about women's secondary place in the Catholic church, but no one made it more emphatically and no one was so unequivocal in linking the priorities of a papacy, as imagined by Burns or as lived by an actual pope, with the enfranchising of Catholic women in their church.

There is no gainsaying Burns. Catholic women quite literally exist within the Catholic faith community as members of a second and a secondary sex, and the situation is a possibly explosive one for the church.

The irony is that, theologically and emotionally, the church is strongly focused on a woman. It glorifies, near-deifies a woman. It has even seemed ready on occasion to declare a woman co-redemptrix of humankind, an action that, had it ever come about, would have elevated her in Catholic theology to a place alongside that of Jesus Christ, son of God, as the redeemer of the world.

This woman, of course, is the Virgin Mary, mother of Jesus Christ and, in the church's view, the epitome of the totally virtuous woman. But Mary's is a special case. The special reverence accorded Mary inevitably conveys a Marian cast to the church. Still, it does not make it a feminist church. No one's keeping precise count, but it is apparent that most of the church's formally declared saints are male; most of its feast days honor males; most of its parish churches are dedicated to males. Maurice Adelman, Jr., a Brooklyn friend of mine with a special interest in Catholic artifacts, brought imbalances between male and female attribution to my attention.

Not long ago, Adelman also randomly checked, on his own initiative, the names of churches and mission chapels in 10 percent of American dioceses to see how many were dedicated to female saints other than the Virgin Mary under one or another of her liturgical titles. Exclusive of Mary, only 10.75 percent were named for female saints, he found. The archdiocese of Anchorage, Alaska, for instance, with eighteen parishes and nine mission chapels (a total of twenty-seven pastoral units) had only one dedicated to a female saint other than Mary. The diocese of Evansville, Indiana, had three out of seventy; the diocese of Memphis, four out of forty-five; the diocese of Salina, Kansas, six out of ninety-six. The highest of his samplings reached only to 18.4 percent, that in the diocese of Wilmington, Delaware, where fourteen of seventy-six parishes and mission chapels were dedicated to female saints besides Mary.

As with church and chapels, so with feast days. Adelman checked the *Missale Romanum* for 1952, the official Roman calendar, which, among other data, lists saints honored on specific days in the church's liturgical cycle. At a time in church history when almost every day carried a dedication, Adelman found only six female saints other than Mary being honored in January, four in February, two in March, one in April, and so forth through the rest of the year.

In accordance with Pope Paul VI's apostolic letter *Mysterii paschalis celebrationem*, the church's calendar of saints was extensively revised in 1969 to allow greater flexibility in arranging liturgical observances. The new calendar left many days unassigned to specific saints, but

those that were assigned went mostly to males. A check
of the 1987 calendar shows male saints outnumbering female saints other than Mary by twelve to two in January, six to two in February, four to two in March, six to
one in April, and once again, so on through the year.

The honoring of Mary, in a word, does not carry
over commensurately to those who shared her gender.
In fact, this woman who is held up as the epitome of the
new and perfect woman, a kind of second Eve repriev-
ing the Eve who was temptress, becomes in the church's
ennobling process a person actually used to humble and
to disenfranchise other women. The exaltation of Mary's
lifelong virginity, for instance, has forever been at the expense of the solemnity and the sacredness of conjugal
love within marriage. For centuries, for instance, after
giving birth, women were expected to present themselves for ''churching,'' a liturgical rite of purification.
It was only in relatively recent years that the ritual was
jettisoned.

Mary's presumed virtues of personality have been
similarly used. The Marian virtue that the church has
traditionally celebrated above all others is her submis-
siveness. Mary was submissive to the will of God as announced by the Angel Gabriel[2]; she was the dutiful
spouse of Joseph; she was submissive, as God's ''instrument,'' to the purpose and mission of Christ's life on
earth. Thus projected as role model and exemplar for
Catholic womankind is one who was generally gentle
and deferential, docile and compliant; a woman who was
seen, but who also belonged to the background. Hers
were the virtues to be striven for; hers the image Cath-

olic womankind should aspire to. The church's view of Mary was and remains that of the perfect female. Further, for centuries, Catholic women themselves looked upon Mary as sum and substance of female perfection. Today, however, isn't quite the same as yesterday. The ancient assessments of what constitutes feminine perfection are no longer acceptable to those they would be recommended to or imposed upon. Nothing is likely to change that situation, at least not in our age—not even encyclicals like John Paul II's *Redemptoris mater* (Mother of the Redeemer), issued 25 March 1987, and describing Mary's life as an image of obedience and freedom, a model of "femininity with dignity," a "point of reference" for all humanity, particularly women.

Catholic women still honor and reverence Mary, but for growing numbers of them, Mary's virtues (to the extent that they ever even existed in the idealized form of their projection) are not necessarily theirs. They reject as belonging to any necessary pattern of perfection those virtues for which Mary is honored. They refuse to be patronized. They demand a stop to their being treated as if they belonged to a second and inferior caste.

This is more than mere assertiveness. As members of the church of Jesus and of Mary, women have just and large grievances. For starters, Catholic women are the objects of sacramental discrimination. All seven of the Catholic sacraments are available to men, but only six to women. Women are barred from Holy Orders, the sacrament of the priesthood, on the tenuous grounds that Jesus did not happen to have any women at the table when the sacrament of Holy Orders was instituted at the Last Supper. Similarly, though some women have been moved into positions of new and greater responsibility in the church, they function nonetheless in secondary roles in what is essentially a man's world. The leadership belongs to men, even in matters where the interests of women are bound up almost exclusively, as in the reformulation of the language of the liturgy to make it inclusive rather than exclusive of women. For centuries, biblical and therefore liturgical language has situated women in the gender that is not theirs, women being addressed as "men" or "sons," or bundled into the term *mankind*, or, just as insulting, called nothing at all. This situation has been ameliorated of late at certain levels of communication within the church. At last working its way into use, for instance, is an updated version of the New Testament, which reflects contemporary American speech and which, with the help of circumlocutions, broadens certain traditional translations in instances where the biblical meaning of the working text, which was in Greek, is inclusive of both sexes. Similarly, in January of 1987, the American bishops announced the formation of a new committee to study possible use in the liturgy of biblical texts edited so that the language is inclusive when the context obviously refers to women as well as men.[3] That committee, not coincidentally, is formed entirely of men: bishop-members of the U.S. Catholic Conference's liturgy committee and committee on doctrine. The staffing, according to the announcement, is also in the hands of men: the priest-directors of the liturgy and doctrine committees' secretariats. Similarly, it is men who do the pronouncing on the reproductive rights of women, just as it was men who were responsible for the March 1987 Vatican statement on procreation and biomedical technologies. The church is a man's world.

There is nothing new about any of this. Women are in the pews in greater numbers than men, but most of the time, they are hardly visible. I think of a confirmation ceremony that I found myself at quite by accident recently in my parish church. The confirming prelate was an auxiliary bishop of the archdiocese of Boston, who delivered a ringing homily before administering the sacrament to the class of twenty-one young boys and girls. The bishop drew on the biblical story of the giant Goliath, the nine-foot-tall Philistine protected by 125 pounds of mail. Goliath terrorized the Israelites before being slain in 1 Kings 17 by the courageous youth with a slingshot, the immortal David. "There are Goliaths out there in the world, giants whom you must slay," said the bishop, and he ticked them off: abortion, drugs and alcohol abuse, absence from mass, cohabitation before marriage, and finally the attitude that religions are all the same. It was a homily that went steadily downhill as the decibels rose in intensity. But that's not the point. The point is that, as the bishop built to his peroration, it wasn't a mixed group of teenagers whom he was addressing, it was "my dear young men about to be confirmed."

It is easy enough to attribute the bishop's misstatement to an unconscious lapse, except such lapses often betray deep-seated attitudes. In the context of the confirmation ceremony, it is virtually unthinkable, for example, that the bishop's lapse could have taken the form "my dear young women about to be confirmed." The Catholic church thinks masculine and so do its leaders— so much so and for so long, in fact, as at last to have created a situation in which those who historically have been the most loyal of the church's members, its women, are rapidly becoming an alienated segment.

That many women are taking a new and jaundiced look at their church is beyond dispute. Rosemary Radford Ruether, professor of theology at Garrett-Evangelical Theological Seminary in Evanston, Illinois, remarked not long ago in her column in the *National Catholic Reporter* that few Catholic feminists of her acquaintance, religious or lay, hold out much hope any longer for the local parish as it exists in the traditional church situation and are busy constructing alternative communities for themselves.[4] The comment came in the course of a story telling how one friend and colleague, Mary Chandler, had passed from enthusiasm to disillusionment about the woman's place in Roman Catholicism. Chandler viewed the local parish as an exciting field of ministry for Catholic women but ended up so disenchanted that she felt impelled to transfer her church membership from Roman Catholicism to Lutheranism. According to Ruether, Chandler progressed in the new and presumably more open Catholic church from a parish lay volunteer, to religious educator, to pastoral assistant, but progress took her only to disappointments, and in the end she walked away, joining a church that she felt offered something the Catholic church never would, at least in her lifetime: parity of opportunity and status. "The Lutheran Church would take her seriously as a church professional."[5]

Ruether's column and Chandler's action clue the reader in to a serious situation, and if the Catholic leadership is blind to it, others are not. The leadership may find it convenient and easy to discount signals coming from women they deem feminist mischief makers, but increasingly, warnings about taking seriously the Catholic feminist movement and its aspirations are coming from men with credentials beyond easy dismissal. Monsignor George G. Higgins, syndicated columnist and adjunct lecturer in the theology department of the Catholic University of America, for one, has sounded a particularly ominous note. He has warned church officials apropos the feminist issue that, by continuing to identify with the rigid, essentially masculine cultural patterns of an era that is dying almost everywhere by the day, they risk having to pay the price on this issue that the church did on the labor issue a hundred years ago at another historical moment of truth. The allusion was to the church's "underestimating the demand of the European proletariat for justice and equality," a miscalculation that lost loyalties to the church and cost it the allegiance of the working class over a period of several generations in nineteenth-century Europe.[6] As with the laborer, cautions Higgins, so could it be with women: the price would be in affection, attention, and, ultimately, church membership itself, and not only among feminist women but also among many dispirited laity, men as well as women, bewildered and exasperated by what is viewed as an obsessive preoccupation with gender.

That is the crux of the issue for growing numbers of Catholic women: gender. Plainly, Catholic women are not taken seriously enough by their church. Many of the old stereotypes of women as baby machines, cake bakers, menders of altar linens, and the like have broken down. But by and large, women remain objects of ecclesiastical patronizing—other Marys, honored but also expected to remain in the background, and to defer to ecclesiastical authority once its dispositions are made known.

Repeating, Catholic women don't respond that way anymore. Geraldine A. Ferraro made that unmistakably clear during the 1984 presidential campaign, when, as the Democratic Party's candidate for the vice-presidency, she stood her feminist ground in the face of challenges from several bishops and, in the process, exposed the essential male chauvinism of the American and the wider church.

The alleged issue so far as the church was concerned was Ferraro's political position on abortion. But only the extremely naive could be expected to believe that gender did not enter, however unconsciously, into the response of some churchmen to her position—indeed, maybe also her candidacy. For as the first woman to have a place on the presidential ticket of a major American political party, Geraldine Ferraro was breaching the walls of one more male preserve and at the same time perhaps burying deeper some old clerical notions about woman's proper place in the world. Whatever the validity of such theories as those, the abortion issue was a convenient club for getting at Geraldine Ferraro.

Throughout the campaign, Ferraro declared that "personally, as a Catholic," she accepted the church's position on abortion.[7] "I am opposed to abortion as a

Catholic," she would affirm—though in all honesty, she would add, she wasn't sure she would be so "self-righteous" and dogmatic if she herself had been raped. But that qualifier wasn't the bone of contention with the bishops who were harassing her, most openly and directly New York's Cardinal O'Connor and Scranton's Bishop James Timlin. That kind of temporizing church officials can understand and make allowances for. What Ferraro's baiters in the hierarchy could not understand, not forgive, was the accommodation within her political philosophy of a general prochoice position on abortion, as well as her persistence in that position in the face of their challenge as members of the magisterium. It mattered not that Ferraro's position was based, not on personal religious convictions, but on the law of the land and on pluralistic considerations of the society. This position was unacceptable, and she came under their intense pressure.

The hypocrisy of it all was that the attacks leveled at Ferraro were spared her male counterpart in the race, Vice-President George Bush, a proabortionist himself, although under a narrower set of circumstances. Bishop Timlin was asked at a press conference, when the campaign was in full swing, why he had singled out Ferraro on the abortion issue and not Bush. He responded, "Because Geraldine Ferraro is a Catholic and is making clear she is a Catholic and Mr. Bush is not."[8] It was a curious remark, which seemed to some to excuse Bush and his position on abortion because he happened not to be a Catholic. Whether Bush was excused or not, it was apparent from the bishop's remark that the issue was Ferraro. The impression was reinforced by the revelation that Timlin, though he had lived in Scranton all his life and had been a priest for thirty-one years, had no idea what positions the two Republican U.S. senators from his own state of Pennsylvania held on abortion. He had never troubled to find out, much less challenge either one of them on the subject. It is a circumstance Ferraro found astonishing because both senators, Arlen Specter and John Heinz, happen to favor choice.[9]

But that's a double standard that's been operative for years in the American church. Maybe Ferraro's citing of Pennsylvania's senators falls short of dramatizing this double standard effectively because neither is a Catholic. But one doesn't have to look far for stronger examples. There are many major Catholic political figures—men—whose political positions on abortion are not substantively different from Ferraro's, yet who have not been similarly subjected to the insulting challenges from the church's leadership—Senator Edward Kennedy of Massachusetts, for example. The politically astute Kennedy maintains a discreet public silence on the abortion issue, but his legislative record makes it abundantly clear that he stands in the company of Ferraro and others like her. But Kennedy is not aggressively challenged by prominent church spokesmen for his stance or his votes on abortion or, at least, has not been yet. Governor Mario Cuomo of New York, on the other hand, has been challenged, though not nearly so intensely and personally as Ferraro was. Throughout the 1984 presidential campaign, Cardinal O'Connor, especially, seemed to

go out of his way to reproach her and in the most public ways possible. The challenges to Cuomo were forever
gentlemanly and generally occurred in refined circumstances, like civilized debates at religious institutions.
That's not the same as a church leader's condemning
and finger-pointing incessantly through the media,
which was Ferraro's lot. In any instance, the willingness
of both Ferraro and Cuomo to defend their intellectual
positions and their respective integrities from the assaults
of church leaders was instructive. It wasn't long ago that
most Catholics in similar circumstances would have
bowed to such unrelenting pressures from church
leaders and would have surrendered their position. If
there was any need for it to be proved that a new Catholic had arrived on the scene, one willing to think for
himself or herself in defiance of church pressure of the
most intensive kind, Ferraro and Cuomo did so in 1984.

It is not my intention to get into a discussion about
the substance and merits of the Cuomo and Ferraro positions on abortion. It is not even to make a judgment
about abortion itself. It is only to say that the abortion
issue has had the effect of sharpening the difference between what it is to be male and what it is to be female
in the church. It has made it unmistakable that, in the
American church, the rules are not the same for women
and for men.

Once again, this is an old story, and a continuing
one. Catholic women are treated differently by their
church and, as the Ferraro case demonstrated, not always gentlemanly. Women venturing outside the home
have forever seemed, in the Catholic scheme of things,

to be venturing into a world where their presence was questioned and their welcome often hostile. There's nothing particularly overstated about that observation. It just happens to be history. Catholic author and activist Gary MacEoin, in the second volume of his autobiography, *Memoirs & Memories*, recalled that, when he married in Ireland in 1937, his bride, Jo, was required, according to the mores of the time, to resign her job in the community because ''woman's place was in the home, and a working woman might be tempted to interfere with the natural law which made procreation the primary end of marriage.''[10] Ireland, with its heavy Catholic traditionalist overlay, is a special case, to be sure. But a quarter century later, it wasn't in Ireland, with its ''quaint laws and conventions imposed on Ireland's civil society by the Catholic Church,'' that one found such a thing. Into the decade of the 1960s, the diocese of Pittsburgh, if no other the United States, was requiring marrying young women to give up their jobs for precisely the same reason that Jo MacEoin had to in Dublin in 1937. The diocese of Pittsburgh may not have been able to extend its edict to women working in the general society, as ecclesiastical authority could in Ireland. But it could—and did—to those women in its employ. It wasn't until a woman reporter of my hiring for the diocesan newspaper made an issue of the policy in the early 1960s that it was finally changed.

The effort to keep women in the home has long been lost by the church, and in the United States at least, church leaders have resigned themselves to the new social reality. Often, though, it seems a reluctant resignation, for the old animus seems never to be far away. This seems particularly to be the case when the Catholic woman is (1) a mother and (2) engaged in an occupation that the church finds objectionable. Then, church leaders can be not only firm, but also ruthless. Women in Providence, Rhode Island, and Toledo, Ohio, can attest to that.

The Providence woman is Mary Ann Sorrentino, executive director of Planned Parenthood of Rhode Island until her resignation on 1 May 1987 to write a book, to act as a consultant, and to explore other career opportunities, including the possibility of public office. Inevitably, the presence of a Catholic woman in so visible a position as hers with an organization viewed so negatively by the church would be a problem for ecclesiastical authorities. Among other services, Planned Parenthood of Rhode Island facilitates abortion for those seeking the procedure. Sorrentino, an advocate of choice, admitted publicly that, on occasion, she was "in the operating suite, holding the hands of women who have had abortions."[11] She had been trained as a social worker, she explained, and had accompanied the women from time to time "to experience the experience of our patients." On the grounds that she was an "accomplice" to abortions, Sorrentino was ruled excommunicated in January 1986 by officials of the diocese of Providence. Several theologians raised questions about the excommunication, expressing doubts whether the articles of canon law dealing with abortion and excommunication (Canons 1389 and 1329) legitimately extended as far as Providence officials had applied them.[12] The questions of the theologians were generally qualified, and in the end, they were totally academic, because those asking them were not actual parties to the case. But even if the circumstances had been otherwise, Sorrentino's excommunication ruling was probably inevitable, given her high profile and the church's intensity on the abortion issue.

If the Sorrentino case had stopped there, the matter might have faded away without further sensationalism. But it didn't. It developed that, at one point during Sorrentino's travail, her fifteen-year-old daughter Luisa was also made the subject of investigation by the church, the pastor of her parish demanding to know her views on abortion before approving her for admission to the sacrament of confirmation. The probing took place two days before the scheduled date of the confirmation, by which time Luisa's dress had been bought, her family invited, and a caterer hired for the festivities following the event. After a half hour's interrogation, the pastor cleared Luisa for confirmation, she, in the meanwhile, having been humbled and reduced to tears. Luisa's confirmation went ahead, and the interrogation was not made public by the parents until another escalation in the Sorrentino story eight months later. But it continued to grate. Sorrentino denounced the interrogation action as "blackmail," her husband called it "unconscionable," and the *Providence Journal* front-paged a story headlined, "They Have to Justify What They Did to That Child."[13]

Many feel that church officials in Toledo, Ohio, also have much to justify in what they did to Sarabeth Eason in the summer of 1986. Eleven years old at the time, Sarabeth was told in August that she could not return to St. Agnes parochial school in the fall because she had publicly supported the right to abortion. It is a fair enough question whether any eleven-year-old minor, however precocious, is mature enough to have a position on an issue for which the consequence would be so grave as that meted out to Sarabeth Eason. But then Sarabeth wasn't just "any" preteen Catholic schoolchild. She was the daughter of the assistant director of a Toledo abortion clinic, Conception Eason, and she made public appearances with her mother in support of abortion. But who knows? Maybe she had been used in a fashion similar to the way antiabortionist activists often use their minor children to advance their adult cause. Young people can make easy pawns. Yet, whether she was or wasn't is beside the point. The fact remains that the church dealt with astonishing, almost unconscionable, severity with one hardly old enough to know her own mind, one only eleven years old, a mere child not yet even in the sixth grade.

The decision affecting Sarabeth Eason was made by the pastor of St. Agnes, Father Richard Miller, but it was far from being an action of an overly zealous man acting on his own. A spokesman for the diocese commented that Toledo's Bishop James F. Hoffman supported the expulsion decision, standing "solidly behind the premise that the church is pro-life and that the spirit of pro-life extends to all its schools and institutions."[14] The spokesman added, "The bishop agrees that we must take a courageous position, although sometimes painful, to witness to the sacredness of human life. This is one of those instances." Father Miller proposed a way of remedying the situation: a letter from Sarabeth to the school's principal saying that she personally did not support abortion. But there would be no letter. Mrs. Eason declared that she would enroll the child in another school. According to the *New York Times*, activists across the country, both for and against abortion, had never before heard of a child's being barred from a Catholic school because of taking a position on abortion. Frances Kissling, executive director of Catholics for a Free Choice, a proabortion, Washington-based organization, called the episode "a very bad civics lesson."[15]

These stories are not daily occurrences, but they happen often enough to demonstrate that the church can play hardball with its women of any age. Of course, the church plays hardball, too, with its men, but a double standard is still operative. The children of Senator Kennedy and Governor Cuomo are well past confirmation or parochial-school age, but it would be unthinkable that any of them would ever have been put to a theological means test such as Mary Ann Sorrentino's and Conception Eason's daughters were. Can one even conceive of a Kennedy child's being called before church authority and asked to disavow the father's legislative record on abortion funding, or a Cuomo child's being asked to abjure his father because the father provided funds in the state budget for artifical birth-control devices and abortions for the poor? Or the child of a notorious mobster's being asked to renounce a parent because of the parent's involvement in crime? In effect, that's what the daughters of Mary Ann Sorrentino and Conception Eason were asked to do: abjure their mothers. That's a hard request to lay on a child, as well as a cruel position in which to place a mother with respect to her own child. The alienation of some women from the church as a result of any of this should not surprise.

Indeed, many have become alienated, but many, too, are hanging tough. Mary Ann Sorrentino, for instance, has made clear that, whatever the church may say about her religious status, she has her own thoughts on the matter. The church says that she is excommunicated, but Sorrentino has declared that she is still a practicing Catholic and still receives Holy Communion.[16] Obviously, she belongs to that new breed of Catholics whom James Carroll spoke of in the previous chapter. The church is hers, too, not just that of the rule makers. She's not going to be booted out.

The regrettable thing about incidents like those involving Mary Ann Sorrentino and her daughter and Conception Eason and her daughter is that they seem to project the church as being blatantly misogynist. It, of course, isn't. But it is so disordinately male-chauvinist as to be insensitive to the feelings and aspirations of the other half of the human race, including those women to whom it quite literally owes the most. These are the church's women religious figures, its nuns and sisters.

There's a fine ecclesiastical difference in meaning between the words *sister* and *nun*. Traditionally, the word *nun* defined one in solemn vows, such as a contemplative or one living in an enclosed group. The word *sister* applied to a religious woman in simple vows and belonging to so-called active orders, such as teaching or nursing communities, or other associations of religious women whose works were carried on outside the convent or enclosure. At one time, a careful distinction was made in the use of the two words, but no longer. The words *nun* and *sister* are today virtual synonyms for one another.

Historically, these women in religious vows kept the church ticking. They taught in the schools, nursed in the hospitals, visited the shut-ins, administered to the poor and afflicted, staffed rectories and episcopal residences, and did such other apostolic and servile work as the church's male leadership ordained or approved for them. They constituted, in sum, an extraordinarily cheap labor pool, as recently as 1966 totaling 182,000 in the United States alone. Without them, the American church would have evolved into a quite different place.

The number of American sisters is much smaller today: 113,000. Obviously, there are fewer hands to do the work that was once theirs. Also, a different attitude prevails among these religious woman, once so thoroughly programmed to respond to the injunctions of the church's male leadership. The women's movement did not bypass the convents. Nuns are not so deferential as before. They, too, have been sensitized by the women's movement to feminist rights and values, so that, even for them, the times are different—and considerably improved. At the least, nuns are taken less for granted than they used to be. This might seem a small gain, but it is progress of a definite sort in the context of a past that was actually something of a scandal. For nuns in the American church were not just taken for granted. They were patronized and frightfully exploited—and accordingly, left vulnerable, as will be detailed later, to major problems of a financial and medical kind once vocations had dried up and old sources of income had thinned out. No sisters ever made very much money. Teaching sisters, for example, were long paid mere token salaries in the parishes and dioceses in which they were engaged, and even after moves were made in the 1960s to upgrade their salaries, thus placing their services on a more professional basis, the sisters remained short-changed. A teaching nun in a parochial school in the United States can expect to be paid from $6,000 to $9,800, according to a sister quoted in 1986 in the *New York Times*, Sister Lois Vanderbeke of the Sisters of St. Dominic in Racine, Wisconsin.[17] This salary is in line with what a diocesan priest is paid, except that·nuns do not have the same perquisites as priests; for instance, there's no stipend or offering for them for tasks performed in the line of duty, as there is for priests when they baptize, witness a marriage, or offer a special mass. Also, unlike diocesan priests, nuns don't get to keep their salaries. Nuns living outside their communities may keep money for their expenses, but by and large the salaries of nuns go into a communal fund, a substantial portion of which helps to support the growing number of community members who are aged, infirm, or otherwise nonproductive of income. The financial squeeze is such that, in some areas, nuns have been forced to sign up for benefits under government programs for persons with limited income and assets, such as Medicaid and Supplementary Security Income (SSI).[18]

It is a blameworthy situation, but no more blameworthy than the church's failure to engage nuns as a group in more meaningful and challenging ways—not that educating (usually at the primary-grade level) and nursing and the like are not meaningful and often challenging occupations. Still, many talents went underutilized. A world of challenges existed besides the traditional apostolates approved for women by the church's leadership. Yet it was left for women religious to discover them for themselves. Thousands did after Vatican Council II, as nuns broke with the set patterns of the past and took their talents and their witness to new and, for them, hitherto strange places. All of a sudden, nuns were teaching on secular university campuses. They were involved in drug and alcoholic rehabilitation programs, in storefront apostolates in the ghetto, in migrant worker camps, in campus ministries, in theological professorships in Catholic colleges and seminaries. They became spiritual directors, and they appeared in pulpits as preachers of missions and at meetings of corporations' directors as champions of corporate responsibilities. These sisters did not reverse the problems of new members and finances endemic these days to orders of religious women, but they gave the sisterhoods a new look and forced the church's leadership to take a new and presumably more appreciative look at them.

The question is whether it is all too late. The problems of the sisterhoods—of vocations, of finances, of morale—are so great that it is a very serious question whether there can be any full recovery from them. The Catholic sisterhoods may not be doomed to the obscure, near-remnant state that the sisterhoods are in Anglicanism, but it is extremely doubtful that they will ever again be in the United States the burgeoning, thriving sisterhoods that they were before the mid-1960s.

If truth be told, the sisterhoods have become a society of geriatrics, of people in need. They are not only without adequate funds, not only without adequate numbers to handle the old apostolates but, in some communities, without adequate numbers to take care of those in need in their own communities, particularly the aged. Nuns of advanced age exist by the tens of thousands. Because of departures from religious life and the inability to attract young recruits, the median age of sisters is in the sixties and climbing. In most communities, the median age of the members is sixty-two to sixty-three years; in some communities, it rises as high as sixty-eight. In the parlance of the social service profession, nuns are a classic instance of a people who slipped between the cracks. Priests became eligible to contribute to Social Security in the 1960s, and in most dioceses, they are covered by diocesan pension plans. The same safety nets do not exist for nuns, or they were set in place so much later as not to be substantially effective. For instance, it wasn't until 1972 that nuns were allowed, under federal regulations, to join the Social Security system.

The welfare of the sisterhoods was obviously based on a premise that the future would duplicate the past. It hasn't.

Traditionally, the sisterhoods took care of their own, and with great and justifiable pride. When a sister retired or became infirm, she went to the motherhouse or to a home specially maintained by the order for its sick and

aged. There, the sister would be supported psychologically, physically, and financially by members of the order for the remainder of her days. But things are
different now. To begin with, the ratio of working sisters to retired sisters has declined; that decline affects income most immediately, because the salaries of the
sisters are commonly turned in to a community treasury.
Thinner at the same time are those bands of young
novices, once in large supply, who did the housekeep-
ing chores and helped take care of the community's
aged sisters, until they moved on to the order's formal
apostolates. Now, veteran sisters have to be recalled or
enticed back from their professional assignments to do
the work once assigned to novices. The reassignment
means, in effect, that sisters at the peak of their professionalism often have to give up careers to become care
providers and convent housekeepers. Some do this will-
ingly out of a spirit of love and dedication; some do it
reluctantly. Either way, it is not a healthy situation, for
career transitions are seldom easy. There must be many
cases in which problems are generated by an attempt to
meet problems.

It is, in sum, a desperate situation, one that promises
to get worse before it gets better. Supporting such a conclusion is the recent study on the retirement needs of religious in the United States completed by the accounting
firm of Arthur Anderson and Company at the request
of the National Conference of Catholic Bishops, the
Leadership Conference of Women Religious, and the
Conference of Major Superiors of Men. According to this
study, Catholic religious communities in the United

States may fall short from $2.5 billion to $3.5 billion in meeting the retirement needs of their aging members.[19] The shortfall hits the sisterhoods the hardest, as their numbers are so much greater than those of the religious-order priests and brothers covered in the study—by 83,839, on the basis of the 113,658 nuns and 29,819 religious-order priests and brothers who were the subjects of the study. (Diocesan, so-called secular, priests were not included in the study because they earn independent salaries and do not pool funds communally, as do nuns and order priests and brothers.)

The financial plight of the men's religious orders and of the sisterhoods more particularly was a startling and sobering surprise. As Archbishop Daniel W. Kucera of Dubuque, chairman of the bishop's liaison committee to the Leadership Conference of Women Religious, remarked, ''We relied solely on the services of religious and never looked to the future where there might not be many religious.''[20] Or any money in their treasuries.

The revelations of the Arthur Anderson and Company study triggered a flurry of activity throughout the American church to help religious orders, of nuns especially, to deal with the financial burdens of their retired and their aging members. The archdiocese of Kansas City, Kansas, for instance, announced in 1986 that it was providing $5.2 million to financially hard-pressed communities of its area, the initial installment of $1.2 million coming as a loan from the priests' retirement fund and from archdiocesan finances.[21] The diocese of Albany, New York, established a Sisters' Retirement Trust Fund and hoped to raise $300,000 in an appeal conducted in

early November 1986; it realized the astounding sum of
$1,046,000, the largest amount ever collected in the di-
ocese's 204 parishes.[22] Diocese after diocese across the
United States took up special collections at masses for
the sisters and announced that these would be annual
events. The archdiocese of Seattle went one better; it
reviewed sister's salaries and drew up guidelines insisting on full parity for the sisters with lay employees by
1 July 1989.[23] Meanwhile, in Silver Spring, Maryland,
outside Washington, a national office was opened under
the direction of Rita Hofbauer, a former director of the
Leadership Conference of Women Religious, to help aging sisters in need. It was launched under the name
SOAR, for "Save Our Aging Sisters," and in less than
four months, it had collected $130,000 in individual do-
nations, according to Hofbauer. "I believe this reflects
a deep gratitude to [women] religious, who through the
years have steadily and devotedly served the Catholic
community, and indeed the wider community," she
commented.

How bad had things become financially for the sisters? The Cincinnati archdiocese's experience answers
that question. Anticipating the support problem of the
nuns earlier than most ecclesiastical jurisdictions, the
archdiocese of Cincinnati announced back in the mid-
1970s the establishment of a retirement fund of $3 mil-
lion for nuns who had worked in archdiocesan schools,
parishes, and institutions and made the final payment
on its pledge in 1985. At the time the fund was set up,
$3 million seemed an adequate sum to meet looming
emergencies. It proved to be short by far. The Sisters of

St. Ursula, for instance, a Cincinnati community of forty-two sisters having a median age of sixty-four, received $70,000 as its retirement allotment. That sum covered only a little more than one year's nursing expenses for five elderly nuns requiring round-the-clock care at St. Ursula Convent.[24]

To be sure, no one is going to abandon the nuns at St. Ursula's to their fate. Cincinnati's Archbishop Daniel E. Pilarczyk has stated that he "stands ready to listen" to communities that feel endangered.[25] It is the same everywhere across the country. The American Catholic community is rallying around the sisterhoods in their time of distress, suddenly aware of their debt to those who formed and enriched them. If consciences are being pricked in the process for having taken women religious so much for granted, and for having neglected their welfare, they should be. The sisters' lot should never have reached the point where they were reduced to being the objects of charity.

But even as the church responds to their plight, the instinct of some people is still to make sport of the sister. For whatever reasons, it's an old game. The sisterhoods have modernized their dress, and many have shed the religious garb entirely. But maybe because sisters went around for so long in medieval or period dress, they became easy marks for those who would associate them, however unfairly, with medievalism of thought, word, and deed. Preconceptions born of that circumstance perhaps help to explain things like Broadway shows holding sisters up to ridicule, and bumper stickers like the one that a clerk in a Casco Bay trading post in

Maine told me was the "hottest item" of the scores in her store: "I SURVIVED CATHOLIC SCHOOL." The bumper stick reflects a complaint that some Catholics have against nuns' being difficult, some maybe even tyrannical. No doubt, some were and still are. But it would be a very small minority who overreacted or were too severe—and maybe some of this response was due to their being exploited themselves. The vast majority of nuns were and remain wholly admirable, dedicated persons. So, naturally, sisters have historically been held in respect by the Catholic community. At the same time, they seem to have been forever vulnerable to those who would choose to make fun of them.

The paradox is that some of the most offensive of these people are well intentioned and are not even aware of their offensiveness—like the Canton, Ohio, priest who launched a program to help aging sisters under the acronym BACON, for "Buy a Catholic Old Nun." It was a Father Robert Reynolds of St. Mary's parish in Canton who conceived the idea, describing it as a counterpart of sorts to programs the sisters themselves once sponsored among school children of adopting or "ransoming" so-called pagan babies in mission lands. Those parochial-school programs largely belong to another age of the conceived responsibility to the church's foreign missions. Reynolds was not content to let the past lie dormant. He resurrected the "ransoming" idea and updated and adapted it in the context of nuns—people of adult dignity, virtually at the Catholic community's mercy, living just down the street. It was an awkward concept from the start, and it didn't help when Reynolds sought to explain things—like what was expected from his parish's "bought" sister for her $800 monthly retirement allowance, or how other parishes might handle their "buy" of an old nun. At St. Mary's in Canton, the "bought" sister was to make a special place for the parish in her prayer life, but she was put on notice. The parish wanted no one who was "going to spend the money on lipstick and dangle earrings." The parish, Reynolds explained, "could submit special petitions for the sister to pray for," but if the prayers weren't "answered promptly, we could cut back on sister's medication."[26] The National Catholic News Service syndicated a tasteless story on Reynolds's offensive idea to the nation's Catholic press.

Now, Reynolds was joking, to be sure. But not everyone appreciated his humor. The *Pilot*, Boston's Catholic weekly, carried the Reynolds story on its front page and was deluged with protesting calls and letters. With only one exception, the protests were from nuns, all of whom felt they were being subjected to cruel and insulting mockery. None of them denied the urgency of their situation, and all were grateful that something was being done to help matters. But each insisted that the methods used to help the sisterhoods should respect them as persons and the serious nature of their situation. Most emphatically, the protestors said, they should not be made the recipients of financial assistance at the expense of their dignity. The *Pilot* was so chastened that, the following week, it printed an editorial apologizing for its insensitivity, adding that no deliberate insult was intended.[27]

Of course, none was—just as no deliberate insult was intended by those stage shows or the "I SURVIVED CATHOLIC SCHOOL" bumper sticker. But somehow, it was easier to excuse the shows and bumper stickers, or at least to understand them. Everything is fair game for satire in entertainment and where there's a buck to be made. One doesn't expect such satire as Reynolds's "Buy a Catholic Old Nun," however, in an emergency situation within the so-called family of the church. Except that, within this family, it is the fate of women, as members of "the second sex," to be treated with condescension.

Along with condescension, there is the problem of place, and that problem belongs to all women, not just those in religious vows. Token recognitions and appointments to secondary positions of responsibility and authority do not begin to get to the heart of the matter. Women are respected in the church, but beyond that, they must be accepted as equals at every level of the Catholic Christian community. Nothing should be denied them because of gender. No doors should be barred to them, not even that of the priesthood. Distinctions based on gender must be wiped out; otherwise, the fears of Monsignor Higgins cited earlier could indeed come to pass. The twentieth-century American church could very well wake up one day and discover that it has lost the allegiance of many of its women, just as the nineteenth-century European church, similarly myopic at another crucial turning point in human affairs, discovered one day that it had lost huge segments of the working class.

It turned out that many of their descendants were lost as well.

This feminist challenge is not unique to the American church. It exists in much of the Western church. It exists, for instance, in Canada, and there Quebec's bishops have shown a particular awareness both of the challenge and of what is to be expected of them. Thus, at a meeting in 1986, they adopted a resolution endorsing the entry of women into all areas of church work and underscored the point with a directive ordering that there be paid coordinators of women's affairs in every diocese by May 1987, one of whose responsibilities would be to advance Catholic sensitivities on women's issues. Quebec's bishops also pledged to remain vigilant and open on the question of women priests, promising even to take the question all the way to Rome.[28] That's a promise that, in the keeping, could prove more quixotic than productive, as least as long as John Paul II is in office. But gestures have their place, too. If truly meaningful change is to come for women in the church, momentum will have to be generated from a multiplicity of sources. None could be more important than momentum originating with the bishops, the very successors of the Apostles.

The American bishops, for their part, have been working for several years on a pastoral letter on the place of women in the church. The letter was supposed to be ready for presentation and final debate by the full episcopal conference in time for its 1987 fall meeting, but the bishop who is chairman of the panel drafting the letter,

Joseph L. Imesch of Joliet, Illinois, has defused that expectation. He declared in December 1986 that it would take a "miracle" to get the letter to the bishops by November 1987.[29] A more realistic timetable, it was indicated, was 1988.

There is nothing surprising about this. Delays are seemingly the rule in the writing of pastoral letters. The bishops' 1983 letter on nuclear weapons ran a year or so behind schedule, and so did the 1986 letter on the economy.

Actually, the bishops are going to be able to use all the delay they can devise on the women's pastoral, for they are in something of a no-win situation. They are caught between Roman intransigence and feminine aspirations on crucial issues that should be addressed in such a pastoral as this, notably that of female ordination; they cannot satisfy one side without alienating the other. It is easy to guess who will be satisfied and who alienated in this instance. Imesch himself intimated this. "We will give positive support to all legislation or initiatives that promote the dignity and the personhood of women, and that promote equal opportunity and rights for women," he said when indicating that a delay was likely in the completing of the pastoral on women. In a separate interview, however, he also signaled that hopes should not be unreined. Noting that women "who were angry before are now angrier," he declared that "women who have expectations of ordination are now having to face it that these expectations are not going to be met. The issues dealt with in the letter will not be the answer to everything."[30]

The women's ordination issue is not, of course, one for the American bishops to settle all by themselves. Decision rests with Rome. But it can be hoped that the bishops will take cognizance of and will dignify the opinions of American Catholics on the subject by at least conveying them to Rome. Rome's mind may be closed as ever on women priests, but those of American Catholics are not. Some eighteen hundred delegates at "Synod '87" regional meetings held recently in the Archdiocese of Milwaukee—priests, religious, and laity from all parishes of the archdiocese—supported the ordination of "all qualified men and women."

The fact is that rank-and-file Catholics are becoming increasingly open-minded on the subject of women priests. A 1986 Catholic University survey, for instance, showed that support for the idea had climbed to 47 percent, up from what was termed "a remarkable 18 percentage points in the eleven years since 1974," when a similar study was conducted.[31] Interestingly enough, in both of those studies, more men than women favored female ordination—by a margin of 51 to 44 percent in the 1986 statistical summary. The finding with respect to men would seem to counter the allegation that women's ordination is primarily a women's issue and that it finds most of its support among militant feminists. Obviously, that is not so.

The Catholic University finding, by the way, is not inconsistent with data from the survey of the 312 American bishops and 122 cardinals worldwide conducted by Father Terrance Sweeney—the same survey that, as discussed elsewhere in this book, cost Sweeney his membership in the Jesuit order. Only ten cardinals responded to Sweeney's inquiry, but a remarkably large number of bishops did—some 145, in fact. Of those respondents, 11 percent favored the ordination of women, and 30 percent said that they would ordain women to the diaconate, the step in Holy Orders immediately below ordination as a priest.[32] Those might seem like modest percentages, but not considering the source. Some American bishops, at least, are not in lockstep with Rome on the issue.

Whether there are enough of them and whether those who exist are strategically enough situated within the hierarchy to make a real difference is the question. One suspects the answer is no on both points, merely because of the careful way in which bishops have been chosen and advanced over the past several years. The safe guys are in control. Even apart from that, with Rome's close overview of so much of what American bishops are doing these days, it is unlikely that the female-ordination issue could or will be broached in a meaningful way in the American bishops' pastoral. Rome won't allow it. Nor are the American bishops likely to press matters very hard. The impulse is to defer. As an assembled body, they did not stand up to Rome on the Hunthausen issue. They are not apt to stand up to Rome on so equally touchy an issue there as female ordination.

Not that you'd expect them to, really. Never mind women priests; most dioceses cannot even decide whether "altar girls" should be allowed to act as servers at Mass—an innocent participation involving little more than answering a few prayers and delivering water and wine and other items to the priest at points in the ceremony. The old 1917 Code of Canon Law contained a specific prohibition against "women approaching the altar," but the new 1983 Code is ambiguous, not using the phrase. Many priests have seized upon the opening to make enterprising, profeminist interpretations of the possibilities, and altar girls are found in their churches. Diocesan policy has been more cautious. Because the altar-girl permission is not specifically stated, the policy in most places in the United States has been to support the controlling norm, which is interpreted as prohibiting female altar servers. One diocese—Worcester, Massachusetts—went so far as to declare it a practical disservice in the pastoral sense even to encourage the idea of "altar girls," the tortured contention being that respect for church law is basic to pastoral practice, and that this disregard of church law is arrogant and confrontational.

The "altar girl" issue will eventually be resolved on the feminist side, perhaps even during the pontificate of John Paul II. What is dismaying, though, is that a matter of secondary significance, which can be so easily resolved, can prove to be so difficult of resolution, and for so long a period of time. It does not encourage optimism about what to expect when discussion moves to weightier issues.

Catholic women, even the most militant, are realistic enough not to expect the church to change overnight on the weightiest of these issues, that of female ordination. But they are also aware that improvement of their place in the church does not await ordination alone. All sorts of changes are demanded in the meantime: women must be accepted as equals in the ecclesiastical community; they must be engaged more seriously in the church's mission; they must enter more into the church's decision-making processes; most especially, they must be released from the sexist baggage heaped on them over the span of centuries. As mentioned earlier, just for women to be called by name in the church's liturgy, rather than being included most of the time in some collective for humankind, or alluded to by way of a circumlocution, would be helpful. The updated text of the New Testament approved by the American bishops in 1987 helps so far as the language factor is concerned. Still much more needs to be done.

Whatever the future brings, however, this is certain: feminist consciousness is going to grow in the church, not wane. Concomitantly, unless the church upgrades the status of its women members, and soon, it is going to lose very many of them. Women have traditionally been the church's most faithful worshipers. But if they become alienated as a group—and the danger is there in the American church—they could render the church's houses of worship empty, echoing halls. The cultural Catholic has moved to the edges of the church's life. Catholic women could be next.

6

THE OLD AND NEW CATHOLIC MINORITIES

Blacks and Hispanics

IN THE AFTERMATH of what the *New York Times* called the "emotionally wrenching" 1986 fall meeting of the U.S. bishops, which was dominated by the Hunthausen affair, a *Times* reporter interviewed several prominent conservative and moderate bishops on the state of American Catholicism and the problem of dissent. Comments touched on a range of topics, from liturgical abuse to dissent from church teaching in matters of sexual morality, such as artificial birth control. At least two bishops stressed that religion was not a democratic process, and they suggested that at least part of the American church's current problems had resulted because of confusion on that point. Some Americans, it was alleged, accustomed to the democratic procedures of the secular society, believed that uncomfortable church teachings could be dealt with and changed much the same way as they are in the state, a possibility the bishops dismissed as impossible. Archbishop Oscar H. Lipscomb of Mobile, Alabama, was one of those interviewed, and he made his argument by drawing a comparison between the issues of segregation and artificial contraception. The church had to decide its approach to artificial contraception and other sexual matters using the same basic principle that it had on integration in the South two decades before: to do what it thought right even if it flew against popular sentiment. "Once we recognized that we would have to be counterculture," Lipscomb said with respect to segregation, "we didn't take any opinion polls to decide whether we would integrate. If we did we might still be segregated."[1]

One might presume from Lipscomb's remark that the Catholic church in the United States had not only fought the good fight and run the good race during the country's tumultuous civil rights period, but also that the church had been a bold leader in the struggle for integration. It would be nice if it had been so, but to imply as much is to fly in the face of history. Archbishop Lipscomb's comment notwithstanding, the last thing that the American Catholic church was during the nation's period of testing on civil rights was "counterculture." To be sure, some church leaders took courageous positions at crucial moments during the civil rights era, people like New Orleans's Archbishop Joseph Rummell and St. Louis's Archbishop Joseph E. Ritter. But the American Catholic church as an institution was hardly out front on civil rights. For decades, the Catholic church in the United States conformed. It conformed until near the very end wherever segregation was institutionalized, which meant that, in the South, even into the middle years of this century, black Catholics had a secondary place in the Catholic community of believers. Blacks sat in the back pews; they came to the communion rail after everyone else; they confessed in segregated confessional boxes. When the pattern was broken in a parish or diocese—as in 1953 when Bishop Vincent S. Waters of the diocese of Raleigh, North Carolina, ordered an end to segregationist practices throughout his jurisdiction—it was a national news story. The American Catholic church, in brief, was about as interested in blacks in America as it was in American Indians, which wasn't very much. Once a year, it thought of them—when it came time for the annual collection, since renamed, but long known as the Collection for the Indian and Negro Missions.

When the moment of truth finally came and the civil rights issue exploded over the land, it wasn't a bishop from this allegedly countercultural institution who did the detonating. The spark was provided by others, and the nation responded to the challenge. The challenge originated with Rosa Parks's refusal on Thursday, 1 December 1955, to give up her seat to a white person on a Montgomery, Alabama, City Lines bus; the challenge was then advanced and carried to triumph by a black Baptist preacher in his first parish assignment in Montgomery, Dr. Martin Luther King, Jr.

Neither was it a "countercultural" Catholic institution nor one of its episcopal leaders who championed the right of the young college students from Negro Agricultural and Technical College to be served at the lunch counter of the F. W. Woolworth store in Greensboro, North Carolina, that February afternoon in 1960.

Neither did Catholic bishops ride freedom buses, nor did they help to staff voter-registration tables in Mississippi.

Catholic bishops and institutional Catholicism were relatively low-profile on the civil rights issue. Neither left to history an immortal example, a ringing, memorable statement or talk. It was not a Catholic bishop, for example, who proclaimed the dream that "one day this nation will rise up, live out the meaning of its creed" that all persons are created equal, thus speeding the day "when all of God's children, black men and white men, Jews and Gentiles, Protestants and Catholics, will be able to join hands and sing in the words of the old Negro spiritual, 'Free at last, Free at last, Great God a-mighty, We are free at last.' "[2]

Leadership and charisma belonged to that Montgomery preacher, Martin Luther King, Jr., and to the black community itself—to the everlasting honor of both. Many Catholics provided a proud witness during the civil rights struggle, but the American Catholic church as an institutional entity was cautious and anything but countercultural, despite Archbishop Lipscomb's statement. The American Catholic church was not only slow in sensing the import and the implications of the civil rights movement; it was slow in responding in dramatically concrete ways to the movement and seemed to do so only after special issues were laid on the church's doorstep. The Catholic church didn't resist the movement; it just didn't embrace the cause of blacks as it has other causes. In 1958, the American bishops published a pastoral letter on the race question in the United States,[3] one that stressed the moral and religious dimensions of racial equality. Still, seven years later, and ten years into the civil rights movement, the secretary of a man regarded as one of the country's most liberal bishops was reprimanded by his employer for taking part in the Selma protest-demonstration that followed the shocking 7 March 1965 clubbing and teargassing incident at that city's Edmund Pettus Bridge. The bishop's worry was that the secretary's presence could have been misinterpreted and could have resulted in the dragging of the bishop's name into news coverage of that sensitive and controversial happening. Incidentally, three years later, that same bishop was foremost among those participating in official obsequies for the slain Dr. King.

If those cognizant of background events like the bishop's censuring of his secretary were and remain skeptical, it should not surprise us. The bishops' 1958 pastoral letter was an important statement for the record; so was the bishops' subsequent pastoral on the subject of civil rights, issued twenty-one years later.[4] Neither changed a page of history, however. Civil rights for blacks was never a Catholic cause, most specially not institutionally. The curious irony is that it turned out to be a Catholic who unmistakably identified the civil rights of black people as a moral issue for Catholics and the rest of the nation. When he did, the story was front-paged in Catholic newspapers across the country. But that person wasn't a bishop, the voice of the magisterium, speaking for the American church. It wasn't a maverick professional Catholic either, brilliantly striking out on his or her own and touching consciences in the act of so doing. It was a born-Catholic, but one educated outside the institution and its formative schools; it was a Choate–Harvard Catholic; it was John F. Kennedy, speaking as president of the country.

The Catholic church got no credit for Kennedy's conscience, and really, it deserved none. But wherever the enlightening initiative of that Catholic president came from, small difference it was likely to make in Roman Catholic–black relationships. Beginning decades, indeed generations, ago, Catholic religious orders of men and women dispatched members on missions of evangelism and social concern to Africa, just as in more recent decades, religious orders have assigned missionaries to Third World countries of Latin America. There is an obvious incongruity in the interest motivating those missions and the lack of interest shown people of those same backgrounds in the United States, but it is explainable. It has forever been easier in the affairs of people to deal with challenges and problems a half-a-world away than with those on one's doorstep. As far as blacks of the United States are concerned, for the Catholic church in the United States they belonged to the ''Other

America''; they were invisible. Which is to say once again that the American Catholic church was never the countercultural force that Lipscomb credited it with being—not in the 1950s, not in the 1960s, not ever in American history. Blacks had never figured prominently in the evangelical goals of the Catholic church in the United States.

The lack of interest was reciprocal, so that whatever the performance of the American church in the 1950s and 1960s, it was not going to atone for history. History isn't corrected by latter-day pangs of conscience or tardy energetic demonstrations of concern and interest, even those arising out of the best and most sincere of motives.

The American Catholic church did not leave its mark on the civil rights movement, but neither did its failures cost the church the interest or loyalties of the American black. It never had them to begin with—again, for the good and obvious reason that the American Catholic church had never particularly concerned itself with the American black.

There are historical and sociological explanations for this. The most obvious is that the strong urban nature of American Catholicism for years minimized contact with American blacks, long a largely rural population. Blacks did not arrive in force in the cities until the Depression and job opportunities stimulated by World War II and the postwar boom made migration easier from rural areas. Of course, by that time, urban white Catholics were on their way to the suburbs—not in flight, at least not most of them, but because they had made it one rung up on the economic ladder.

Another factor accounting for the distance between American Catholicism and the American black community is that, in sinking roots in its beginnings, the American Catholic church had its hands full just seeing to the spiritual welfare of its Catholic emigrants. Except for the early period of Spanish exploration and colonialization, the Catholic church was never strongly evangelical on the American continent, and even colonial Spanish evangelism was itself limited in time and scope. Spanish Catholicism waned with Spanish political hegemony, and little was left behind of either except memories largely bound up with mission chapels and the names of cities in the West and the Southwest: Los Angeles, San Francisco, San Diego, San Antonio, and the like. A Hispanic Catholicism would arrive again in the United States from Latin American and Caribbean areas, but much later. By that time, American Catholicism would have a distinctly Western European flavor, the church being dominated in numbers and leadership by the descendants of those who had arrived on the nineteenth-century waves of emigration from Ireland and from central and southern Europe. That church was not nearly as strong in its early periods as it is now. When it arrived on American shores, Protestantism was firmly established as the religion of the majority. The Catholic objective was to sink its own roots and survive, not to evangelize those already here, blacks included—the more so because the blacks were mainly in the South, where the church's future did not lie at the time.

Still, if the Catholic church in the United States did not or could not evangelize the members of the black community in a serious way, it never seemed particularly to agonize over the fact. It did not go out of its way to make blacks feel welcome as Catholics, and it did not encourage black vocations. In 1890, for example, there was only one black priest in the entire United States.[5] Indeed, black candidates for the priesthood and the sisterhoods were generally not even accepted into American Catholic seminaries and convents during the 1920s and 1930s.[6]

Given this background, we can see why today there are fewer than 300 black priests out of some 57,000 in the United States, and out of some 113,000 sisters, fewer than 800 who are black.[7] Similarly, it is easy to understand why, out of an American black population of some 25 million, only 1.3 million are Catholic.[8] This is a 41 percent increase since 1975, but it still leaves black Catholics comprising barely 3 percent of the national Catholic population of more than 52 million. Further, even though the black Catholic poulation has grown since 1975, analysts are not certain that this growth signals anything markedly significant for the American Catholic church. For instance, in reporting the growth, the *Wall Street Journal* discounted it almost in the same breath: "Scholars say some blacks join the Catholic Church because they view it as proof of their upward mobility, a way of distinguishing themselves from some of the more traditional black denominations such as Baptists or Pentecostals."[9]

Whatever the validity of that observation, we can safely say that such growth as has occurred has been largely free of initiative on the part of white Catholics.

True, evangelization of those already evangelized runs counter to the ecumenical spirit of the times. Even allowing for that fact, however, no particular effort has been made by the American Catholic church to make blacks the objects of its apostolic affections. Nor has there been any concerted effort to recruit vocations to the religious life from among those blacks who are Catholics.

If the truth be faced, over the years the black Catholic minority has often been far more concerned with the spiritual welfare and standing of blacks as Catholics than the white Catholic majority has been. Which is to say that credit for such advances as have been made in areas of the black Catholic presence belongs largely to blacks themselves. Just recently, for instance, the Baltimore-based National Black Catholic Congress, in developing a black Catholic agenda for evangelization looking to the year 2000, created a new post to administer the organization and to direct its concerns. Its objectives include the witnessing and affirming of the Catholic faith among black Catholics and the shaping of practical evangelical methods within the context of the ''social and economic conditions of black Americans.'' The administrator is expected to work closely with U.S. black Catholic bishops and the memberships of the principal black Catholic organizations: the National Association of Black Catholic Administrators, the National Black Sisters' Conference, the National Black Clergy Caucus, and the Knights and Ladies Auxiliary of St. Peter Claver.

This is not to imply that black Catholics are being left on their own to do whatever they can for themselves in the American church. The official church is cooperating, markedly so in recent years. The year 1986, for instance, saw such innovations as these:

1. The introduction in the archdiocese of Chicago of a new hymnal aimed at making Catholic worship services and music more meaningful to black parishioners. Entitled "Lead Me, Guide Me," the hymnal made available for the first time in a publication approved by Catholic officials gospel favorites like "What a Friend We Have in Jesus."[10]

2. The inauguration in dioceses like Pittsburgh of special features or supplements to the diocesan newspaper focusing on news and information of special interest to blacks. The Pittsburgh project, an initiative of the diocese's Office of Black Catholic Ministeries, took the form of a supplement in the *Pittsburgh Catholic*.[11] Coincidentally, a new national Catholic newspaper for the black Catholic community was making its debut about the same time out of Nashville. Named the *National Catholic Mentor*, the paper announced that it will serve to showcase the talents of black Catholic writers and will aim to overcome the persistent lack of what was described as "black input" into the Catholic press.[12] The publisher is James W. Pebbles, a convert to Catholicism, founder and president of Winston-Derek Publishers, a Nashville-based publishing house.

3. The establishment by the U.S. Bishops Conference of a new standing committe for black Catholics, the first chairperson of which will be elected in November 1987, and, as of 1988, a new Office for Black Catholics at the headquarters of the National Conference of Catholic Bishops. (*Crux of the News*, a weekly newsletter pub-

lished especially for priests, deacons, and religious, described the actions as "demonstrating future directions and priorities" of the American Catholic church.[13])

The question is whether actions such as these, impressive though they certainly are, have come too late to make much of a difference. They probably have. Collectively, they do not seem to have changed, at least not yet, the perception among blacks, black Catholics included, that the Catholic church is essentially a white ethnic European institution, which continues to come up short of the universality it proclaims for itself. Such at least is the opinion of one prominent black priest, Father Edward K. Braxton, director of Calvert House, the Catholic student center at the University of Chicago. Though the American Catholic church includes among its members blacks and other minorities, Braxton commented not long ago at a forum in Chicago, "a growing number of black Catholic lay leaders, clergy and religious in various parts of the country believe that the church does not really wish to expand in the black community."[14] The church is seen by blacks, he said, as "the special home of the great ethnic and national groups from Europe. It is the custodian of their customs, their traditions, and their mores—and is in some way incompatible with the black experience in America." Further, Braxton declared, "When we reflect on the scars of the past, we need no longer wonder why there are so few black Catholics. The wonder is that there are so many."

This is blunt language, but no blunter than that which the ten American black bishops (their number recently grew to eleven) used in their historic pastoral letter

of 9 September 1984, "What We Have Seen and Heard."
The pastoral hailed the maturity of black Catholic Christianity in the United States in the context of what it
described as the four major characteristics of black
spirituality: it is contemplative, holistic, joyful, com-
munitarian. However, the black bishops observed, the
black Catholic community of believers still labored under the handicap of racism. "Unhappily, we must acknowledge that the major hindrance to the full
development of black leadership within the church is still
the fact of racism," the bishops declared in their pastoral.
"This racism, at once subtle and masked, still festers
within our church as within our society."[15]

A year later, at a day-long symposium at St. Charles
Borromeo Church in Harlem commemorating the first
anniversary of the pastoral letter, the black bishops saw
no reason to change their assessment. Auxiliary Bishop
Emerson J. Moore of New York noted that "many black
Catholics as individuals have met resistance" when they
sought to join white parishes. "Racism is a sin and must
always be on the agenda of the church," he remarked.
Auxiliary Bishop James P. Lyke of Cleveland, echoed the
pastoral's stress on the "gift of spirituality" that blacks
offered the church, but he declared that the old challenge
remained: "We have to dispel the myth that black
Catholics belong to a white church."[16] The black
bishops' pastoral was supposed to educate and challenge, but even New York's Cardinal O'Connor conceded at the symposium that "very little" had been done
in the year since the issuance of the pastoral to bring
about the changes sought by black Catholics.[17]

Black Catholics have an agenda for improving their role and influence in the church. Among much else, the black bishops would like to see increased representation of blacks in the church's hierarchy. With the appointment in January 1987 of Josephite Father Carl Fisher as an auxiliary bishop in Los Angeles, there are now eleven black American bishops. But currently in the United States there is only one black ordinary, or head of a diocese, Bishop Joseph L. Howze of Biloxi, Mississippi.

For his part, Braxton recommended—again, among much else—a serious commitment to Catholic education for blacks, a greater effort to get into black hands church documents that pertain to them, and a deepening of the church's dedication to evangelization in the black community. "Couldn't there be two or three million black Catholics in the United States by the year 2000?" he asked at the Harlem symposium.[18]

Possibly there could be, particularly if Bishop Moore's prediction at the Harlem symposium proves true that, in time, "things *will* get better" as far as racism in the institution and in the body of Catholics is concerned.

On the other hand, black Catholicism would not seem, as they say on Wall Street, a promising growth stock in the church's future. The interest of the church's white leadership remains tepid at best, and even were it to heat up, it would very likely encounter the problem of black indifference to such a change. That should be no surprise. The history of the past hangs too heavily over the present for matters to be otherwise.

Quite a different story is that involving Hispanics. Hispanics are not the nation's newest minority by any means; most certainly, they are not the newest Catholic minority. Catholic Germans, Irish, French and French-Canadians, Italians, and Slavs of middle and eastern Europe—they arrived in various stages, staked out their hegemonies, and solved their problems of relocation in the late nineteenth and early twentieth centuries, thanks to the melting pot; coexistence, neighborliness, and finally intermarriage helped improve the blend. As mentioned, Spanish Catholicism of the colonial period became a remnant faith. Subsequently there was a long history of Hispanic immigration, though these immigrants settled in the main along the border regions of the southwestern United States and in pockets along the Atlantic and Pacific coasts. Today it is different, both in terms of the numbers of Hispanic immigrants and their distribution. Hispanics are immigrating to cities and towns everywhere in the United States, and are rapidly becoming one of the largest, if not the largest, of the nation's minorities. In fact, so large and continuing is Hispanic immigration that some observers speak of what they call the "Latinization" of America. California, worried that the language of these new immigrants, Spanish, might one day replace English as the first language of its area, even approved a referendum in 1986 formally designating English the official language of the state.

The precise size of the Hispanic population in the United States is a matter of considerable speculation. Bishop Ricardo Ramirez of Las Cruces, New Mexico, speaks of the U.S. Catholic church having 21 million Hispanic members.[19] However, U.S. Census Bureau figures released in 1986 estimated the numbers of Hispanics living in the United States—Catholics, Protestants, whatever—to be only 17.3 million. One says "only," but the number is nonetheless very large, and growing. The Census Bureau projects that, by the year 2020, the number of Hispanics living in the United States will more than double to 36.5 million and will continue upward, reaching 51 million by 2046. This statistic means by extrapolation that the Hispanic population, which was 6.4 percent at the time of the 1980 census, will rise to 12 percent nationally in 2020, to 16 percent in 2050, and then to 19 percent by 2080.[20] What's more, these are "conservative" estimates, according to Census Bureau official William Matney. They represent a so-called middle-range scenario of what bureau experts believe is likely to happen in the interaction between fertility, immigration, and the death rate.

Admittedly, those projections, like all such figures, are subject to revision. Any number of factors could come along to alter them upward or downwards—from changes in immigration laws, to tougher policing of the nation's boundaries and ports of entry, to new preferential attitudes of the Immigration and Naturalization Service, to different migratory impulses on the part of Hispanics. For one reason or another, the United States could lose its attractiveness to Hispanics as a place to which to emigrate, although it is difficult to conceive of that happening anytime soon. Hispanic immigration is currently a very real, very large fact of American life, and undoubtedly, it will continue as such for the indefinite future.

The implications are enormous for the country, and also for the Catholic church, as the vast majority of

Hispanic immigrants are Catholics—some 90 percent, as a matter of fact. Accordingly, if Hispanic immigration has the potential for changing the face of secular America, it has the same potential for the American Catholic church, maybe even more so, given American Catholicism's still strong urban focus and Hispanic immigration's essentially urban character. About 85 percent of Hispanics reside in metropolitan areas.[21] At least twenty-five American cities have Hispanic communities of fifty thousand people or more, and most are cities where the Catholic church is well established and strong, places such as Hartford, Philadelphia, Chicago, New York, and Los Angeles. In many of these and other cities, the Hispanic population may be much larger because of illegal immigration; in fact, it no doubt is. It would follow that the church's Hispanic element is correspondingly larger, and maybe more in the neighborhood of Bishop Ramirez's figure after all. Some church officials agree with him at any rate. By way of example, the archdiocese of Los Angeles—a jurisdiction embracing the counties of Los Angeles, Ventura, and Santa Barbara—officially places its total membership at 2.6 million Catholics. But, because of unreliable estimates of illegal aliens in the region, it is believed that the total is more like 3 million, according to an archdiocesan spokesman, Father Joseph Battaglia.[22]

The archdiocese of New York, an ecclesiastical composite of some 2 million Catholics who live in three of New York City's boroughs and seven upstate counties, may now be as much as 35 percent Hispanic. The great concentrations of Hispanics are in the Bronx and Manhattan, so that in New York City alone, one of every three Catholics is Hispanic. Further, four of every ten Hispanics are under thirty years old, a demographic statistic indicating that Hispanics could become the majority in the Catholic church in New York by the turn of the new century.[23]

From the standpoint of religion, there seems to be nothing preplanned about Catholic Hispanics' arriving at established centers of Catholic strength and influence. Maybe, once upon a time, immigrants of a particular religious persuasion sought out communities of kindred souls where, if nothing more, there were the assurances and psychological consolations of a life continued among a people who shared the same religious beliefs and values as themselves. But immigration history has not repeated itself in the same way with Hispanics. Today's Hispanic immigrants do indeed tend to congregate and group into enclaves, but the reasons are apparently far more cultural and economic than they are religious.

Hispanics are obviously a religious people, but so far as their Catholicism is concerned, they are keeping a distance from the organized Catholic church of the United States. Maybe some feel themselves strangers in the American Catholic church. Many Hispanics, for example, are reported to be uncomfortable with the rigidities and formalisms of American Catholicism, such as the stress on regular worship, the importance placed on being on time for church services, and what they consider petty expectations like staying in one's pew until the priest has made his exit from the altar. Maybe some Hispanics feel culturally unwelcome in the American church. Or maybe some view the American church and its officials with a suspicion, lingering from their past, that the church and its officials are counterparts of the authoritarian apparatus they knew in the old country. Whatever the reasons, studies show that members of this great tide of Catholic immigration are turning out to be far less identified with the church that was theirs back in their countries of origin. Whether they were, in fact, close to the church in their old situation is another question; for many—indeed, most—Hispanics, the Roman Catholic option was the only one they had in their native country. One was Catholic or one was nothing. In any instance, as the *Daily News* remarked of New York's Hispanics in a special report published in 1986, "Hispanics overwhelmingly consider religion important in their lives." However, the paper added, in their new situation "they feel no great identification with the Catholic church."[24] Apparently, neither spiritually nor culturally do they view the American church with the same sense of intimacy that they did the Catholic church in the lands of their origin.

Undoubtedly, part of the problem is that, unlike earlier groups of Catholic immigrants—the Irish, Italians, and Germans, most notably—the new Hispanic immigrants have not arrived with their own priests, individuals who could help to foster Catholic religious bonds and to ease Hispanics into the mainstream of American Catholic life. As the experience of earlier immigrant groups indicates, the latter is not an automatic and frictionless process. There was considerable competition in some areas of the country, for instance, between early German and Irish Catholic immigrant communities on such issues as language and episcopal appointments. Would the essential flavor of this American church be German, or would it be Irish? The Irish achieved the initial ascendancy in influence and numbers, and for half a century or more, much of the American church was dominated by that ethnic group. The Irish hegemony began to wane around 1960, however, as appointments to the hierarchy began to include, as a matter of conscious papal policy, individuals from ethnic groups that, until then, had been largely bypassed. As a result, at the hierarchial level, if no other, the American church is today a far more ethnically balanced church, in which the various groups generally relate well to one another as Catholics.

It is in this church that Hispanics have to find a place. But as Hispanics have not arrived with priests, neither do they seem to have arrived with any reservoir of young vocations to the priesthood. The lack of a sizable Hispanic clergy is a problem for them. It is also an additional complication for the institutional church of the United States. For at a time when its own resources are strained because of a shortage of priests, the American church must now minister to many more Catholics arriving in its midst. Italian popes of the nineteenth century insisted that priests and nuns accompany Italian immigrants to ensure that their faith would be protected; it is how Sister Frances Xavier Cabrini, for one, happened to come to America.[25] That's what is not happening now. Hispanics, indeed, are not only arriving priestless, but as Catholics from a different religious tradition from Catholics already here, and speaking a language still foreign to most in the official church.

Further, if religious illiteracy, as argued earlier, is a problem among Catholics already living here, it is now compounded. For Hispanic immigrants are not arriving with what would seem to be a particularly strong working knowledge of the formal faith or of current Catholicism. About two-thirds, according to one study, cannot name a single one of the seven sacraments. A 1986 survey of 1,010 Hispanic Catholics across the United States found a high level of support for certain tenets of the church, such as the divinity of Christ and the intercessory power of the saints, but at the same time, it found that more than half the respondents had never heard of Vatican Council II or the American bishops' pastoral letter on war and peace. Three out of four said they did not know of "liberation theology," a movement centered in Latin America, and thus of Hispanic origins.[26] This same study confirmed the *Daily News* observation that Catholic Hispanics do not feel close to the official church. It produced the statistic that 86.7 percent of Hispanics do not involve themselves in parish activities. The survey, entitled "The Hispanic Catholic in the United States," was conducted by the Reverend Roberto O. Gonzalez and Michael La Velle, and its findings were made public in New York by the Northeast Pastoral Center for Hispanics.

Passing current-events quizzes is not a test of faith, to be sure. But lack of awareness about events and movements shaping the church, such as Vatican II and liberation theology, carries sobering implications. A shaky knowledge and grasp of denominational goings-on could reflect a shaky hold of the faith itself. This might not be a problem in a country where religion is something of a closed Catholic shop, but it could be in a country like the United States, where so many more religious options exist. Not "could be," it is. In its 1986 study of religion in New York, the *Daily News* reported Catholic leaders to be "clearly uneasy about the appeal of fundamentalist storefront churches" to Hispanics.[27] In the context used, *fundamentalist* translates as "Protestant."

The unease does not appear to be misplaced. George Gallup, Jr., and Jim Castelli reported in their book *The American Catholic People: Their Beliefs, Practices and Values* that 74 percent of Hispanics have been contacted by proselytizing Evangelicals, Pentecostals, or Jehovah's Witnesses.[28] Similarly, the Gonzalez–La Velle study revealed that eight out of every ten Hispanic Catholics were being approached for conversion by Pentecostals, Evangelicals, and other sects, and that a majority of Hispanic Catholics had a favorable view of these groups.[29] So favorable, indeed, that many Catholic Hispanics are converting to other faiths. At least, one might so surmise on the basis of the *Daily News* study, which showed that 14 percent of New York City's Hispanic population—1.4 million persons, not counting illegal residents—now describes itself as Protestant. According to the poll, about 5 percent are Pentecostal, 3 percent Jehovah's Witnesses, 3 percent Baptists, and 3 percent "other."[30]

Obviously, the situation in New York is not unique. Speaking last year in San Diego, Bishop Ramirez warned that the American church is in danger of losing its Hispanic members if it cannot halt their flow into fundamentalist groups. The leakage of Hispanic Catholics to Protestantism is due, he remarked, to "the proselytism of fundamentalist groups," but he conceded that "we" in the Catholic church haven't done a whole lot to counter the flow.[31] It is a "sad" phenomenon, Ramirez remarked, sad not just because Hispanics are leaving the church, but also because they are "losing the vision" the church offers, including the fullness of sacramental life. One tragedy is that families are being divided in the process. Ramirez told of a Hispanic family—some of whom were Catholic, others Protestant—that gathered for the grandmother's funeral. The denominational differences caused such friction at the funeral that some of the family refused to sing certain songs or to recite given prayers.

But things are changing at the institutional level. The church that once took the Catholicism of Hispanics for granted is aware now that it must reach out to them if that Catholicism is to be preserved. The U.S. bishops' *ad hoc* committee on Hispanic affairs, accordingly, is now a permanent one, and the bishops are working on a Hispanic pastoral plan, which they expect to issue in 1988. Also, individual dioceses are initiating programs aimed at helping Hispanics feel at home in the United States, both as Catholics and as Americans. The archdiocese of Los Angeles, for example, announced in 1986 a five-year plan that will bring the power of the church to bear in a concerted advocacy for the Hispanic majority of its area. One of the diocese's first actions in the context of the plan was to express opposition to a government plan to evict illegal aliens from public housing.

American Catholic leaders obviously appreciate that there is an urgency involved, and that, among much else, the urgency includes winning the trust of Hispanics, and also developing a greater familiarity with their culture and language. The latter is seen as particularly important for those ministering to Hispanics. As Ramirez noted, the outreach must be done in Spanish: "We can't wait for [Hispanics] to learn English." In a word, American Catholics are advised by Ramirez to take a page from the book of the fundamentalists. Two of the reasons that Protestants have been so successful in converting Hispanics, he contended, is that they took the trouble both to learn Spanish and to recruit Hispanics as ministers.[32]

Ramirez's observations and actions such as those of the Los Angeles archdiocese have a strong ring of practicality to them. At the very least, they coincide with recommendations originating with the 190 priests from twenty-four states who met in 1986 in San Antonio as the National Convention of Hispanic Priests in the United States. They urged increased diocesan interest and parish involvement in questions of refugees, immigrants, undocumented aliens, and poverty; greater efforts to train Hispanic lay ministers and leaders; the creation of a federation of Hispanic priests with recognition from the U.S. bishops; and broader seminary training to include Hispanic-oriented liturgical customs and practices.[33]

To the extent that familiarity with the Spanish language is important in all of this, a few parts of the

American church are in a much better position than others. The archdiocese of New York, for one, has promoted the learning of Spanish by its priests since back when Cardinal Spellman was alive and sending seminarians to Puerto Rico for a portion of their training, specifically so that they would learn the language. Spellman saw the Hispanic future of his archdiocese better than most, and this is one reason that, today, it is possible for the Mass to be celebrated in Spanish in more than two hundred parishes of the archdiocese of New York.[34] But the same foresight did not exist in other dioceses where, today, Hispanics are settling in great numbers. New York may not be an example of a brilliantly bilingual archdiocese, but it is ahead of most of the country's ecclesiastical jurisdictions.

But language is only one element of the equation. The Catholic loyalties of the Hispanic people will be quickened, but they are not going to be cemented for all time just by non-Hispanic people's being able to speak Spanish. Language and common tongues could not ensure the ascendancy of Catholicism over Lutheranism, Calvinism, or other Protestant creeds in northern and middle Europe at the time of the Reformation.

If the experience of ethnic groups in the United States is any criterion, the Catholicism of Hispanics will be put here to other tests, specifically, cultural and intellectual tests born of the society's pluralism and the multiplicity of religious options that exist in the country. The testing is already occurring.

This is a circumstance not necessarily to be deplored; belief is a matter of mind as well as soul, or should be. The problem is that certain disadvantages are built into the situation as it applies to Hispanic Catholics. Because of a combination of circumstances, Hispanic Catholics may be more vulnerable to proselytism now that they are outside the protective precincts of the totally Catholic society that was theirs. This is not to say that, in the United States, Catholic Hispanics will eventually be lost to the traditional Catholic church. It is only to repeat that they are vulnerable, and that maybe it isn't a good time for them or any other segment of American Catholicism to be vulnerable when so much else exists to claim the attention and concerns of the church's leadership—in Rome and the United States.

7

THE CURRAN SYNDROME

FROM THE OUTSET, Rome's action against Father Charles Curran of the Catholic University of America's faculty was difficult to fathom. On the human level, the action displayed a sorry, even cruel, insensitivity toward a man of high integrity and great personal loyalty to the church; on the bureaucratic level, it evidenced, at best, a lack of knowledge and, at worse, a contempt for the intellectual and statutory independence of American colleges and universities—particularly those that are Catholic. Curran is a theologian attached to a university with pontifical ac-

237

creditation; the pontifical association is an impressive Catholic credential. But at the same time, it rendered Curran—as it would almost anyone on the Catholic University faculty—vulnerable to the displeasure of Rome, an open target to anyone with the will and in a position to invoke pontifical authority against him. Through such authority, Cardinal Ratzinger did in Father Charles Curran.

But Curran is only one theologian teaching on one Catholic campus. There are scores, indeed hundreds, more theologians on the 242 Catholic campuses of the United States. What happens to Charles Curran to one degree or another affects them, too, as professors within the Catholic discipline. It also affects the intellectual climate of each and every one of those Catholic colleges and universities. Whether Rome's challenge to Curran took that factor into account is impossible to say. The guess is that it did; challenge and disciplining can be effective inhibiting factors, and if Curran is a lesson to others, so much the better in Rome's view. Nevertheless, the net result of Rome's challenge to and disciplining of Father Charles Curran—begun by Rome and then pursued in Rome's name by the archbishop of Washington, James A. Hickey, in his role as university chancellor—is certain to diminish the academic standing not only of Catholic University, but also of every American Catholic campus as a place of free inquiry and of scholarship.

And that's only one of the consequences. The challenge to Curran could also have severe financial repercussions for many Catholic institutions of higher learning. American Catholic colleges and universities receive almost a half-billion dollars annually in federal and state aid, and the criteria for receiving this aid are established by law, are overseen by educational accrediting agencies, and in contested cases, are adjudicated by the courts. If campus principles are impinged on, academic freedom among them, the institution risks the withdrawal or curtailment and denial of funds; in such a circumstance, the whole institution suffers, not merely the department or departments in violation of a particular code. The assertion of will in the name of orthodoxy could, therefore, be a very expensive exercise of authority.

Beyond personal and institutional considerations, there are likewise those of morale—not just Curran's morale; not just the morale of Curran's students and his colleagues at Catholic University; not just the morale of Catholic campus people all over the United States; but the morale of the American Catholic community generally. To be sure, many Catholics whole-heartedly approve the disciplining of Father Charles Curran for daring to depart from traditional Catholic thought on birth control and other issues of sexual morality. But many others are dismayed. For them, the issue is not just one of thought control. It is also one of intrusion on the concept of freedom of conscience developed at Vatican II and assimilated by many Catholics within their Catholic situations.

From the start, therefore, only the most naive could believe that the implications of the Curran case involved one man, a moral theologian, teaching in one department, the theology department, at one university, the

Catholic University of America. Obviously, the case involved, and continues to involve, much more. It is probable that Rome has had not so much as a second thought about the wisdom of its action. Nonetheless, the Curran affair looms at the moment as the church's own 1980s Contragate. It was an action rashly conceived, hastily adopted, and pressed on ahead with little thought about the consequences if one small detail fell apart. And one did: Curran refused to play according to Rome's code and triggered a controversy of huge dimensions. That controversy has cost Curran his theological and academic place at Catholic University, at least temporarily; it could cost him his very future as a teacher within official Catholicism. But if it does, it is going to cost official Catholicism even more. Maybe Rome believes that no price is too high to pay in its pursuit of orthodoxy on the Catholic campus. But it is painfully apparent that the Curran controversy is not neatly contained. The implications spill over, and so will the consequences. Damage control will not be an easy exercise.

Even beyond the Catholic community, the Curran case carries considerable implications.

Specifically, the Curran case has large ecumenical dimensions. Inevitably, those engaged in friendly contact and dialogue with the Catholic church are marking carefully the progression of the case for the signals it emits, however obliquely, to the wider Christian community. And the Curran case is sending strong signals, particularly to Protestants. As each new chapter in the Curran story has unfolded, the Protestant press has been heavy with coverage and discussion. Its viewpoints and sympathies are predictable, indeed inevitable. But then, how could they be otherwise when Protestants see a person disciplined for broaching ideas held as matter of course in most of their mainline Protestant denominations? Though one must be true to one's own religion, it is a circumstance that does not bode well for the ecumenical movement and the often-expressed hope of Christian reunion.

But it is the Catholic intramural issues that are of immediate concern. How could the Curran case have happened? How could it have mushroomed to the extent it did? How could Rome's timing have been so inept? The timing was curious almost beyond belief. Rome had appeared to have extricated itself at last from the awkward situation it had created for itself by its ultimatum to the twenty-four nuns who had signed the controversial paid statement on Catholics and abortion in the *New York Times* of 7 October 1984—eighteen of the twenty-four nuns by then having submitted to Rome acceptable clarifications of their positions on abortion (the number of nuns under Rome's ultimatum was subsequently reduced to two). But then, Rome allowed its ultimatum to Curran, festering on and off since 1979, to come to a denouement in March 1986, and with that action, Rome took on a sweeping set of additional issues in moral and behavioral areas that were far less cosmic in their theological, moral, and behavioral significance than the abortion issue involving the twenty-four nuns.

To be sure, as with the nuns, Rome had its problems with Curran's view about abortion.

Rome would disagree with Curran, for instance, on the question of the moment when human life begins. Curran's proposition is that ''truly individual human life begins at the time of individuation which occurs between the fourteenth and twenty-first day.''[1] Rome would again part company on exceptions that Curran would allow for abortion. Curran would not require Rome's absolute prohibition of abortion; still, he would not come under the heading of being an abortion liberal. Curran holds, for instance, that ''one can be justified in taking truly individual life only for the sake of the life of the mother or for a value commensurate with life itself.''[2] He is not, in a word, a radical on the subject of abortion, or even what a prochoice person would call much of progressive. But he is nuanced, and he is not a stickler for certain of the theological niceties that his more strictly orthodox colleagues would insist upon. He made that clear during an appearance on the ''Firing Line'' program of William F. Buckley, Jr., taped in New York City on 20 November 1986, and later telecast nationally on the Public Broadcasting System.

Asked for an example to demonstrate how moral proportionality, a Curran concept, could ever enter into abortion, Curran cited the instance of ectopic pregnancy. This is a situation in which pregnancy occurs outside the womb, in the Fallopian tube. The church has historically allowed the ending of such a pregnancy under the principle of the double effect. In other words, to save at least one of the lives—that of the mother—the church would permit the evil of the death of the fetus. However, four criteria would have to be strictly met: the evil effect could not be wished, and every reasonable effort would have to be made to avoid it; the immediate effect would have to be good in itself (in this instance, the saving of the life of the mother); the evil could not be a means of obtaining a good effect (ends can never be used to justify means); and the good effect would have to be at least as important as the evil that followed. The problem is that, based on these ground rules, the terminating of an ectopic pregnancy entails removal of the Fallopian tube. Curran's proposition when such cases occur is that "it might be much better at times to attack the embryo. Therefore you save the [Fallopian] tube for future childbearing and [thus] I would justify at times the possibility of directly attacking the embryo."[3] He could conceivably have added that such a medical strategy would also eliminate the problem of mutilating the body of the mother, a discussable point, because unnecessary mutilation likewise is a procedure proscribed in the Catholic canon. Admittedly, however, to have added such a comment would have been to lead the discussion afield and into another area entirely of medical ethics.

But Rome, in challenging Charles Curran, had much more on its mind than abortion alone. It also targeted him for viewpoints on such subjects as divorce, artificial contraception, masturbation, premarital intercourse, and homosexuality.

The subject categories would seem to suggest strongly that Curran is something of a freewheeling libertine, a professor and writer who would free students and readers from all moral restraints. In point of fact, he is anything but that. As "Xavier Rynne," nom de plume for the Redemptorist priest who was the *New Yorker's* literary ghost at Vatican Council II, commented in the *Boston Globe* at the height of the Curran controversy, "He does not advocate abortion or sterilization; . . . he does not justify homosexuality as such; nor does he exonerate masturbation. He does disagree with papal teaching on contraception; but here he enjoys the support of a majority of theologians and no small number of bishops."[4]

Curran's views, again, are not radical, and though they may often depart from the views of the official church, they do so in areas where the church's infallibility is not involved. This is Curran's contention, and most of his colleagues would support him on it. Father Charles Curran, in other words, dissents from authoritative but noninfallible teachings of the church.

NC News Service, the news arm of the United States Catholic Conference, summarized the respective opinions of the church and of Curran on a number of subjects in August 1986. The précis are interesting for the clues they provide to who is the zealot and who is intruded upon. A selection of the précis follows:

Masturbation: The church holds that masturbation "is an intrinsically and seriously disordered act." Curran holds that masturbatory acts "are ordinarily not very important or significant and usually do not involve grave matter. Such actions are generally symptomatic of other realities and should be treated as such."

Premarital intercourse: The church holds that sexual relations outside marriage are always intrinsically and seriously wrong. Curran would admit exceptions "only in very rare and comparatively few situations."

Artificial contraception: The church holds that "every marital act must remain open to the transmission of life," and that, therefore, actions aimed at obstructing that purpose "are forbidden as intrinsically wrong." Curran's contention is that this approach ties moral judgments too closely to the physical or biological structure of the act, rather than to a broader moral framework of intentions, meanings, and relationships. He holds further that artificial contraception and direct sterilization "are not intrinsically evil but can be good or evil insofar as they are governed by the principles of responsible parenthood and stewardship."

Indissolubility of marriage: The church holds that a sacramental, consummated marriage is indissoluble. Curran holds that New Testament teaching on marital indissolubility represents an ideal to be striven for and not an absolute norm binding on all, and thus, he urges that the church allow divorce in certain limited instances. (The church, of course, grants annulments, but they are based on finding that no marriage existed in the first place because of one or another impediment.)

Homosexual acts: The church holds that homosexual acts "lack an essential and indispensable finality and must therefore always be considered gravely wrong." Curran holds that homosexual relationships fall short of the full meaning of human sexuality. But he proposes that, "for an irreversible, constitutional or genuine homosexual, homosexual acts in the context of a loving relationship striving for permanency can in a certain sense be objectively morally acceptable."

NC News Service's summary of Curran's views[5] extended through several more areas, but the point is clear for those willing to accept it. On the basis of positions appearing in the précis, Curran is nothing at all of an extremist but is a moderate, certainly by today's standards. If he is breaking new ground in some areas of behavioral morality, he is, as more than one observer remarked, only performing the normal function of a theologian. *Boston Globe* columnist and former ambassador to Ireland William V. Shannon summed up Curran as one who "made theological distinctions to take account of difficult situations and gray areas of human conduct,"[6] and Dr. John C. Bennett, senior contributing editor of the Protestant-oriented journal *Christianity and Crisis*, evaluated him there as one who is "in no way an aggressive rebel," but one who came "to his conclusions involving dissent after the most careful and fair exposition of the alternatives in his many books."[7]

Increasing the wonder over the action against Curran was the fact that, apart, perhaps, from the abortion issue, he was not venturing into those sacrosanct territories that Rome has traditionally been zealous about guarding. In recent years, Rome has instituted ecclesiastical measures against European theologians like Father Hans Küng and Dominican Edward Schillebeeckx, but those theologians were raising fundamental questions on issues of dogma, the organization of the church, and papal infallibility, the very bedrock of the church's teaching authority. But none of this has been Curran's preoccupation. Curran is a moral theologian; he is concerned with the moral as distinct from the dogmatic dimensions of problems. Though he has come to be regarded as a specialist in matters of sexual morality, and though it is for his views in these matters that he is being disciplined, the fact is that he has not even taught sexual ethics in the classroom for fifteen years. In addition, as most would concede, Curran's stature is of a different kind from that either of Küng or of Schillebeeckx. Curran is the author of sixteen books; he is enormously popular on campus; he is credited with being very effective in the classroom, where he teaches moral theology, primarily on the masters and doctoral levels; his courses are filled almost as soon as they are announced. Yet Curran's name is not linked in a triumvirate with those of Küng and Schillebeeckx. Curran's books, for instance, have not had the great international impact that Küng's and Schillebeeckx's have had—though, again, perhaps only because the dogmatic implications of the subject matter are less momentous. Why, then, was Curran singled out?

One early possibility seemed to be that Curran was being made something of an example for other teachers on American Catholic campuses. The Vatican's Sacred Congregation for Catholic Education was readying its document on the identity and role of the Catholic university, and it could perhaps have made sense to Rome to have a few things understood about orthodoxy, authority, and the precedence of the teaching authority of the magisterium over any other thought of a moral, ethical, or theological kind on campus. In such a scenario, the "straightening out" of a situation involving a well-known theologian with relatively liberal views at a conservative Catholic educational institution would send out a much clearer signal than the censuring, disciplining, or firing, say, of a so-called radical theologian on a Catholic campus of more liberal reputation. In a word, it could have made more sense to go after a Father Charles Curran at Catholic University than a Dr. Daniel Maguire at Marquette University. Maguire, a former priest, is a board member of Catholics for a Free Choice and a man of such controversial views that he is not welcome as a lecturer on many Catholic campuses in the country. Besides, it was easier to go after Curran because Catholic University is a pontifical university, whereas Marquette has a certain Catholic autonomy as a Jesuit university.

Certainly, there appeared to be more logic to that theory than that Rome was evening the score for the embarrassment that Curran had caused church authorities back in 1967, when, under public pressure, they had been forced to reverse Curran's firing from Catholic University. On 17 April 1967 Curran learned that, rather than being promoted to associate professor, he had been fired by the university's trustees—without public explanation, but obviously because of his progresive views on artificial birth control. The birth control issue, still under official ecclesiastical reexamination at the time, presumably could have been considered something of an open question. But not by the trustees. They acted against Curran, and the action touched off a totally unprecedented five-day strike by Catholic University students and faculty. The strike closed the university and was effective in full. Curran was reinstated and given his promotion.

At a press conference following the Ratzinger ultimatum to retract his views on sexual morality or be disciplined, Curran conceded the probability that revenge for 1967 had motivated the new moves against him.[8] But almost twenty years had passed since the 1967 incident, and the connection seemed tenuous. For one thing, most of those involved in a major way in the 1967 events had moved on, many having died or been retired. Indeed two papacies had come and gone. Admittedly, Rome's memory is long, and vindictiveness is not exactly an unknown element in its history. Still, it was difficult to believe that so personal a vengeance could be harbored so long after an incident, then resurrected. It became less hard to believe as the Curran case unfolded. Rome, as the saying goes, can remind elephants. Its dossiers go back a long way, and twenty years isn't so long a time to have to remember in an institution that has been around for nearly two millennia and thinks in terms of eternity.

So, in 1986, the Vatican declared Curran no longer "suitable nor eligible to exercise the function of a professor of Catholic theology." Curran contested, as we know, first through academic channels. When success seemed precluded, or at least prejudiced, there, he turned to the civil courts and, on 27 February 1987, filed a civil suit at the Superior Court of the District of Columbia to overturn his suspension. The case is still pending.

Catholic University "unilaterally" had removed Curran's name during the fall of 1986 from class schedules for the next semester. Curran, on sabbatical leave at the time, protested the action as a violation of the university's own procedures. The university defended the action as one taken in order not to "mislead students."[9]

Curran threatened to teach anyway when the next semester opened, but he abandoned those plans after he said Archbishop Hickey threatened to invoke an article of canon law (Canon 812), which exerts church authority over anyone teaching theology in a Catholic college or university anywhere.[10] Curran feared that his action would put theological colleagues at unnecessary risk, because it would increase the likelihood that the canon would be invoked again and more extensively. He also noted that invocation of the rule posed a danger to the "academic freedom and autonomy" of Catholic colleges and universities, and that its use "would have serious consequences for academic accreditation, government funding, and a host of other issues important to Catholic higher education in the country."[11] Thus, Curran thought it better to blink than to force the issue. Robert McAfee Brown, the Protestant theologian, protested the threat against Curran in the *Christian Century*, as "outright blackmail."[12] "It is a way of telling Curran," Brown added, "that the heaviest guns of the ecclesiastical artillery will no longer be pointed simply at him, but at all of his theological colleagues everywhere." Though Curran withdrew his plans to teach in defiance of higher authority, he did not withdraw his plans to fight for his eventual return to the Catholic University classroom, where he taught for twenty-two years. Nor is his determination to fight for reinstatement affected by his acceptance of a one-year visiting professorship at Cornell University, beginning with the 1987 fall semester.

Obviously, Curran's campaign to resolve his rights as a tenured professor was not off to a promising start at Catholic University. Whether his prospects will improve as he pursues his case through the university's academic channels remains to be seen. So far as academic channels are concerned the cards appear to be heavily stacked against him there. Which then leaves the civil courts. Curran could win or lose a civil suit. His grievance is real. However, the courts could walk wide of the issue, electing to hand the matter back to the church through a reverse application of the separation-of-church-and-state clause of the Constitution. If it happens, it wouldn't be the first time the courts did such a thing. The courts generally have been sensitive to the consideration that if church should not intrude on state, neither should state intrude into the affairs of church.

But whatever happens, whether the Curran case is resolved through the appeals procedures of academe or in the civil courts, the outcome will affect many more people than this one priest brought to account by church authority and deciding to defend himself. It will affect much more than the university of Curran's association. If the case goes to the civil courts and is decided there in Curran's favor, American jurisprudence may force on Rome a painful review of its relationship to Catholic education in the United States on the college and university level. For Rome's challenge to Curran ultimately tests the cherished American values of academic freedom and due process, both of which are written into most university statutes, including those of Catholic institutions, and supported by legal protections. Much is at stake, finally, for faculty members at every Catholic college and university in the land. A showdown has been avoided for now on the literal implications of Canon 812, but most professors on Catholic campuses must be aware that Curran's lot could conceivably be any one of theirs, as Rome presses the issue of conformity. Indeed, Curran's lot, in one way or another, is already that of a growing list of people. Theirs may not be household names, as Curran's has become, but they have made news. Some of them are:

1. Father Terrance A. Sweeney, mentioned earlier. He was forced to resign from the Jesuit order because church officials objected to his survey of bishops and cardinals on the questions of priestly celibacy and women clergy. Presumably, all was fine until word of the survey reached high levels. When the pronuncio in Washington, Archbishop Pio Laghi, inquired about Sweeney's project, cautions went into effect, and Sweeney was ordered to suppress his work. He refused and took his leave of the order rather than submit to what he called ''authority destructive of the very foundations of the church, and religious and academic freedom.''[13] Sweeney was subsequently offered the priestly faculties of the archdiocese of Los Angeles, but he turned them down because of restrictions that went with the offer. Specifically, he said, he would have to discontinue his research into attitudes of U.S. bishops on such controversial issues as priestly celibacy and women priests, and to refrain from talking to reporters about his work.[14]

2. Father John J. McNeill. He had expulsion proceedings from the Jesuits initiated against him after he disregarded a Vatican directive forbidding him to comment publicly on issues of homosexuality or to minister to

homosexuals. McNeill spoke out against the Vatican's homosexual guidelines issued in 1986, saying on 2 November 1986 that, in conscience, he could not remain silent. The directive restricting McNeill's activities as a priest had come from the head of the Jesuits, Father Peter-Hans Kolvenbach, on orders from Cardinal Ratzinger of the Congregation for the Doctrine of the Faith, and it reinforced an earlier ban that had followed the publication of McNeill's book *The Church and the Homosexual*.[15] Paradoxically, the book had originally been published with ecclesiastical approbation. McNeill described the document containing the Vatican's new homosexual guidelines as "almost diabolical," adding, "We desperately need the church's moral authority. But by putting all its energies into this lost cause, it is being prevented from having the impact on the community that it should have and that we desperately need."[16] McNeill's dismissal from the Jesuits became official on 2 January 1987 when a decree was signed branding McNeill "pertinaciously disobedient" and charging him with spreading teachings "condemned by the magisterium of the Catholic Church." McNeill said he would appeal the decree and make a "public appeal to all those who have been influenced by my ministry to let you know if that influence was helpful or injurious to their relationship to the Roman Catholic Church." McNeill claimed that "hundreds, even thousands" of gay men and lesbian women had returned to the church as a result of his writings.[17]

3. Father Michael Buckley. Another Jesuit, Buckley found his appointment as executive director of two committees of the National Conference of Catholic Bishops

coming under fire in 1986 for a statement that he and twenty-two other theologians had signed nine years earlier, in 1977, dissenting from a Vatican declaration issued that year rejecting the ordination of women to the priesthood. The 1977 statement objected to "the faulty nature of its [the declaration's] argumentation and conclusions."[18] A three-member panel of bishops, headed by Archbishop Daniel Pilarczyk of Cincinnati, was named to investigate the suitability of Buckley's appointment, after reports circulated in the conservative religious press questioning Buckley's orthodoxy. The panel concluded that there was no evidence that Buckley had ever publicly dissented from the teaching of church authority "or was in any way disloyal to the church, the Holy Father or the Holy See."[19] His appointment stood, but Buckley's future was touch-and-go to the very end.

4. Father James Provost. A canon lawyer on the faculty of the Catholic University of America, Provost came under fire after the Vatican raised questions about his writings. Under question were the conditions under which divorced and remarried Catholics may receive the sacraments of the church, and those under which Catholics generally may probe the limits of theological dissent and press the right of laypersons to hold church office. Also at issue for Rome were reports that Provost had held that the church "discriminates" against women, as well as Provost's alleged emphasis of community over hierarchy in his understanding of the church. At stake for Provost was his application for tenure on the Catholic University faculty. A majority of the university's eighteen trustee-bishops eventually granted Provost his tenure. However, the announcement by

Archbishop James Hickey of Washington, the university's chancellor, included the declaration that Provost had agreed to publish "clarifying articles," which could allay the concerns of church authorities.[20] He was the same archbishop, incidentally, who declared in announcing the sanctions against Father Charles Curran on 19 August 1986 that "there is no right to public dissent" in the church.[21]

The litany of disciplinary actions could go on, but the common denominators would not change. The church might be preoccupied with Father Hans Küng's ideas on infallibility and whether, as Küng maintains, it belongs only to God or whether, as the church maintains, it belongs also to the pope. The church might be deeply concerned about Father Edward Schillebeeckx's interpretation of the "real presence" of Christ in the Eucharist. But as far as the American church is concerned, what matters most for Rome are the issues of sexual morality and public dissent from the church's teaching authority. When the two elements are combined in the one case, the impulse of Rome is to act decisively.

Preoccupation with sexual morality is so longstanding in the Catholic church that almost nothing invoked or initiated in this regard by the church particularly surprises rank-and-file Catholics anymore. It might annoy and anger, but it doesn't shock. *Humanae vitae* appears to have immunized Catholics to the fact that when sexual ethics are involved, the most reactionary response is possible from the church's leadership.

Dissent? That is another matter. It is such a new thing within the church that no one is comfortable with it, including, no doubt, many dissenters themselves. In-

deed, dissent is such a new thing within the Catholic religious family that no graceful method has yet been
established for living or coping with it, much less chan-
neling it toward constructive ends. In 1968, the American bishops adopted norms for dealing with dissent, but
these were abruptly dismissed as "simply not workable"
by Archbishop Hickey at the time he made public the
Vatican's decision that it no longer considered Curran
"suitable nor eligible to exercise the function of a professor of Catholic theology." In place of the bishops' 1968
norms, Hickey, in effect, passed on the mandate of
Ratzinger and the Vatican's Congregation for the Doctrine of the Faith that "the authentic teachings of the
church, enunciated by the Holy Father and the bishops
in communion with him, although not solemnly defined,
require a religious submission of intellect and will." The
infallible teachings of the church do not stand alone,
Hickey argued in defense of Rome: "They are intimately
related to all official church teachings and together, form
an organic unity of faith."[22] More explicitly, as Cardinal
Ratzinger said in a letter to Curran, "The church does
not build its life upon the infallible magisterium alone
but on the teaching of its authentic, ordinary magisterium as well."[23] Curran is not alone in labeling
this concept "creeping infallibilism" or "creeping infallibility." Many see the Ratzinger–Hickey move as an attempt to blur the classical theological distinctions
between infallible church teachings and those teachings
that are authoritative but not infallible and, therefore,
open to questioning and development.

Curran's position—again, surprisingly cautious—is
that, under certain conditions, there is room for theolog-

ical dissent within the church on matters "of ordinary, non-infallible teaching." There is nothing revolutionary in the least in such a position. It is one of the reasons that the church's understanding has been able to develop on a host of issues once considered theologically acceptable—issues such as the use of torture against persons suspected of heresy and, as a correspondent in the *Tablet* of London not long ago recalled, "the simonical selling of ecclesiastical benefices," a practice so long enshrined in the Code of Canon Law as to become, in the opinion of a papal commission in the time of Paul III (1534–1549), the origin of all the Reformation evils.[24]

That the problem of dissent is on the church's mind in a major way is without question. At a meeting of theologians in Rome in April 1986, Pope John Paul II issued what the press described as a "particularly severe rebuke" to theologians who dissented from the church's traditional view of sexuality, saying that unorthodox teachings were "spreading confusion in the conscience of the faithful."[25] It was not the first time the pope had made the point, and his concern was quickly felt in the United States. A few months later, Archbishop Daniel Pilarczyk of Cincinnati issued a pastoral letter in which he said that theologians may dissent from some church teachings, but that "they do so at their own risk."[26] Pilarczyk added that church authority ultimately "has the right and the responsibility to make a prudential judgment, case by case, about the limits of such tolerance." Again, in a few months, Cardinal Joseph Bernardin of Chicago followed with a pastoral letter warning against the dissemination of dissenting views on moral issues. Addressed to parish staffs, Catholic schoolteachers, and catechists, the pastoral advocated traditional methods of presenting moral issues and stressed, "It is essential that we, who teach in the name of Christ, present clearly and without ambiguity what the magisterium teaches. We are not to teach dissent."[27]

But it was not just individuals who were the focus of attention. The church's overview of Catholic publishing houses and their books continued. In 1984, the Paulist Press was forced to halt circulation of its popular adult education text *Christ among Us*, under pressure from the Vatican, the Congregation for the Doctrine of the Faith having judged the book "not suitable as a catechetical test." In 1986, the publishing house found another of its titles in trouble with the same source. This time, the Congregation for the Doctrine of the Faith "expressed reservations" to Bishop Matthew H. Clark of Rochester, New York, about a local sex-educational manual, *Parents Talk Love: The Catholic Family Handbook about Sexuality*, a book to which he had extended an imprimatur, or permission for the book to be printed. The congregation said the book did not deserve the *imprimatur*—the word is Latin for "Let it be printed"—because it was seriously "defective on the church's moral teaching on human sexuality both in and out of marriage." The congregation's objection cited chapter and verse, including what it termed "dissent" from the church's teaching on contraception and failure to stress the important of sacramental marriage as a condition for the legitimate sexual expression of love. Of course, the imprimatur was speedily rescinded. The authors—Father Matthew A. Kawiak, a Rochester diocesan priest, and

Susan K. Sullivan, a science teacher in a Catholic high school—were magnanimous in their disappointment. They told the Rochester diocesan newspaper, the *Courier-Journal*, that they had written the book not to argue with church teaching but to help parents "find the courage" to talk to their children about sex. They assured Bishop Clark that they realized he was without options. They didn't see this as a "personal affront," they explained. "This is just the atmosphere of our times."[28]

It is, to be sure, and that is what so many persons find disconcerting—and dangerous. As Milwaukee's Archbishop Rembert Weakland noted in the remarkable pair of commentaries in his archdiocesan newspaper questioning the Vatican's attempts to impose a stricter orthodoxy on the American church,[29] the fervor for orthodoxy, which has periodically come and gone in Catholicism, has often coincided with fertile growth periods for the church: "People were excited about and cared about religion." But, remarked Weakland, even though some of those times of travail may have led to growth, they also produced division. "In honesty one has to admit...that in these struggles many human beings were treated inhumanely and with excessive cruelty," wrote Weakland. "The Inquisition and the periodic witch hunts for heretics were not the most glamorous part of the history of the Catholic Church. On the contrary, too many innocent people suffered. It does no good to poor Galileo to vindicate and exonerate him today. The list, alas, is endless."[30] He reminded his readers that, as recently as the 1940s and 1950s, theologians like Yves Congar, Henri de Lubac, Teilhard de

Chardin, and John Courtney Murray had been silenced by the church, but that most of these men ''were rehabilitated and vindicated by Vatican Council II.'' The obvious point is that today's pariah could turn out to be tomorrow's prophet. In any instance, in the pursuit of purity of doctrine, Weakland said, there is a need ''to avoid the fanaticism and small-mindedness that has characterized so many periods of the church in its history—tendencies that lead to much cruelty, suppression of theological creativity and lack of growth.''

Is there a better way of proceeding? Has history taught the church anything? Those were Weakland's questions, and he responded to them by recalling Pope John XXIII's famous opening speech at Vatican II: ''Often errors vanish as quickly as they arise, like fog before the sun. The church has always opposed these errors. Frequently she has condemned them with the greatest severity. Nowadays, however, the spouse of Christ prefers to make use of the medicine of mercy rather than that of severity. She considers that she meets the needs of the present day by demonstrating the validity of her teaching rather than by condemnations.''

Was good Pope John being naive? ''Many, I fear, think so,'' concluded Weakland.

Was Weakland himself being naive if he expected his cautions to be embraced in Rome and, by extension, to be taken to heart by his fellow bishops in the United States? Maybe so. The early signs were not encouraging. The *New York Times* quoted an unnamed but ''influential'' Vatican source as being surprised by the Weakland commentaries. ''I would have expected him to voice sup-

port for the Vatican if he was going to say anything,''
said the official.[31]

In the United States, meanwhile, no archdiocese or
diocese seemed in a rush to reverse controversial policies of its own in response to Weakland's cautions. In
the archdiocese of New York, for example, officials were
standing firm on a decision to exclude as speakers at
parish-sponsored events individuals ''whose public position is contrary to and in opposition to the clear, un-
ambiguous teaching of the church.'' The policy drew the
ire of a number of Catholic politicians, at whom it was
obviously aimed, including Governor Cuomo himself.
The policy was also criticized as impolitic in *America*
magazine, the influential Jesuit journal, by a former
chancellor of the archdiocese. ''For churchmen to cross
the line between, on the one hand, instructing and in-
forming conscience and, on the other hand, trying to
force a legislative position on an officeholder by a
speaker's ban is a very dangerous political game,'' said
Monsignor Harry J. Byrne, now pastor of Manhattan's
Epiphany Church on East Twenty-first Street. ''It can result in the nonelectibility of Catholics.''[32]

Should that ever come to pass, it would be a tragedy
of enormous proportions—for the country and for
Catholics themselves. It is nice for American Catholics
to be able to believe that, as a people, they came fully
of age politically with the election of John F. Kennedy,
a Catholic, to the presidency. It would be a pity if they
discovered themselves rendered politically immature,
and again politically suspect, because of self-serving impulses that weren't supposed to exist anymore—like

church pressure on Catholic politicians to enact Catholic positions into civil law, followed by speaking bans on those who do not respond as the church would have them.

Admittedly, the New York speakers' directive belongs to only one of the church's territorial jurisdictions. Nonetheless, it is symptomatic in a larger sense of the insecurity prevailing today in much of Roman Catholicism. Evidence of insecurity certainly abounds in the American church. It displays itself in actions such as those taken against Seattle's Archbishop Hunthausen; against Fathers Curran, Sweeney, and McNeill, among other priests; against writers and publishers; against Geraldine Ferraro, Mary Ann Sorrentino, and Conception Eason's preteenage daughter Sarabeth; against the nuns of the 7 October 1984 abortion ad—in a word, against any who stray from the narrowing path of orthodoxy.

The irony is, of course, that the disciplinings and suppressions are likely only to exacerbate the church's problems. For in excluding even the possibility of responsible theological dissent and by persisting in the tendency to make public examples of those who depart from orthodoxies, the church not only squanders such authority as it has remaining to it but also invites more of the very fragmentation that its actions are intended to arrest. Moreover, the mavericks attract new people and many of the disenfranchised. The alternative, be it said, is not for church leaders to throw up their hands and let the church become a community where any kind of theological public or private position is forever possible. Rather, as *Commonweal* magazine perceptively remarked, it is "to find a way of maintaining the church's identity and proclaiming a truth not in the tow of cultural fashion, while simultaneously recognizing that fidelity to this truth itself requires constant and courageous self-questioning."[33] That's more easily said than done, particularly in an institution where self-questioning has never been fostered—nor welcomed when forced upon it.

On the other hand, maybe there is hope for a church situated in a country like the United States, where political and cultural self-questioning has been developed both to an art and a strength. Should self-questioning ever be adopted as a proper mode for the church, it would not be the first time that the church was able to draw a profitable lesson from a secular source. But for that to happen with the American church, the American church's leadership must be willing to assert an ecclesiastical maturity of its own by having the courage to stand up to a leadership in Rome that would keep it forever docile and responsive to Roman will. A few of the American church's leaders are obviously willing to be assertive; a few, as Archbishop Weakland demonstrated in his columns on the price of orthodoxy, are not afraid to speak out and act in independent ways. If these individuals appear at times to be overly oblique and cautious in their ways, it could be that they perceive this as the only method of being able to make their point and expecting to survive. In the controlled environment of

Roman Catholicism, even cautious steps can be very bold ones. The question is whether there will be enough courageous church leaders around to make a difference after the hierarchy is remade to conform to the concepts of orthodoxy currently championed by Rome.

Perhaps the May 1987 compromise in the Hunthausen case is reason for optimism. Under the settlement worked out between Rome, Hunthausen, and a three-bishop commission named four months earlier by Rome to assess the situation in Seattle, Hunthausen's authority was largely restored to him, though he must now work with a coadjutor archbishop, or assistant with right of succession, Thomas J. Murphy, formerly of the diocese of Great Falls–Billings, Montana.[34] Removed from office for reassignment elsewhere was Auxiliary Bishop Wuerl, the man whose appointment to Seattle had produced the unworkable situation, embarrassing to Rome and maddening to many Catholics.

One is inclined to pass out high marks—to the bishops' commission for daring to confirm Rome in its misjudgments; to Rome for its sensitivity to public opinion and for utilizing the principle of episcopal collegiality in resolving matters. Rome did listen, after all, to the commission it named to look into the case. But at least one narrow Roman interest may also have come into play to help rescue the situation for Hunthausen. As the *New York Times* observed, the resolution of the Hunthausen affair "defused" one problem that had "threatened to provoke confrontations" when Pope John Paul II came visiting in the United States a few months hence.[35]

8

AND NOW WHERE?

A Look to
the Future

SOON AFTER THE Vatican's disciplining of Father Curran
and its stripping of areas of authority from Seattle's
Archbishop Hunthausen, Archbishop Weakland of Milwaukee warned in a lecture at Union Theological Seminary in Manhattan that disciplinary actions by the
Vatican against prominent Catholic figures in the American church were alienating ordinary Catholics from the
institutional church and causing many of them to drift
away.[1] A month later, the outgoing president of the National Conference of Catholic Bishops, Bishop James W.
Malone of Youngstown, Ohio, picked up the theme at

the opening session of the U.S. bishops' 1986 fall meeting. There was "a growing and dangerous disaffection" between some American Catholics and the Vatican, Malone declared, announcing at the same time that he was seeking an audience with Pope John Paul II to discuss the tensions in hopes of clearing some air before the pope visited the United States the following fall.[2] A month later came yet another warning that the American church was being seeded with disaffection. Catholic University's Monsignor John Tracy Ellis, the American church's preeminent historian, spoke at Seton Hall University in Newark, New Jersey, of a rift between "conservatives and liberals," and he declared that this rift posed a real threat to the church.[3] Storm warnings seemed to be going up all around.

The alarm of these and other prelates was easy enough to understand, for it did seem in the fall of 1986 that the Hunthausen and Curran cases were about to trigger an angry, emotional explosion in the American church, one that could possibly involve thousands of rank-and-file Catholics in direct and defiant protest. A steady stream of disciplinary cases involving figures of lesser prominence than Hunthausen and Curran was fueling the situation. Anything seemed possible. The protest did not happen, however, even though the Hunthausen and Curran cases were not isolated.

The relief of church officials could be sensed—it was almost tangible—that there was no popular protest among Catholics across the country. American Catholics, by and large, stayed amazingly calm.

This calm gave rise to a phenomenon of another kind. Suddenly, different voices were being heard in the land, voices saying that the contentions of the American church had been magnified and that the image of a fractured church was largely the creation of the media.[4] Archbishop Roger M. Mahony of Los Angeles, for one, was quoted by the *New York Times* as saying that Catholics of his jurisdiction were not particularly upset by the Vatican's rebuke of Hunthausen or the church's stripping of Curran's Catholic University professorship. "You hardly ever hear these kinds of concerns," Mahony said. "I really feel people who have voiced concern may represent a fraction of our church and in our diocese a very, very small fraction of our people."[5]

Even John Paul II seemed anxious to downplay the significance of events in the American church, saying in response to questions about the American situation from reporters covering his visit to Asia in November 1986 that sometimes "divisions which don't exist are created."[6]

The fact, however, is that divisions of a serious kind do exist in the American church.

The further fact is that no one should take consolation that the Vatican's 1986 disciplinings of several well-known and respected members of the American church did not produce the open rupture some prelates seemed to be anticipating. There is a calm, but that calm may only demonstrate the distance that has grown between the church's leaders and the church's people, as well as the detachment that many Catholics feel from what transpires in the institution itself. Catholics are aware of what is going on, to be sure; they read the papers. They are not oblivious to what the Roman and American church leadership does. By the same token, they are anxious that justice be served in the church, and that individuals of honor be treated honorably. However, many Catholics are so disaffected, so vexed by the church's leaders and by what many of them regard as their petty, intramural games, that they cannot be bothered to be involved. The issues and resolves that are important to the hierarchs are not shared in the same way by the rank-and-file. Often, those matters of concern appear to belong to another time frame. They seem to have minimal importance or relevance to life as it is lived in the 1980s.

In reporting Archbishop Weakland's Union Theological address, the *Times* representative took the liberty of interpreting the message behind the words. The archbishop "seemed to be saying," in the opinion of the reporter, that the Vatican's actions had already had an impact on lay Catholics, disenchanting many and prompting many of them to pursue their faith privately in their own fashion.[7] That's probably true enough, except that the condition is of considerably longer standing than was intimated. Rank-and-file Catholics began turning off years ago and pursuing their faith privately long before the disciplinings of 1986, when many of them came to realize that, no matter what they did or how they involved themselves in what was happening in the church, they weren't going to make much of a difference. The church wasn't going to change. It would still be run in the same way and by the same types. So the drift began. By now, so many have completed the turning-off process that prelates like Mahony of Los Angeles can apparently mistake the sound of their silence, the calm sea, for approval of how events are transpiring and how the leadership is steering Peter's bark. It could be a serious delusion.

It is not so long ago that the situation was quite different, and that the church's disciplining of an individual of noble intention and praiseworthy undertakings could stir the indignation of Catholics not ordinarily given to demonstrating against ecclesiastical authority. It happened, for instance, in November 1965, when Cardinal Spellman and the local Jesuit superiors thought it best to cool the ardor of Father Daniel Berrigan, S.J. Vietnam was heating up and so was antiwar sentiment. A pacifist of such high visibility and impassioned feelings as Berrigan did not seem the best person to have around, ruffling the feathers of a hawkish church, so Berrigan was summarily shipped off on an indefinite writing assignment to Latin America for *Jesuit Missions*, a nonideological magazine of innocent contents. It was an action that enraged Catholics near and far. In Manchester, New Hampshire, a Catholic went on a hunger strike in St. Joseph's Cathedral to protest the exiling. Students at Notre Dame University began a fast, and in New York, pickets—most of them Catholic—marched outside Cardinal Spellman's residence on Madison Avenue, immediately behind St. Patrick's Cathedral, carrying placards reading, "End Power Politics in the Church" and "Merry Christmas, Dan Berrigan, Wherever You Are."[8]

Those were thought to be the worst of days. Catholics weren't supposed to take to the streets like this; they weren't supposed to confront their church leaders boldly and defiantly. They deferred. For the

American church, those days were awkward, embarrassing, and no doubt annoying—and the demonstration on behalf of Berrigan was only one of many such public assertions of grievance. But one thing would seem to be certain. They were better than these days of silence.

The silence is not absolute, be it said. The official diocesan Catholic press is characteristically cautious in its comments, but those elements of the Catholic press able to express themselves freely—newspapers like the *National Catholic Reporter* and magazines like *Commonweal* and *America*—are speaking out energetically and boldly in defense of those whom Rome is disciplining and, at the same time, are raising questions about the wisdom of the essentially conservative redirection of the American church occurring under John Paul II.

On the other hand, however, the students at Catholic University have not marched out of their classrooms to protest the suspension of Father Curran, as their counterparts did in 1967, when they literally shut the university down for several days after Curran was denied promotion and was served notice that his services were being terminated with the completion of his current contract. (Incidentally, Curran has been a tenured full professor at the university since 1971.) Admittedly students of the 1980s are generally less demonstrative as a group than were students of the 1960s. Nonetheless, the contrast is striking, and one has to wonder how much the seeming student detachment on a Catholic campus like Catholic University, when an issue like the Curran one is involved, reflects a detachment, too, from the wherefores of institutional religion itself.

Similarly, in Seattle, Catholics of the archdiocese did not take to the streets in the 1980s in support of Archbishop Hunthausen, as Catholics of New York did in the 1960s in support of Father Daniel Berrigan. Abigail McCarthy, in her *Commonweal* column, wrote impressively of the "encouraging numbers" she encountered on a visit there who were "willing to sign letters questioning the Vatican's actions and to attend protest meetings and supportive liturgies."[9] She was in Seattle just before the 1986 November meeting of the National Conference of Catholic Bishops, and to be in Seattle then, she said, "was to have a sense of having returned to the liveliness of the early days of Christianity when bishops were chosen by acclamation and battles over theology and church governance were waged in the public forum."[10] Seattle's overwhelmingly sensitive response and refined demeanor in the face of what had every appearance of being a historic injustice done a good man and an admirable church leader were probably best for the circumstances. If nothing else, the local response accented, as it complemented, the character of Archbishop Hunthausen himself, who is patient and civilized, pastoral rather than emotional. The response, in a single phrase, was so genuinely Christian as to become a rebuke to the rebukers.

One admires the response of Seattle's Catholics in the time of crisis for the church there. It had a gospel quality about it—precepts of the Sermon on the Mount brought virtually to life. It was restrained and persuasive, and helped produce the rehabilitation of a man who still has nine years before he reaches the mandatory retirement age of seventy-five for bishops. Hunthausen underwent cancer surgery in 1986, but his overall health appears to be good. Barring the unforeseen, physical or ecclesial, he should last the course.

Yet as one complements Seattle Catholics, one wonders about Catholics elsewhere. There was much hand-wringing over Hunthausen's treatment, but there were no demonstrations such as those generated by the Berrigan exiling. Closest things to them were convention resolutions and a signed newspaper ad asking the return of Hunthausen's authority.

Nor have such disciplinary actions as the expulsions of Fathers McNeill and Sweeney from the Jesuit order sparked the public protests that they assuredly would have a few years ago.

These are different days, to be sure. The issues are different and, for many people, not as clear-cut as during the periods of the civil-rights and antiwar movements of the 1960s and 1970s. The issues are more narrowly ecclesiastical. They do not involve large issues of patriotism and national public policy, as the Berrigan case did, for instance. Because the issues are more intramural, they do not touch as many people. There's no supporting cast beyond the Catholic community itself. Furthermore, many Catholics are not comfortable with some of the issues themselves. They are strongly sexual in their content and, accordingly, appeal more to the private than to the demonstrative side of many Catholics.

An example would be issues such as abortion and homosexuality and the questions that arise from them. Does the church really suffer from a case of homophobia, and if so, as has been asked by the novelist James Carroll, does this homophobia indeed contribute to the culture of impermanent, and now deadly, transient relationships among gay men by not extending to them the same rights that everyone has to blessed, supported, openly monogamous love—marriages, that is—and safe sex?[11] Is it self-righteous for the church to condone abortion without also openly advocating birth control, which would lessen the probability of at least some abortions?—asked Carroll again.[12] These are weighty questions, and there are hosts more in these same and other areas of human sexuality. They are anything but academic, topics that just about anyone can comfortably theorize about in some detached, purely intellectual way. They are deeply personal questions, for they involve one's own sexuality. Their answers demand a sophisticated and nuanced knowledge of human biology, the behavioral sciences, and moral theology. It is easy to see how they could intimidate. Also, they are issues that some people don't find it easy to talk about in mixed society and the public forum. Despite the so-called sexual revolution, people do still have sexual inhibitions. So it is, in any case, that issues of moment in the church can render some people inarticulate and undemonstrative at the same time that these issues quietly divide the Catholic community.

But beyond genital sex, there are for the church other urgent issues of sexuality—women's role in the church, for instance, including questions such as those of women priests, a married male priesthood, and the return to the active ministry of priests who have married. The church cannot hide from these matters. It is going to have to come to grips in a meaningful way with these and other questions very soon.

It is likewise going to have to come to grips with the matter of the new generations of Catholics. A large percentage of these younger Catholics are disengaged, uninterested, and detached from much that keeps the senior generations religiously loyal and dutiful. Theirs is not a formula faith. Theirs is not the orthodoxy of their parents and grandparents. They are independent rather than obedient Catholics. They are also the future, people whom the church must recognize and provide for. If it doesn't, then there most certainly will be no escaping the split of American Catholicism into that of the institution and that of the culture. As I argued earlier, the process is already at work. With no response from the church hierarchy to these boiling issues, the prognosis for the institutional church's surviving in a healthy way is not promising.

The tragedy in the present situation is that the church is purging the very persons who could help ensure its institutional survival. It is purging the people who inspire the disenfranchised, the people who hold out such hope as can be held out that the American church will one day again be the live, vibrant, exciting, relevant, and holy place it was so short a time ago as the Vatican II years, 1962–1965. Specifically, it is the Hunthausens, Currans, and others of the put-upon who bring back auras of those yesterdays. If anyone is going to close the gap between the institutional church and the disenfranchised, the detached, the indifferent, and the alienated, it is people such as these. Effectively purge or neutralize them, and the American church can kiss much of its future good-bye.

But then, maybe that future wasn't bright to begin with. The problems of disappearing vocations to the religious life, of private and public dissent from doctrinal orthodoxy, of increasingly casual religious observance on the part of American Catholics—these all predated Rome's confronting figures in the American church.

That's the supreme irony in the current crisis. While the church was losing ground, it unwittingly greased the skids.

Hunthausen, Curran, and other men and women like them, could turn out to be only bit players in the ecclesiastical drama of the times, footnotes to the chapter detailing Rome's confrontation with modern American Catholicism. It would be nice if the script revealed them to be movers and shakers, individuals who made a positive difference at a memorable turning point of church history. That seems to be wishing for a lot, however. Still, this much is certain: If they and people like them continue to be harassed in the church that is theirs as much as the leadership's, this church is in extremely deep trouble. The older generations are going to die off. The church has to hold the generations coming along. It has to win back those stepping aside or to the sidelines. If it does not get them back in the pews, so to speak, it is going to end up a shell of an organization. How many, however, are going to step back into what now could be perceived to be something of an ecclesiastical gulag?

The tragedy of the church's times is reflected in the image of the female figure in the Rockwell Kent lithograph, "And Now Where?" described in this book's preface. Her head is turned, her eyes focus backward. This is so much the turn of the church's head, too. The church should be looking ahead, planning for a twenty-first century in which, in the United States, there won't be nearly enough priests to staff parishes' churches; nor nearly enough nuns to help continue the apostolates of justice and social morality; nor nearly enough laity, men and women, to plug the gaps of ministry and religious education; nor nearly enough Catholics, in a word, to do God's work.

But mainly, the church is looking back, preoccupied with codes and disciplines that belong to another age. Chances are, for example, that despite legitimate concerns the church is looking backward in declaring its unequivocal moral opposition to so many of the new and already routine biomedical procedures and technologies relating to human reproduction, as it did in its doctrinal statement of March 1987 on procreation and the origin of life. The fear is that, when the church finally turns around, much of the flock will by then have wandered away.

It would be an utter pity if this were to happen, but it could. In addressing the Catholic University community several months after his censure by Rome, Father Curran predicted that tensions between the American church and Rome would intensify, and that they would continue until "proper education and appropriate structures" can "overcome the strident, destructive and negative" relationship that currently exists between the two.[13]

This may be placing too much hope in the enlightenment of the leadership in both places and, for some, too much stress on the importance of the institution and church structures—especially in a period of history when the old structures, certainly the organizational ones, have come to mean so little. It may also be hoping for too much when so much of faith has been internalized and appropriated to the individual conscience. But it is a start.

ENDNOTES

PREFACE

1. "The Pope Gets Tough," *U.S. News & World Report*, 17 Nov. 1986, 64ff.
2. Rembert G. Weakland, O.S.B., "The Price of Orthodoxy," *Catholic Herald*, Milwaukee, 18 Sept. 1986, 3.
3. Ibid.
4. "Instruction on Respect for Human Life in Its Origins and on the Dignity of Procreation: Replies to Certain Questions of the Day," a doctrinal statement issued 10 Mar. 1987 by the Vatican's Congregation for the Doctrine of the Faith, with the approval of Pope John Paul II.

CHAPTER 1

1. William Shakespeare, *Henry the Fourth*, Part I, Act I, Scene 3, line 224: "I'll have a starling shall be taught to speak."
2. John Cooney, *The American Pope: The Life and Times of Francis Cardinal Spellman* (New York: Doubleday, 1984), 256.
3. Robert Suro, "Vatican Asks Help to Meet Increasing Deficit," *New York Times*, 26 Oct. 1986, 9.
4. *Testem benevolentiae*, 22 Jan. 1899.
5. Walter Elliott, C.S.P., *The Life of Father Hecker* (New York: 1891). The French translation appeared in 1897 under the title *Le Père Hecker Fondateur des "Paulistes" Americains*. The French edition was sensationalized by a preface by Abbé Felix Klein of the Institut Catholique de Paris, which placed Hecker in a pantheon with Franklin, Lincoln, Augustine, and St. Thérèse of Lisieux.
6. Published annually by P. J. Kenedy & Sons, New York.
7. Andrew M. Greeley, *The American Catholic: A Social Portrait* (New York: Basic Books, 1977), 167.
8. Andrew M. Greeley, *The Catholic Priest in the United States: Sociological Investigations* (Washington, DC: United States Catholic Conference, 1972), 287.
9. Richard A. Schoenherr and Annemette Sorensen, "From the Second Vatican to the Second Millennium: Decline and Change in the U.S. Catholic Church," CROS Report #5 (Madison: University of Wisconsin Department of Sociology, 1981); Richard A. Schoenherr and Annemette Sorenson, "Social Change in Religious Organizations: Consequences of Clergy Decline in the U.S. Catholic Church," *Sociological Analysis* 43 (1982): 23–52.
10. *Sacrosanctum concilium*, Vatican Council II's Constitution on the Sacred Liturgy, 10.
11. Anna Quindlen, "Life in the 30's," *New York Times*, 18 June 1986, C-12.
12. John Courtney Murray," *National Catholic Reporter*, 23 Aug. 1967, 10; Donald E. Pelotte, S.S.S., *John Courtney Murray, Theologian in Conflict* (New York: Paulist Press, 1976), 100.
13. Walter M. Abbott, S.J., general editor, *The Documents of Vatican*

II (New York: Guild Press, America Press, Association Press, 1966); quotes from John Courtney Murray's introduction to the Declaration on Religious Freedom, 672–674.

14. Ibid.
15. Ibid.
16. Joseph Berger, "Catholic Dissent on Church Rules Found," *New York Times*, 25 Nov. 1985, A-7.
17. "The Protestant Push," *Newsweek*, 1 Sept. 1986, 63.
18. "French Church Looks for Boost from John Paul," *Catholic Free Press*, Worcester, MA, 3 Oct. 1986, 1.
19. "Attendance at Sunday Mass Still Declining," OSV/Gallup Poll Report, *Our Sunday Visitor*, Huntington, IN, 27 Jan. 1985, 5.
20. Ed Wilkinson, "Here's a Sneak Preview of a New Tablet Mini-Series," *Tablet*, Brooklyn, New York, 13 Sept. 1986, 16.
21. "Attendance at Sunday Mass."
22. Declaration on Religious Freedom, 1:2.
23. "Pope Tells Brazilians: Don't Play Politican," *New York Times*, 14 Mar. 1986.
24. *New York Times*, Week in Review section, 7 Oct. 1984, 7.
25. Archbishop Raymond G. Hunthausen in a 1983 letter to Catholics of the archdiocese of Seattle, cited in *Progress*, official newspaper of the archdiocese, 28 Nov. 1985, 1.
26. Archbishop Pio Laghi, letter to Archbishop Hunthausen, *Progress*, 28 Nov. 1985, 3.
27. Bishop Donald W. Wuerl, at a press conference in Seattle, 31 Jan. 1986, as reported by National Catholic (henceforth NC) News Service.
28. Carlos Andres Pedraza, "Archbishop of Seattle Loses Some Authority," Associated Press (henceforth AP) story, *Boston Globe*, 5 Sept. 1986.
29. "Another Dispute between the Pope and U.S. Catholics," *New York Times*, Week in Review section, 7 Sept. 1986, 6.
30. Madonna Kolbenschlag, "Sister Mansour Is Not Alone," *Commonweal*, 17 June 1983.
31. John Deedy, "U.S. Church under Scrutiny," *Tablet*, London, 12 Nov. 1983, 1104, quoting from *Newsweek* magazine.

32. Ibid.
33. *Gaudium et spes,* the Pastoral Constitution on the Church in the Modern World, 81–82.

CHAPTER 2

1. Gerald P. Fogarty, *The Vatican and the American Hierarchy, From 1870 to 1965* (Wilmington, DE: Michael Glazier, 1985), 115.
2. John Tracy Ellis, ed., *Documents of American History* (Milwaukee: Bruce, 1962), 509.
3. Fogarty, 117.
4. Operative at the time was a 25 July 1916 decree of the Sacred Consistorial College stating that, every two years, bishops should send a list of priests to their metropolitan, or the archbishop of their geographical area, whom they regarded as worthy to be bishops. The metropolitans were then to send the screened results to the apostolic delegate, who, in turn, would forward the list to the Sacred Consistorial Congregation, where it would be recorded for the guidance of the pope in due course. The Sacred Consistorial Congregation has since been reconstituted as the Sacred Congregation for Bishops, and the nomination procedures have been modified. Bishops, for instance, may now counsel more systematically with priests, religious, and laity with respect to nominees.
5. Andrew M. Greeley, *Confessions of a Parish Priest* (New York: Simon & Schuster, 1986), 176.
6. Fogarty, p. 356. In his autobiography, *Mine Eyes Have Seen* (New York: McGraw-Hill, 1959), p. 256, Daniel A. Poling gave the date of the incident as ''fall of 1950.'' Poling's son Clark was one of the chaplains to go down on the *Dorchester,* and the senior Poling directed the campaign for a Chapel of the Four Chaplains. However, Fogarty's appears to be the more accurate date and identification of principals, as he worked from correspondence in the archives of the archdiocese of Boston between then-Auxiliary Bishop Wright of Boston and the Reverend Cletus Benjamin of the archdiocese of Philadelphia's chancery office. For

a Kennedy version of the episode, see Theodore C. Sorensen's *Kennedy* (New York: Harper & Row, 1965), 191–192.

7. Greeley, 183–184.

8. Albert J. Menendez, *John F. Kennedy: Catholic and Humanist* (Buffalo, NY: Prometheus Books, 1978), 53.

9. John Tracy Ellis, *American Catholicism*, 2nd ed., rev. (Chicago: University of Chicago Press, 1969), 220.

10. William Bole, "Upholds Parents' Complaints against Sex Ed Series," *The Wanderer*, 21 Aug. 1986, 1, Religious News Service (henceforth RNS). The story contains a statement released to RNS by Archbishop Daniel W. Kucera.

11. Ibid.

12. E. J. Dionne, Jr., "Vatican Sees Bar to Anglican Pact," *New York Times*, 1 July 1986, A6.

13. James L. Franklin, "Cardinal Names Lay Activist as Editor of Pilot," *Boston Sunday Globe*, 23 Nov. 1986, 44.

14. Ibid.

15. "Cardinal Backs Speaker's Guidelines," *Catholic Free Press*, Worcester, MA, 19 Sept. 1986, 2.

16. Jerry Filteau, "Vatican–U.S. Relations," NC News Service story in *Pittsburgh Catholic*, 10 Oct. 1986, 1.

17. As cited in NC News Service story appearing in Catholic newspapers the weekend of 11–13 July 1986.

18. Ibid.

19. E. J. Dionne, Jr., "Vatican Embracing Third World and Battling Marxist Influences," *New York Times*, 25 Dec. 1986, 1.

20. John Deedy, "Defections from Authority and the Institution Itself," *New York Times*, Week in Review section, 16 Dec. 1973.

21. Ibid., quoting from the Chicago newsletter *Overview*.

22. Andrew Greeley, "Andrew Greeley Responds," commentary in a symposium, "Is There an American Catholic Literature?" *Critic*, Summer 1986, 57.

23. *Our Sunday Visitor*, 27 Jan. 1985, 5.

24. NC News Service quotation in reporting the transfer of F. Scott Fitzgerald's remains from Union Cemetery in Rockville, Maryland, to St. Mary's Cemetery across the road on 8 Nov. 1975. Moved at the same time were the remains of Fitzgerald's

wife, Zelda, who had outlived him by seven years and died in a sanitarium fire. When Fitzgerald died in 1940, decisions relating to his burial resided with the archdiocese of Baltimore. In 1947, Washington was separated from the archdiocese of Baltimore, and in 1965, it was constituted a metropolitan see. St. Mary's Cemetery became part of the Washington archdiocese in the process, and thus, it was the archdiocese of Washington that reviewed and redecided the matter of Fitzgerald's resting place. Father William J. Silk of St. Mary's Church in Rockville conducted the liturgy of recommital. Reflecting softened ecclesiastical attitudes, Washington's archbishop, then Cardinal William Baum, issued a statement citing Fitzgerald's Catholic background and crediting him with finding in the Catholic faith ''an understanding of the human heart caught in the struggle between grace and death,'' while in his own life he experienced ''the mystery of suffering and. . .the power of God's grace.'' Fitzgerald's daughter, Frances Scott Smith, died 18 June 1986 in Montgomery, Alabama, and she was buried next to her parents in St. Mary's Cemetery.

25. Ari L. Goldman, ''Man with AIDS Is Denied a Wedding at St. Patrick's,'' *New York Times*, 9 Jan. 1987, B1.

26. Ibid. Also, Roberto Suro, ''Vatican Reproaches Homosexuals with a Pointed Allusion to AIDS,'' *New York Times*, 31 Oct. 1986; and John Thavis, ''Vatican Warns against Church Support for 'Pro-Homosexual Movement,' '' NC News Service story in *Church World*, Portland, ME, 6 Nov. 1986, 10.

27. ''Sandinista Cleric Defends His Stand,'' *New York Times*, 11 Dec. 1984, A3.

28. Marlise Simons, ''Friar Says He Prefers 'to Walk with the Church,' '' *New York Times*, 21 Mar. 1985, A18.

29. Jerry Filteau, ''Fr. Curran Says He Would Go to Court,'' NC News Service story in *Catholic Free Press*, Worcester, MA, 21 Mar. 1986, 9.

30. The dogmatic constitution *Pastor aeternus* of Vatican Council I, 1869–1870.

31. Apropos slavery, it is of note that at the Congress of Vienna (1814–1815), it was Great Britain, not the Papal States, at whose

great urging it was declared that the slave trade was to be abolished. Apropos usury, the twelfth canon of the first Council of Carthage (345) and the thirty-sixth canon of the Council of Aix (789) declared it reprehensible for laity to make money by lending at interest. The principle was reinforced by Benedict XIV's encyclical *Vix pervenit* 1 Nov. 1745, addressed to the bishops of Italy on usury and other dishonest profit.

32. Not only did Pope Boniface VIII circumscribe the availability of salvation, but he also wrote in 1302, "We declare, state, define and proclaim (*declaramus, dicimus, definimus, et pronuntiamus*) that it is absolutely necessary for salvation that every human creature should be subject to the Roman Pontiff," a proposition that not even a pope would attempt to argue today. In any case, applying the first of the propositions, *extra ecclesiam nulla salus*, in its most literal sense, Father Leonard Feeney, S.J., led a number of Boston-area young people in the 1940s into what became known as the Boston heresy. Feeney was serving as chaplain at St. Benedict Center, a gathering place in Cambridge for Catholics attending Harvard, Radcliffe, and other nearby colleges. The atomic bombing of Hiroshima and the advance of communism confirmed for him the utter corruption of the world, and salvation became, in turn, an all-consuming preoccupation. For Feeney, this had to be through Roman Catholicism. His theories grew stridently anti-Semitic and anti-Protestant and a cause of open scandal as on Sunday afternoons he took his campaign to Boston Commons. Feeney was expelled from the Jesuits in 1949, then excommunicated by Rome in 1953. He and his followers moved to Still River, Massachusetts, where remnants of the community, some reconciled with Rome, still exist. Feeney himself was reconciled, and ecclesiastical censures against him were removed in 1972. He died in 1978.

33. Bede Griffiths, O.S.B., "The Case of Fr. Curran," *Tablet*, London, 20 Sept. 1986, 983.

34. "Pope: Church Only Authentic Interpreter of Bible," NC News Service story in *Pittsburgh Catholic*, 25 July 1986, 6.

35. The Synod of Bishops is a central ecclesiastical institute, permanent by nature, and convened on a periodic basis to deal with

matters of moment in the church. It was chartered in 1965 by Pope Paul VI.

36. Francis X. Murphy, C.SS.R., *The Papacy Today* (New York: Macmillan, 1981), 2. Murphy is commonly identified as Xavier Rynne, pseudonym for the astute commentator on Vatican Council II, whose writings appeared in the *New Yorker* and later in book form.

37. Ibid., 3.

38. Ibid., 5–6.

39. Cardinal Joseph Ratzinger, "The Church and the Theologian," *Origins*, 8 May 1986, as quoted by Father Richard P. McBrien in his syndicated column for 17 July 1986 in *Church World*, Brunswick, ME.

40. Greeley, *Confessions*, 31.

41. Jean-Guy Vaillancourt, *Papal Power, A Study of Vatican Control over Lay Catholic Elites* (Berkeley: University of California Press, 1980), 31.

42. Pedraza, "Archbishop of Seattle," *Boston Globe*, 5 Sept. 1986.

43. Ari L. Goldman, "Prelates Endorse Steps by Vatican on Seattle Bishop," *New York Times*, 13 Nov. 1986, 1.

44. Richard P. McBrien, "The Bishops and Archbp. Hunthausen," *Church World*, Brunswick, ME, 4 Dec. 1986, 18.

45. Kevin H. Gunning, "Catholic Bishops Play It Safe," *Boston Globe*, 16 Nov. 1986, Focus section, A30.

46. Ari L. Goldman, "Jewish Groups Fault O'Connor on Mideast Trip," *New York Times*, 11 Jan. 1987, 1.

CHAPTER 3

1. Jerry Filteau, "The Diminishing Priest," *Catholic Messenger*, Davenport, IA, 5 Apr. 1984, 1, the first of a three-part series from NC News Service on the priest shortage in the United States.

2. Ibid.

3. "New Guidelines Issued for Priests' Assignments," *Pilot*, Boston, 19 Dec. 1986, 1.

4. Parish bulletin, St. Peter the Apostle Church, Provincetown, MA, 2 Nov. 1986.

5. *The John Carroll Papers*, Notre Dame, 1976; I, 180, 183, as cited in "John Carroll and Interfaith Marriages," by Robert F. McNamara, *Studies in American History*, edited by Nelson H. Minnich, Robert B. Eno, and Robert F. Trisco (Wilmington: Michael Glazier, 1985), 31–32.

6. *Immensae caritatis*, an instruction on facilitating the availability of the Eucharist in particular circumstances.

7. "Sister Rita-Mae, Vice Chancellor," *Church World*, Brunswick, ME, 8 Jan. 1987, 1.

8. "Nun to Head Seminary Board," *Pittsburgh Catholic*, 9 Jan. 1987, 6.

9. "Report Says Priest Decline Slows, Ordinations Rise," *Pittsburgh Catholic*, 1 Aug. 1986, 6.

10. Jerry Filteau, "U.S. Seminary Enrollments Down," NC News Service story in *Church World*, Brunswick, ME, 6 Nov. 1986, 23.

11. Ibid.

12. "Research on Men's Vocations to the Priesthood and Religious Life," a study by Dean R. Hoge, Raymond H. Potvin, and Kathleen M. Ferry, under the direction of Eugene Henrick; United States Catholic Conference, Washington, DC, 1984.

13. Eugene C. Kennedy, "What Boat or Barque Can Rescue the Priest from a Sea of Discontent?" *National Catholic Reporter*, Kansas City, MO, 4 Apr. 1986, 9–10.

14. Ibid.

15. Greeley, *The American Catholic: A Social Portrait* (New York: Basic Books, 1977), 155–156.

16. Ibid.

17. John Cogley, *Catholic America* (New York: Dial Press, 1971), 129.

18. Ibid.

19. Stephen Nash (pseudonym), "Speaking Out: I Am a Priest, I Want to Marry," *Saturday Evening Post*, 12 Mar. 1966. The article was subsequently expanded under James Kavanaugh's own name into the book *A Modern Priest Looks at His Outdated Church* (New York: Trident Press, 1967).

20. Father William Wells (pseudonym), "I'd Like to Say: 'If I Had a Son, I Wouldn't Want Him to Be a Priest!' " *St. Anthony Messenger*, Aug. 1986, 8–12. Circulation figures for the magazine are from the *Catholic Press Directory* for 1986.

21. The quotes are from Pope John Paul II in an address at an audience 23 May 1986 with Angolan bishops making their *ad limina* visit to the Vatican, as reported by NC News Service. *Ad limina* translates from the Latin as the phrase "to the threshold," and describes the periodic visit, usually every five years, that bishops are expected to make to Rome.

22. Joseph Martos, *Doors to the Sacred* (New York: Doubleday, 1981), 485.

23. Herbert Thurston, "Celibacy of the Clergy," *The Catholic Encyclopedia*, vol. 3 (New York: Gilmary Society, 1913), 481.

24. Vatican Council II's Pastoral Constitution on the Church in the Modern World, *Gaudium et spes*, 48, 49.

25. Michael Miles, *Love Is Always* (New York: Morrow, 1986).

26. Tim McCarthy, "Author Repels Prelates' Attack on Book," *National Catholic Reporter*, 15 Aug. 1986, 6. Miles allowed in the *NCR* story that, "at the outset of events," Hunthausen may have seen things one way and he another—that is, that he was a lay minister, not a priest minister—but he claimed still to have been allowed to concelebrate the Eucharist and to preach. He told *NCR* that he had tried to make clear in his book "where [Hunthausen] is coming from, but at the same time to make equally clear how I, along with my wife and the people of Resurrection, saw and felt those same events, which produced a unique, unprecedented situation." Miles responded to Curtiss by saying that "a statement from on high can't erase what happened."

27. Wells, 10.

28. Jonathan Friendly, "Catholic Church Discussing Priests Who Abuse Children," *New York Times*, 4 May 1986, 26.

29. Ibid.

30. Ibid.

31. Kennedy, 9.

32. The First Friday of each month is a devotion that has long been popular among Catholics, although that popularity has gone into something of an eclipse in recent years with the shift of the Catholic away from a devotional and toward a sacramental piety. The First Friday devotion began in 1675 with professed revelations to St. Margaret Mary Alacoque promising a happy death to those

who received communion on the first Friday of nine consecutive months.

33. Dogmatic Constitution on the Church, *Lumen gentium*, 10.
34. Father Richard P. McBrien, "Today's Seminarians," *Church World*, Brunswick, ME, 19 June 1986, 18.
35. "Attitudes of American Priests in 1970 and 1985 on the Church and the Priesthood," Report No. 4 in a study on future church leadership by Dean R. Hoge, Joseph J. Shields, and Mary Jeanne Verdieck, March 1986, supported by a grant from the Lilly Endowment, Inc. The study replicated topics of a 1970 National Conference of Catholic Bishops survey conducted by the National Opinion Research Center of Chicago. Hoge, Shields, and Verdieck were all from the Catholic University of America.
36. Wells, 11.
37. Ari L. Goldman, "Priests Gather to Ponder Their Dwindling Ranks," *New York Times*, 8 Mar. 1986.
38. "Fewer Here Share More Work," *Catholic Messenger*, Davenport, IA, 5 Apr. 1984, 1.
39. " 'Columbia' Features Vocations Coming from Thomas Aquinas College," *Wanderer*, St. Paul, MN, 15 Jan. 1987, 1.
40. "New Study Lists Reasons for Drop in U.S. Vocations," *Pittsburgh Catholic*, 8 June 1984, 3.; NC News Service story on the study "Research on Men's Vocations to the Priesthood and the Religious Life," cited in note 12, this chapter. Father Richard P. McBrien's observations appeared as an interpretive commentary as part of the study's final chapter.

CHAPTER 4

1. Fran Schumer, "A Return to Religion," *New York Times Magazine*, 15 Apr. 1984, 90ff.
2. Dirk Johnson, "Students Turning to Spiritual Life at Campuses in New York Area," *New York Times*, 25 Dec. 1985, 1.
3. Jerry Filteau, "Says Fr. Hesburgh: Priesthood Is 'The Core of My Life,' " NC News Service story in *Pittsburgh Catholic*, 18 July 1986, 1.

4. Nancy P. McMillan, "Letter from the Editor," *Boston Business*, Winter 1986, 4.

5. Johnson, 36.

6. John Deedy, "The Catechism Crisis: Can Catholics Pass Religion 101?" *U.S. Catholic*, Aug. 1984, 20–24.

7. Andrew M. Greeley, *Crisis in the Church* (Chicago: Thomas More Press, 1979), 157.

8. Ibid., 176.

9. Andrew M. Greeley, *Confessions of a Parish Priest* (New York: Simon & Schuster, 1986), 213.

10. Matt Scheiber, "Mass Confusion on a Catholic Campus," *U.S. Catholic*, Aug. 1984, 25–27.

11. Ibid.

12. Theodore M. Hesburgh, "The Vatican and American Catholic Higher Education," *America*, 1 Nov. 1986, 247ff.

13. Pontifical universities are institutions of higher learning that have been canonically erected and that are authorized by the Vatican's Sacred Congregation for Catholic Education to confer degrees in specific fields of study. There are forty-six such universities in twenty-eight countries of the world. Three are located in the United States: Catholic University of America and Georgetown University, both in Washington, and Niagara University in Niagara Falls, New York.

14. "Bingo Second Only to Mass in Parishioner Participation," NC News Service story summarizing Report No. 8 in a University of Notre Dame study of Catholic parish life, written by sociologist David Leege, senior research director of the study; *Pittsburgh Catholic*, 22 Aug. 1986, 3.

15. Grace Mojtabai, *Blessed Assurance: At Home with the Bomb in Amarillo, Texas* (Boston: Houghton Mifflin, 1986).

16. "Living with Apocalypse," an interview with Grace Mojtabai conducted by David Toolan, *Commonweal*, 26 Sept. 1986, 499.

17. Greeley, *Crisis*, 103.

18. Greeley, *Confessions*, 256.

19. John Deedy, *What a Modern Catholic Believes about Conscience, Freedom and Authority* (Chicago: Thomas More Press, 1972), 61ff. The

Thomas More series explored contemporary Catholic thought on a range of subjects, among them God, sex, sin, marriage, women, death, suffering, and evil.

20. Andrew M. Greeley, *The Communal Catholic: A Personal Manifesto* (New York: Seabury Press, A Crossroad Book, 1976).
21. Andrew M. Greeley, *The American Catholic: A Social Portrait* (New York: Basic Books, 1977) and *Crisis in the Church* (1979).
22. Greeley, *Crisis*, 109–110.
23. Robert McClory, "New Breed of Laity Takes Religion on the Job," *National Catholic Reporter*, 26 Sept. 1986, 19.
24. John Deedy, "Catholic Social Action: Does It Measure Up to Yesterday?" *America*, 5 Oct. 1985, 195. The Cort quote has been altered here to restore a word—*bitch* in the phrase "bitch goddess success"—that was dropped in the editing of the article.
25. Richard McBrien, "How Do We Reach 'Cultural Catholics'?" *Church World*, Brunswick, ME, 24 July 1986.
26. Agostino Bono, "Pope Recommits Church to Peace, Ecumenism. . . during Visit to France," *Catholic Free Press*, Worcester, MA, 10 Oct. 1986, 1.
27. Greeley, *Communal Catholic*, 17.
28. Ibid.
29. William P. Coughlin, "Fr. Jim Young, 46, Ministered to Divorced, Separated Catholics," *Boston Globe*, 17 Sept. 1986, obituary page.
30. James Carroll, "The Lord of Unbelief," text of address delivered to priests, sisters and lay ministers of the archdiocese of Chicago, Quigley Seminary, 11 Oct. 1986. The text was made available to me by Carroll.
31. Dan Wakefield, "The Passions of James Carroll," *Boston Business*, Winter 1986, 64.
32. Carroll, "The Lord of Unbelief."
33. Ibid.
34. Wakefield, "Passions."
35. Greeley, *Communal Catholic*, 198.
36. James R. Kelly, "The New Roman Church: A Modest Proposal," *Commonweal*, 3 Dec. 1971, 222.
37. *Unitatis redintegratio*, The Decree on Ecumenism, 1.

CHAPTER 5

1. Candida Lund, editor, *If I Were Pope* (Chicago: Thomas More Press, 1987). Robert E. Burns's contribution is on page 165.
2. In Catholic understanding, the Angel Gabriel was the messenger from God who announced to Mary that she had been chosen to be the mother of the Redeemer, Jesus Christ, who had been miraculously conceived in her womb. Hers, thus, was to be a virgin birth. The account of the angel's appearance, Mary's bewilderment (''How can this be, for I know not man?''), and her acquiescence (''Be it done unto me according to thy word'') is narrated in the Gospel of St. Luke, 1:26ff.
3. Jerry Filteau, ''Bishops to Scan Gender Use in Bible,'' NC News Service story in *Catholic Free Press*, Worcester, MA, 13 Feb. 1987, 2.
4. Rosemary Radford Ruether, ''Why Mary Chandler Left the Church She Loved,'' *National Catholic Reporter*, 26 Sept. 1986, 14.
5. Ibid.
6. George G. Higgins, ''The Women's Challenge,'' *America*, 10 Jan. 1987, 3ff.
7. Geraldine A. Ferraro, *Ferraro: My Story*, with Linda Bird Francke (New York: Bantam Books, 1986), 137.
8. Ibid., 227.
9. Ibid., 227–228.
10. Gary MacEoin, *Memoirs & Memories* (Mystic, CN: Twenty-Third Publications, 1986), 10.
11. Matthew L. Wald, ''Church Calls Excommunicated Catholic Abortion 'Accomplice,' '' *New York Times*, 25 Jan. 1987.
12. Joe Michael Feist, ''Theologians Disagree on R.I. Excommunication,'' NC News Service story in *Catholic Free Press*, Worcester, MA, 31 Jan. 1986, 3.
13. Mark Patinkin, ''They Have to Justify What They Did to That Child,'' *Providence Journal*, Providence, RI, 23 Jan. 1986, 1.
14. Ari L. Goldman, ''Catholic School Expels Girl over Abortion Stand,'' *New York Times*, 16 Aug. 1986, 24.
15. Ibid.
16. ''People,'' *Christian Century*, 17 Dec. 1986, 1145.
17. Joseph Berger, ''Retiring Priests and Nuns Lack Adequate

Fund," *New York Times*, 30 May 1986, 1.

18. Ibid.

19. Ibid.

20. Pat Windsor, "Entire Church Must Meet Religious Retirement Needs," NC News Service story in *Catholic Free Press*, Worcester, MA, 12 Sept. 1986, 1.

21. "Kan. Archdiocese to Aid Retired Nuns," *Pittsburgh Catholic*, Pittsburgh, 1 Aug. 1986.

22. "Aging Nuns: Dioceses Finding Ways to Meet Retirement Needs of Religious," *Church World*, Brunswick, ME, 4 Dec. 1986, 19.

23. Ibid.

24. Marianne Ciancuolo, "Archdiocese's $3 Million for Nuns May Not Be Enough," NC News Service story in *Catholic Free Press*, Worcester, MA, 6 June 1986, 5.

25. Ibid.

26. Sue Schreiber, "Parish 'Adopts' Nun to Meet Retirement Needs," *Pilot*, Boston, 7 Nov. 1986, 1.

27. "Footnote," *Pilot*, Boston, 14 Nov. 1986, 4.

28. Walter Poronovich, "Quebec's Bishops 'Open' on Women in Priesthood," RNS story in *Catholic Messenger*, Davenport, IA, 13 Mar. 1986.

29. Liz Schevtchuk, " 'Miracle' Needed to Get Women's Pastoral to Bishops in 1987, Bishop Says," NC News Service story in *Pilot*, Boston, 12 Dec. 1986, 12.

30. Ibid.

31. "Women Priests Favored by 47% of Catholics in the United States," NC News Service story reporting research by sociologist Dean Hoge of the Catholic University of America; *Catholic Free Press*, Worcester, MA, 13 June 1986, 2.

32. "Priests vs. Authority," *Christian Century*, 27 Aug.–3 Sept. 1986, 736; also, "The Sweeney Case," column by Richard P. McBrien in *Church World*, Brunswick, ME, 16 Oct. 1986, 26.

CHAPTER 6

1. Joseph Berger, "Dissent Magnified, U.S. Prelates Say," *New York Times*, 1 Dec. 1986, 1.

2. Charles Osborne *et al., I Have a Dream—The Story of Martin Luther King in Texts and Pictures* (New York: Time-Life Books, 1968), 57.
3. ''Discrimination and Christian Conscience.''
4. ''Brothers and Sisters to Us.''
5. Elinor G. Walter, ''Black Catholic Congress Seen Facing Challenges Similar to Century Ago,'' NC News Service story in *Pilot*, 9 Jan. 1987, 5.
6. Edward K. Braxton, ''Black Catholics in America: Where Do We Go from Here?,'' *America*, 2 Nov. 1985, 273ff.
7. Ibid.
8. Michael Days, ''Black U.S. Catholics Make Big Changes in Ways of Worship,'' *Wall Street Journal*, 5 Nov. 1985, 1.
9. Ibid., 20.
10. ''New Roman Catholic Hymnal Aimed at Black Parishioner,'' *New York Times*, 10 Nov. 1986.
11. ''Black Catholic Ministries,'' vol. 1, no. 1, *Pittsburgh Catholic* Supplement, Pittsburgh, Winter 1986.
12. ''New Catholic Paper to Focus on Blacks,'' *Catholic Free Press*, Worcester, MA, 11 July 1986, 2.
13. *Crux of the News*, Albany, NY, 10 Nov. 1986, 1.
14. ''Blacks Still Feel Alienated in 'European' Church, Priest Says,'' NC News Service story in *Pilot*, Boston, 9 May 1986.
15. ''Pastoral Presents Characteristics of Black Spirituality,'' *Progress*, Seattle, 5 Sept. 1986, 8–9.
16. Carlyle C. Douglas, ''Bishops Seeking Larger Role for Black Catholics,'' *New York Times*, 10 Sept. 1985, B3.
17. Ibid.
18. Ibid.
19. ''Hispanics Moving Out?'' *Catholic Messenger*, Davenport, IA, 1 May 1986, 1.
20. Kenneth Reich, ''19% Hike in Hispanic Population Seen by 2080,'' *Boston Globe*, 26 Sept. 1986, 3.
21. Thomas B. Morgan, ''The Latinization of America,'' *Esquire*, May 1983.
22. Judith Cummings, ''Los Angeles Archbishop Leads Drive to Aid Hispanic Catholics,'' *New York Times*, 15 June 1986.
23. ''The Church's Future Has a Spanish Accent,'' *Daily News*, New York, 31 Mar. 1986, 22.

24. Charles W. Bell, "City of Faith: What We Believe," *Daily News*, New York, 31 Mar. 1986, 22.

25. Frances Xavier Cabrini at first aspired to be a Catholic missionary to the Far East. In the floodtide of Italian emigation to the United States, however, there was such great concern in Italy about the immigrants' temporal and religious welfare that church authorities suggested she go instead to New York and work among those immigrants. At first she refused. Her mind was changed by Pope Leo XIII, who said to her, "Not to the East, but to the West. . . . You will find a vast field for labor in the United States." She shipped to New York and landed in March 1889. Mother Cabrini later became an American citizen. She was canonized a saint of the Catholic church in 1946, the first naturalized American citizen to be so honored.

26. Joseph Berger, "Hispanic Catholics Found to Hew to Tradition," *New York Times*, 9 Feb. 1986, 33. The study was published as *The Hispanic Catholic in the United States: A Social, Cultural and Religious Profile*, Roberto O. Gonzalez and Michael La Velle (New York: Northeast Pastoral Center for Hispanics, 1985). Foreword to the book was writted by Cardinal John O'Connor.

27. "Church's Future."

28. George Gallup, Jr., and Jim Castelli, *The American Catholic People: Their Beliefs, Practices and Values* (New York: Doubleday, 1987), as quoted in a news story announcing the book's publication by Dawn Gibeau in *National Catholic Reporter*, 30 Jan. 1987, 16.

29. Berger, "Hispanic Catholics."

30. "Church's Future."

31. Veronica Garcia, "Church in Danger of Losing Hispanics, Says Bishop Ramirez," NC News Service story in *Pilot*, Boston, 9 May 1986.

32. Ibid.

33. *Crux of the News*, Albany, NY, 1 Dec. 1986, 2.

34. "Church's Future."

CHAPTER 7

1. "Where Church, Fr. Curran Differed on Theological Issues," NC News Service story in *Pittsburgh Catholic*, 22 Aug. 1986, 3.

2. Ibid.

3. "Firing Line," transcript of program taped in New York City, 20 Nov. 1986, and telecast later on the Public Broadcasting Service, as a production of the Southern Educational Communications Association, Columbia, South Carolina. The program featured William F. Buckley, Jr., as host. The other guest, along with Father Curran, was Monsignor Eugene V. Clark, pastor of St. Agnes Church in New York City and once personal secretary to Cardinals Francis Spellman and Terence Cooke. Curran's comment appears on page 19 of the program's transcript.

4. Xavier Rynne (pseudonym), "The Curran Controversy and the Vatican's Obsession with Conformity," *Boston Globe*, 24 Sept. 1986, 19.

5. "Church, Fr. Curran."

6. William V. Shannon, "Silencing a Catholic Theologian Who Dares to Dissent," *Boston Globe*, 27 Aug. 1986, 15.

7. John C. Bennett, "The Vatican Moves to Repress Dissent," *Christianity and Crisis*, 6 Oct. 1986, 33.

8. Joseph Berger, "Priest Is Told to Retract His Views on Sex Issues," *New York Times*, 12 Mar. 1986.

9. "Curran Complains against C.U. Action," RNS story in *Wanderer*, St. Paul, 4 Dec. 1986, 1.

10. Robin Toner, "Censured Priest Drops Teaching Plans for Spring," *New York Times*, 16 Jan. 1987, A15.

11. Ibid.

12. Robert McAfee Brown, "Father Charles Curran and Canon 812," *Christian Century*, 4–11 Feb. 1987, 100.

13. "People vs. Authority," *Christian Century*, 27 Aug.–3 Sept. 1986, 736.

14. "Ex-Jesuit, Citing 'Restrictions,' Turns Down Archbishop's Offer," *Wanderer*, St. Paul, 25 Dec. 1986, 7.

15. Published by Sheed, Andrews & McMeel, Kansas City, MO, 1976.

16. Dick Ryan, "Jesuits to Expel Rebel Gay Priest," *National Catholic Reporter*, 14 Nov. 1986, 1, 6.

17. "Fr. McNeill Dismissed from Jesuit Order," *Pilot*, 27 Feb. 1987, 8.

18. Jerry Filteau, "Fr. Buckley, Named to NCCB, to Be Reviewed," NC News Service story in *Catholic Free Press*, Worcester, MA, 25

July 1986, 6.

19. David E. Anderson, "Jesuit Critic of Vatican to Get Key Doctrinal Post," UPI story in *Boston Globe*, 28 Aug. 1986.

20. "Canon Lawyer Critical of Rome Wins Tenure at Catholic U.," UPI story in *Boston Globe*, 29 Aug. 1986, 64.

21. Jerry Filteau, "Archbishop James Hickey: 'No Right to Public Dissent,' " *Pittsburgh Catholic*, 23 Aug. 1986.

22. "Archbishop Supports Vatican Decision," NC News Service in *Progress*, Seattle, 28 Aug. 1968, 15.

23. "Explanation of Curran's, Vatican Views on Issues," *Progress*, Seattle, 28 Aug. 1986, 14.

24. Canon T. K. A. Walsh, "The Case of Fr. Curran," *Tablet*, London, 10 May 1986, 486.

25. "Pope Rebukes Dissent on Sexual Issues," *New York Times*, 11 Apr. 1986, A5.

26. "Dissent a Risk," NC News Service story in *Catholic Free Press*, Worcester, MA, 4 July 1986, 2.

27. Robert McClory, "Bernardin Writes Pastoral against Teaching Dissent," *National Catholic Reporter*, 24 Oct. 1986, 3.

28. Karen M. Franz, "Bishop Withdraws Imprimatur from Sex Education Book," NC News Service story in *Church World*, Brunswick, ME, 4 Dec. 1986, 10.

29. Archbishop Rembert G. Weakland, O.S.B., "The Price of Orthodoxy," *Catholic Herald*, Milwaukee, 11 Sept. 1986 and 18 Sept. 1986, p. 3 in both issues.

30. Ibid.

31. Roberto Suro, "The Vatican and Dissent in America," *New York Times*, 27 Sept. 1986, 9.

32. Joseph Berger, "Church Directive on Speakers Is Questioned," *New York Times*, 6 Dec. 1986, 29. The story concerned the cover article, "Thou Shalt Not Speak," by Monsignor Harry J. Byrne, in *America* magazine for 6 Dec. 1986.

33. "The Curran Effect," *Commonweal*, 12 Sept. 1986, 451.

34. Joseph Berger, "Catholic Compromise Is Reached in Dispute on Seattle Archbishop," *New York Times*, 27 May 1987, 1. The three-bishop commission that worked out the agreement comprised Cardinal Joseph Bernardin of Chicago, Cardinal John O'Connor of New York, and Archbishop John Quinn of San Francisco.

35. Joseph Berger, "Catholics Reach Accord in Seattle Case," *New York Times*, 31 May 1987, Week in Review section, 30.

CHAPTER 8

1. Joseph Berger, "Archbishop Warns Vatican May Alienate Many in U.S.," *New York Times*, 9 Oct. 1986, A22.
2. Ari L. Goldman, "U.S. Bishop Urges a Papal Audience on 'Disaffection,'" *New York Times*, 11 Nov. 1986, 1. A delegation of American bishops eventually traveled to Rome in March 1987, both to brief Vatican officials on plans for Pope John Paul II's September 1987 tour of nine U.S. cities, and to hold talks aimed at "easing tensions caused by a Vatican crackdown on dissent from orthodox views": "U.S. Clerics Will Meet at Vatican on Tension," Reuters dispatch in *New York Times*, 13 Mar. 1987, A20.
3. Bob Dylak, "Rift of Left/Right Threat to Church, Msgr. Ellis Says," NC News Service story in *Catholic Free Press*, Worcester, MA, 12 Dec. 1986, 1.
4. Joseph Berger, "Dissent Magnified, U.S. Prelates Say," *New York Times*, 1 Dec. 1986, 1.
5. Ibid.
6. "Pope Plays Down Rift with Bishops," *New York Times*, 20 Nov. 1986, A3.
7. Berger, "Archbishop Warns Vatican."
8. John Deedy, "Apologies Good Friends," *An Interim Biography of Daniel Berrigan, S.J.* (Chicago: Claretian Publications, 1981), 67ff.
9. Abigail McCarthy, "Spirit of Seattle," *Commonweal*, 5 Dec. 1986, 649.
10. Ibid.
11. Carroll, "Lord of Unbelief."
12. Ibid.
13. Maryclaire Dale and Jim McManus, "Curran Predicts Tensions with Rome Will Intensify," *National Catholic Reporter*, 12 Dec. 1986, 4.

INDEX

299